Kubernetes in Production Best Practices

Production Best Practices

Build and manage highly available production-ready
Kubernetes clusters

Aly Saleh

Murat Karslioglu

BIRMINGHAM—MUMBAI

Kubernetes in Production Best Practices

Group Product Manager: Wilson D'souza

Publishing Product Manager: Vijin Boricha

Senior Editor: Arun Nadar

Content Development Editor: Romy Dias

Technical Editor: Yoginee Marathe

Copy Editor: Safis Editing

Project Coordinator: Neil Dmello

Proofreader: Safis Editing

Indexer: Tejal Daruwale Soni

Production Designer: Prashant Ghare

First published: February 2021

Production reference: 1110221

Published by Packt Publishing Ltd.

Livery Place

35 Livery Street

Birmingham

B3 2PB, UK.

ISBN 978-1-80020-245-0

www.packt.com

To the doctors, nurses, public health officials, and first responders who are protecting us from COVID-19.

Contributors

About the authors

Aly Saleh is a technology entrepreneur, cloud transformation leader, and architect. He has worked for the past 2 decades on building large-scale software solutions and cloud-based platforms and services that are used by millions of users. He is a co-founder of MAVS Cloud, a start-up that empowers organizations to leverage the power of the cloud.
He also played various technical roles at Oracle, Vodafone, FreshBooks, Aurea Software, and Ceros.

Aly holds degrees in computer science, and he has gained multiple credentials in AWS, GCP, and Kubernetes, with a focus on building cloud platforms, app modernization, containerization, and architecting distributed systems. He is an advocate for cloud best practices, remote work, and globally distributed teams.

> *I want to thank my wonderful wife, Rabab, my sons, Adham and Adam, and my big family for giving me the encouragement and support I needed to write this book, even while the COVID-19 global pandemic was raging around us.*

Murat Karslioglu is a distinguished technologist with years of experience using infrastructure tools and technologies. Murat is currently the VP of products at MayaData, a start-up that builds data agility platform for stateful applications, and a maintainer of open source projects, namely OpenEBS and Litmus. In his free time, Murat is busy writing practical articles about DevOps best practices, CI/CD, Kubernetes, and running stateful applications on popular Kubernetes platforms on his blog, Containerized Me. Murat also runs a cloud-native news curator site, The Containerized Today, where he regularly publishes updates on the Kubernetes ecosystem.

> *I want to thank my wife, Svetlana, and the rest of my family for their continuous support, patience, and encouragement throughout the whole difficult process of book-writing.*

About the reviewers

Renzo Tomà is a seasoned cloud engineer. He has built enterprise cloud infrastructures that empower 100+ scrum teams with self-service cloud and Kubernetes capabilities.

His Kubernetes experience stems from building multi-cluster setups and dealing with large-scale problems. At home, he runs Kubernetes on a Raspberry Pi to support home automation.

Marcos Vale is a software engineer with more than 20 years in the IT industry with a focus on DevOps, product architecture, design and development in many different languages (mainly Java), and databases.

He has completed a PhD and a master's degree in data mining and a postgraduate course in analysis, project, and management systems. He has graduated as a systems engineer and is also Java certified (SJCP).

He has worked as a DevOps specialist for the last 6 years, working on many different projects in Brazil, the United States, and across Europe, implementing DevOps with a focus on IaC, Kubernetes, and CI/CD processes.

I wish to thank my family for supporting me, and I would like to express my very great gratitude to Aly and Murat and the publisher for giving me the opportunity to be a part of this great book.

Table of Contents

7

Managing Storage and Stateful Applications

8

Deploying Seamless and Reliable Applications

9

Monitoring, Logging, and Observability

10
Operating and Maintaining Efficient Kubernetes Clusters

Other Books You May Enjoy

Index

Preface

Kubernetes is an open source container orchestration platform originally developed by Google and made available to the public in 2014. The popularity of Kubernetes helped to make the deployment of container-based, complex, distributed systems simpler to manage for developers. Since its inception, the community has built a large ecosystem around Kubernetes, with many open source projects that have made the automation of management functions possible.

This book is specifically designed to quickly help Kubernetes administrators and **site reliability engineers** (**SREs**) to build and manage production-grade Kubernetes infrastructure following industry best practices and well-proven techniques learned from early technology adopters of large-scale Kubernetes deployments.

While we use Amazon **Elastic Kubernetes Service** (**EKS**) to deliver the practical exercises in this book, we believe that the explained Kubernetes design, provisioning, and configuration concepts and techniques remain valid for other cloud providers. Regarding the selection of provisioning and configuration tools, we decided to use cloud-agnostic tools such as Terraform and Ansible to ensure portability across cloud providers.

Kubernetes in Production Best Practices gives you the confidence to use Kubernetes to host your production workloads, having the comprehensive infrastructure design knowledge to build your clusters and a clear understanding of managing and operating them efficiently.

Who this book is for

This book is ideal for cloud infrastructure architects, SREs, DevOps engineers, system administrators, and engineering managers who have a basic knowledge of Kubernetes and are willing to apply cloud industry best practices to design, build, and operate production-grade Kubernetes clusters.

A basic knowledge of Kubernetes, AWS, Terraform, Ansible, and Bash will be beneficial.

What this book covers

Chapter 1, Introduction to Kubernetes Infrastructure and Production-Readiness, teaches you about the basics of Kubernetes infrastructure, then explains the principles of infrastructure designing, and finally the characteristics of production-ready clusters.

Chapter 2, Architecting Production-Grade Kubernetes Infrastructure, teaches you about the various aspects, trade-offs, and best practices that you need to consider while designing Kubernetes infrastructure.

Chapter 3, Provisioning Kubernetes Clusters Using AWS and Terraform, teaches you how to use AWS, Terraform, and infrastructure as code techniques to provision Kubernetes infrastructure.

Chapter 4, Managing Cluster Configurations with Ansible, teaches you how to use Ansible to build a flexible and scalable configuration management solution for Kubernetes clusters.

Chapter 5, Configuring and Enhancing Kubernetes Networking Services, teaches you how to configure and improve Kubernetes cluster networking, and the essential Kubernetes networking add-ons to use.

Chapter 6, Securing Kubernetes Effectively, teaches you about Kubernetes security best practices, and how to validate and ensure the security of clusters.

Chapter 7, Managing Storage and Stateful Applications, teaches you how to overcome storage challenges in Kubernetes using the best storage management solution in the ecosystem.

Chapter 8, Deploying Seamless and Reliable Applications, teaches you container and image best practices, as well as application deployment strategies to achieve scalable service in production.

Chapter 9, Monitoring, Logging, and Observability, teaches you Kubernetes observability best practices, important metrics to watch for, as well as the monitoring and logging stacks available in the market, and when to use each of them.

Chapter 10, Operating and Maintaining Efficient Kubernetes Clusters, teaches you Kubernetes operation best practices, as well as cluster maintenance tasks such as upgrades and rotation, backups, and disaster recovery, and the solutions available to improve the quality of clusters.

To get the most out of this book

To use this book, you will need access to computers, servers, AWS, or other cloud provider services where you can provision virtual machine instances. To set up the lab environments, you may also need larger cloud instances that will require you to enable billing.

Software/hardware covered in the book	OS requirements
Terraform v0.14.5, Python v3.9, pip3, virtualenv, kubectl, and Helm	Windows, macOS, or Linux

If you are using the digital version of this book, we advise you to type the code yourself or access the code via the GitHub repository (link available in the next section). Doing so will help you avoid any potential errors related to the copying and pasting of code.

Download the example code files

You can download the example code files for this book from GitHub at `https://github.com/PacktPublishing/Kubernetes-in-Production-Best-Practices`. In case there's an update to the code, it will be updated on the existing GitHub repository.

We also have other code bundles from our rich catalog of books and videos available at `https://github.com/PacktPublishing/`. Check them out!

Code in Action

Code in Action videos for this book can be viewed at `http://bit.ly/36JpElI`.

Download the color images

We also provide a PDF file that has color images of the screenshots/diagrams used in this book. You can download it here: `https://static.packt-cdn.com/downloads/9781800202450_ColorImages.pdf`.

Conventions used

There are a number of text conventions used throughout this book.

`Code in text`: Indicates code words in text, database table names, folder names, filenames, file extensions, pathnames, dummy URLs, user input, and Twitter handles. Here is an example: "As a best practice, we recommend that you limit any privileged pods within the `kube-system` namespace."

A block of code is set as follows:

```
terraform {
  required_version = "~> 0.12.24"
}
```

When we wish to draw your attention to a particular part of a code block, the relevant lines or items are set in bold:

```
provider "aws" {
  region = var.aws_region
  version = "~> 2.52.0"
}
```

Any command-line input or output is written as follows:

```
$ cd Chapter03/terraform/shared-state
$ terraform init
```

Bold: Indicates a new term, an important word, or words that you see on screen. For example, words in menus or dialog boxes appear in the text like this. Here is an example: "Select **System info** from the **Administration** panel."

> **Tips or important notes**
> Appear like this.

Get in touch

Feedback from our readers is always welcome.

General feedback: If you have questions about any aspect of this book, mention the book title in the subject of your message and email us at customercare@packtpub.com.

Errata: Although we have taken every care to ensure the accuracy of our content, mistakes do happen. If you have found a mistake in this book, we would be grateful if you would report this to us. Please visit www.packtpub.com/support/errata, selecting your book, clicking on the Errata Submission Form link, and entering the details.

Piracy: If you come across any illegal copies of our works in any form on the internet, we would be grateful if you would provide us with the location address or website name. Please contact us at copyright@packt.com with a link to the material.

If you are interested in becoming an author: If there is a topic that you have expertise in and you are interested in either writing or contributing to a book, please visit authors.packtpub.com.

Reviews

Please leave a review. Once you have read and used this book, why not leave a review on the site that you purchased it from? Potential readers can then see and use your unbiased opinion to make purchase decisions, we at Packt can understand what you think about our products, and our authors can see your feedback on their book. Thank you!

For more information about Packt, please visit packt.com.

1
Introduction to Kubernetes Infrastructure and Production-Readiness

With more and more organizations adopting Kubernetes for their infrastructure management, it is becoming the industry de facto standard for orchestrating and managing distributed applications both in the cloud and on premises.

Whether you are an individual contributor who is migrating their company's applications to the cloud or you are a decision-maker leading a cloud transformation initiative, you should plan the journey to Kubernetes and understand its challenges.

If this book has a core purpose, it is guiding you through the journey of building a production-ready Kubernetes infrastructure while avoiding the common pitfalls. This is our reason for writing about this topic, as we have witnessed failures and successes through the years of building and operating Kubernetes clusters on different scales. We are sure that you can avoid a lot of these failures, saving time and money, increasing reliability, and fulfilling your business goals.

In this chapter, you will learn about how to deploy Kubernetes production clusters with best practices. We will explain the roadmap that we will follow for the rest of the book, and explain foundational concepts that are commonly used to design and implement Kubernetes clusters. Understanding these concepts and the related principles are the key to building and operating production infrastructure. Besides, we will set your expectations about the book's scope.

We will go through the core problems that this book will solve and briefly cover topics such as Kubernetes production challenges, a production-readiness characteristics, the cloud-native landscape, and infrastructure design and management principles.

We will cover the following topics in this chapter:

- The basics of Kubernetes infrastructure
- Why Kubernetes is challenging in production
- Kubernetes production-readiness
- Kubernetes infrastructure best practices
- Cloud-native approach

The basics of Kubernetes infrastructure

If you are reading this book, you already made your decision to take your Kubernetes infrastructure to an advanced level, which means you are beyond the stage of evaluating the technology. To build production infrastructure, the investment remains a burden and it still needs a solid justification to the business and the leadership within your organization. We will try to be very specific in this section about why we need a reliable Kubernetes infrastructure, and to clarify the challenges you should expect in production.

Kubernetes adoption is exploding across organizations all over the world, and we expect this growth to continue to increase, as the **International Data Corporation (IDC)** predicts that around 95 percent of new microservices will be deployed in containers by 2021. Most companies find that containers and Kubernetes help to optimize costs, simplify deployment and operations, and decrease time to market, as well as play a pivotal role in the hybrid cloud strategies. Similarly, Gartner predicts that more than 70 percent of organizations will run two or more containerized applications in production by 2021 compared to less than 20 percent in 2019.

Kubernetes components

> *"Kubernetes (K8s) is an open-source system for automating deployment, scaling, and management of containerized applications."*
>
> *– kubernetes.io*

As we are concerned about building a reliable Kubernetes cluster, we will cover an overview of the Kubernetes cluster architecture and its components, and then you will learn about production challenges.

Kubernetes has a distributed systems architecture – specifically, a client-server one. There are one or more master nodes, and this is where Kubernetes runs its control plane components.

There are worker nodes where Kubernetes deploys the pods and the workloads. A single cluster can manage up to 5,000 nodes. The Kubernetes cluster architecture is shown in the following diagram:

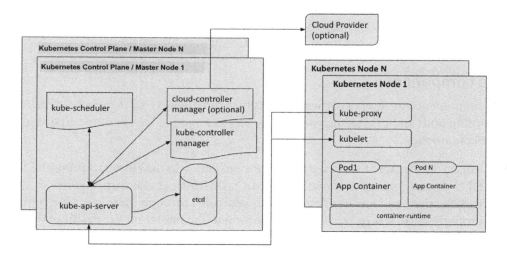

Figure 1.1 – Kubernetes cluster architecture

The preceding diagram represents a typical highly available Kubernetes cluster architecture with the core components. It shows how the Kubernetes parts communicate with each other. Although you have a basic understanding of the Kubernetes cluster architecture, we will need to refresh this knowledge over the next section because we will interact with most of these components in deeper detail when creating and tuning the cluster configuration.

Control plane components

Control plane components are the core software pieces that construct the Kubernetes master nodes. All of them together belong to the Kubernetes project, except `etcd`, which is a separate project on its own. These components follow a distributed systems architecture and can easily scale horizontally to increase cluster capacity and provide high availability:

- `kube-apiserver`: The API server is the manager of the cluster components and it is the interface responsible for handling and serving the management APIs and middling the communication between cluster components.

- `etcd`: This is a distributed, highly available key-value data store that acts as the backbone of the cluster and stores all of its data.

- `kube-controller-manager`: This manages the controller processes that control the cluster – for example, the node controller that controls the nodes, the replication controller that controls the deployments, and the endpoint controller that controls services endpoints exposed in the cluster.

- `kube-scheduler`: This component is responsible for scheduling the pods across the nodes. It decides which pod goes to which node according to the scheduling algorithm, available resources, and the placement configuration.

Node components

Node components are a set of software agents that run on every worker node to maintain the running pods and provide network proxy services and the base runtime environment for the containers:

- `kubelet`: An agent service that runs on each node in the cluster, this periodically takes a set of pod specs (a manifest file in YAML format that describes a pod specification) and ensures that the pods described through these specs are running properly. Also, it is responsible for reporting to the master on the health of the node where it is running.

- kube-proxy: This is an agent service that runs on each node in the cluster to create, update, and delete network roles on the nodes, usually using Linux iptables. These network rules allow inter-pod and intra-pod communication inside and outside of the Kubernetes cluster.

- **Container runtime**: This is a software component that runs on each node in the cluster, and it is responsible for running the containers. Docker is the most famous container runtime; however, Kubernetes supports other runtimes, such as **Container Runtime Interface (CRI-O)** and containerd to run containers, and kubevirt and virtlet to run virtual machines.

Why Kubernetes is challenging in production

Kubernetes could be easy to install, but it is complex to operate and maintain. Kubernetes in production brings challenges and difficulties along the way, from scaling, uptime, and security, to resilience, observability, resources utilization, and cost management. Kubernetes has succeeded in solving container management and orchestration, and it created a standard layer above the compute services. However, Kubernetes still lacks proper or complete support for some essential services, such as **Identity and Access Management (IAM)**, storage, and image registries.

Usually, a Kubernetes cluster belongs to a bigger company's production infrastructure, which includes databases, IAM, **Lightweight Directory Access Protocol (LDAP)**, messaging, streaming, and others. Bringing a Kubernetes cluster to production requires connecting it to these external infrastructure parts.

Even during cloud transformation projects, we expect Kubernetes to manage and integrate with the on-premises infrastructure and services, and this takes production complexity to a next level.

Another challenge occurs when teams start adopting Kubernetes with the assumption that it will solve the scaling and uptime problems that their apps have, but they usually do not plan for day-2 issues. This ends up with catastrophic consequences regarding security, scaling, uptime, resource utilization, cluster migrations, upgrades, and performance tuning.

Besides the technical challenges, there are management challenges, especially when we use Kubernetes across large organizations that have multiple teams, and if the organization is not well prepared to have the right team structure to operate and manage its Kubernetes infrastructure. This could lead to teams struggling to align around standard tools, best practices, and delivery workflows.

Kubernetes production-readiness

"Your offering is production-ready when it exceeds customer expectations in a way that allows for business growth."

– Carter Morgan, Developer Advocate, Google

Production-readiness is the goal we need to achieve throughout this book, and we may not have a definitive definition for this buzzword. It could mean a cluster capable to serve production workloads and real traffic in a reliable and secure fashion. We can further extend this definition, but what many experts agree on is that there is a minimum set of requirements that you need to fulfill before you mark your cluster as production-ready.

We have gathered and categorized these readiness requirements according to the typical Kubernetes production layers (illustrated in the following diagram). We understand that there are still different production use cases for each organization, and product growth and business objectives are deeply affecting these use cases and hence the production readiness requirements. However, we can fairly consider the following production-ready checklist as an essential list for most mainstream use:

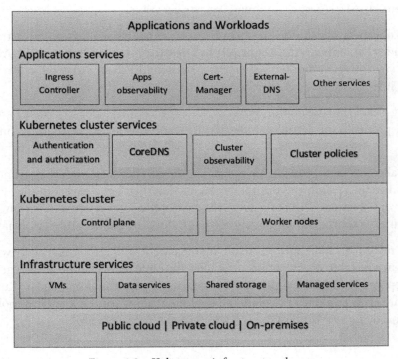

Figure 1.2 – Kubernetes infrastructure layers

This diagram describes the typical layers of Kubernetes infrastructure. There are six layers, which include physical, on-premises, or cloud infrastructure; the infrastructure services layer; the cluster layer; the cluster services layer; the applications supporting services layer; and finally, the applications layer. You will learn about these layers in depth while navigating this book and see how to design a Kubernetes production architecture that brings these layers seamlessly together.

The production-readiness checklist

We have categorized the production-readiness checklist items and mapped them to the corresponding infrastructure layers. Each checklist item represents a design and implementation concern that you need to fulfill to consider your cluster a production-ready. Throughout this book, we will cover the checklist items and their design and implementation details.

Cluster infrastructure

The following checklist items cover the production-readiness requirements on the cluster level:

- **Run a highly available control plane**: You can achieve this by running the control plane components on three or more nodes. Another recommended best practice is to deploy the Kubernetes master components and `etcd` on two separate node groups. This is generally to ease `etcd` operations, such as upgrades and backups, and to decrease the radius of control plane failures.

  Also, for large Kubernetes clusters, this allows `etcd` to get proper resource allocation by running it on certain node types that fulfill its extensive I/O needs.

  Finally, avoid deploying pods to the control plane nodes.

- **Run a highly available workers group**: You can achieve this by running a group or more of worker nodes with three or more instances. If you are running these workers groups using one of the public cloud providers, you should deploy them within an auto-scaling group and in different availability zones.

  Another essential requirement to achieve worker high availability is to deploy the Kubernetes cluster auto scaler, which enables worker nodes to horizontally upscale and downscale based on the cluster utilization.

- **Use a shared storage management solution**: You should consider using a shared storage management solution to persist and manage stateful apps' data. There are plenty of choices, either open source or commercial, such as AWS **Elastic Block Store (EBS)**, **Elastic File System (EFS)**, Google Persistent Disk, Azure Disk Storage, ROOK, Ceph, and Portworx. There is no right or wrong choice among them, but it all depends on your application use case and requirements.

- **Deploy infrastructure observability stack**: Collecting logs and metrics on the infrastructure level for nodes, network, storage, and other infrastructure components is essential for monitoring a cluster's infrastructure, and also to get useful insights about the cluster's performance, utilization, and troubleshooting outages.

  You should deploy a monitoring and alerting stack, such as Node Exporter, Prometheus, and Grafana, and deploy a central logging stack, such as ELK (Elasticsearch, Logstash, and Kibana). Alternatively, you can consider a complete commercial solution, such as Datadog, New Relic, AppDynamics, and so on.

Fulfilling the previous requirements will ensure the production-readiness of the cluster infrastructure. Later in this book, we will show you in more detail how to achieve each of these requirements through infrastructure design, Kubernetes configuration tuning, and third-party tools usage.

Cluster services

The following checklist items cover the production-readiness requirements on the cluster services level:

- **Control cluster access**: Kubernetes introduces authentication and authorization choices and lets the cluster's admin configure them according to their needs. As a best practice, you should ensure authentication and authorization configuration is tuned and in place. Integrate with an external authentication provider to authenticate cluster's users, such as LDAP, **OpenID Connect (OIDC)**, and AWS IAM.

  For authorization, you need to configure the cluster to enable **Role-Based Access Control (RBAC)**, **Attribute-Based Access Control (ABAC)**, and webhooks.

- **Hardening the default pod security policy: Pod security policy (PSP)** is a Kubernetes resource that is used to ensure a pod has to meet specific requirements before getting created.

  As a best practice, we recommend that you limit any privileged pods within the `kube-system` namespace. For all other namespaces that host your apps pods, we recommend assigning a restrictive default PSP.

- **Enforce custom policies and rules**: Rules and policy enforcement are essential for every Kubernetes cluster. This is true for both a small single-tenant cluster and a large multi-tenant one. Kubernetes introduces native objects to achieve this purpose, such as pod security policies, network policies, resource limits, and quotas.

  For custom rules enforcement, you may deploy an open policy agent, such as OPA Gatekeeper. This will enable you to enforce rules such as pods must have resource limits in place, namespaces must have specific labels, images must be from known repositories, and many others.

- **Deploy and fine-tune the cluster DNS**: Running a DNS for Kubernetes clusters is essential for name resolution and service connectivity. Managed Kubernetes comes with cluster DNS pre-deployed, such as CoreDNS. For self-managed clusters, you should consider deploying CoreDNS too. As a best practice, you should fine-tune CoreDNS to minimize errors and failure rates, optimize performance, and adjust caching, and resolution time.

- **Deploy and restrict network policies**: Kubernetes allows all traffic between the pods inside a single cluster. This behavior is insecure in a multi-tenant cluster. As a best practice, you need to enable network policies in your cluster, and create a deny-all default policy to block all traffic among the pods, then you create network policies with less restrictive ingress/egress rules to allow the traffic whenever it is needed for between specific pods.

- **Enforce security checks and conformance testing**: Securing a Kubernetes cluster is not questionable. There are a lot of security configurations to enable and tune for a cluster. This could get tricky for cluster admins, but luckily, there are different tools to scan cluster configuration to assess and ensure that it is secure and meets the minimum security requirements. You have to automate running security scanning tools, such as `kube-scan` for security configuration scanning, `kube-bench` for security benchmarking, and Sonobuoy to run Kubernetes standard conformance tests against the cluster.

- **Deploy a backup and restore solution**: As with any system, Kubernetes could fail, so you should have a proper backup and restore process in place. You should consider tools to back up data, snapshot the cluster control plane, or back up the `etcd` database.

- **Deploy an observability stack for the cluster components**: Monitoring and central logging is essential for Kubernetes components such as `control-plane`, `kubelet`, container runtime, and more. You should deploy a monitoring and alerting stack such as Node Exporter, Prometheus, and Grafana, and deploy a central logging stack, such as EFK (Elasticsearch, Fluentd, and Kibana).

Fulfilling the previous requirements will ensure the production-readiness of the cluster services. Later in this book, we will show you in more detail how to achieve each of these requirements through Kubernetes configuration tuning and third-party tools usage.

Apps and deployments

The following checklist items cover the production-readiness requirements on the apps and deployments level:

- **Automate images quality and vulnerability scanning**: An app image that runs a low-quality app or that is written with poor-quality specs can harm the cluster reliability and other apps running on it. The same goes for images with security vulnerabilities. For that, you should run a pipeline to scan images deployed to the cluster for security vulnerabilities and deviations from quality standards.

- **Deploy Ingress Controller**: By default, you can expose Kubernetes services outside the cluster using load balancers and node ports. However, the majority of the apps have advanced routing requirements, and deploying an Ingress Controller such as Nginx's Ingress Controller is a de facto solution that you should include in your cluster.

- **Manage certificates and secrets**: Secrets and TLS certificates are commonly used by modern apps. Kubernetes comes with a built-in `Secrets` object that eases the creation and management of secrets and certificates inside the cluster. In addition to that, you can extend secrets object by deploying other third-party services, such as Sealed Secrets for encrypted secrets, and Cert-Manager to automate certificates from certificate providers such as Let's Encrypt or Vault.

- **Deploy apps observability stack**: You should make use of Kubernetes' built-in monitoring capabilities, such as defining readiness and liveness probes for the pods. Besides that, you should deploy a central logging stack for the applications' pods. Deploy a blackbox monitoring solution or use a managed service to monitor your apps' endpoints. Finally, consider using application performance monitoring solutions, such as New Relic APM, Datadog APM, AppDynamics APM, and more.

Fulfilling the previous requirements will ensure the production-readiness of the apps and deployments. Later in this book, we will show you in more detail how to achieve each of these requirements through Kubernetes configuration tuning and third-party tool usage.

Kubernetes infrastructure best practices

We have learned about the basics of Kubernetes infrastructure and have got a high-level understanding of the production readiness characteristics of the Kubernetes clusters. Now, you are ready to go through the infrastructure best practices and design principles that will lead you through the way building and operating your production clusters.

The 12 principles of infrastructure design and management

Building a resilient and reliable Kubernetes infrastructure requires more than just getting your cluster up and running with a provisioning tool. Solid infrastructure design is a sequence of architecture decisions and their implementation. Luckily, many organizations and experts put these principles and architectural decisions into real tests.

The following list summarizes the core principles that may lead the decision-maker through the Kubernetes infrastructure design process, and throughout this book, you will learn about these principles in detail, and apply them along the way:

1. **Go managed**: Although managed services could looks pricier than self-hosted ones, it is still preferred over them. In almost every scenario, a managed service is more efficient and reliable than its self-hosted counterpart. We apply this principle to Kubernetes managed services such as **Google Kubernetes Engine (GKE)**, **Azure Kubernetes Service (AKS)**, and **Elastic Kubernetes Service (EKS)**. This goes beyond Kubernetes to every infrastructure service, such as databases, object stores, cache, and many others. Sometimes, the managed service could be less customizable or more expensive than a self-hosted one, but in every other situation, you should always consider first the managed service.

2. **Simplify**: Kubernetes is not a simple platform, either to set up or operate. It solves the complexity of managing internet scale workloads in a world where applications could scale up to serve millions of users, where cloud-native and microservices architectures are the chosen approach for most modern apps.

   For infrastructure creation and operation, we do not need to add another layer of complexity as the infrastructure itself is meant to be a seamless and transparent to the products. Organization's primary concern and focus should remain the product not the infrastructure.

Here comes the simplification principle; it does not mean applying trivial solutions but simplifying the complex ones. This leads us to decisions such as choosing fewer Kubernetes clusters to operate, or avoiding multi-cloud; as long as we do not have a solid use case to justify it.

The simplification principle applies to the infrastructure features and services we deploy to the cluster, as it could be very attractive to add every single service as we think it will make a powerful and feature-rich cluster. On the contrary, this will end up complicating the operations and decreasing platform reliability. Besides, we can apply the same principle to the technology stack and tools we choose, as unifying the tools and technology stack across the teams is proven to be more efficient than having a set of inhomogeneous tools that end up hard to manage, and even if one of these tools is best for a specific use case, simplicity always pays back.

3. **Everything as Code (XaC)**: This is the default practice for modern infrastructure and DevOps teams. It is a recommended approach to use declarative **infrastructure as code (IaC)** and **configuration as code (CaC)** tools and technologies over their imperative counterparts.

4. **Immutable infrastructure**: Immutability is an infrastructure provisioning concept and principle where we replace system components for each deployment instead of updating them in place. We always create immutable components from images or a declarative code, where we can build, test, and validate these immutable systems and get the same predictable results every time. Docker images and AWS EC2 AMI are examples of this concept.

This important principle leads us to achieve one of the desired characteristics of Kubernetes clusters, which is treating clusters as cattle instead of pets.

5. **Automation**: We live in the era of software automation, as we tend to automate everything; it is more efficient and easier to manage and scale, but we need to take automation with Kubernetes to a further level. Kubernetes comes to automate the containers' life cycle, and it also comes with advanced automation concepts, such as operators and GitOps, which are efficient and can literally automate the automations.

6. **Standardization**: Having a set of standards helps to reduce teams' struggle with aligning and working together, eases the scaling of the processes, improves the overall quality, and increases productivity. This becomes essential for companies and teams planning to use Kubernetes in production, as this involves integrating with different infrastructure parts, migrating services from on-premises to the cloud, and way more complexities.

Defining your set of standards covers processes for operations runbooks and playbooks, as well as technology standardization as using Docker, Kubernetes, and standard tools across teams. These tools should have specific characteristics: open source but battle-tested in production, support the other principles, such as Infrastructure as code, immutability, being cloud-agnostic, and being simple to use, and deploy with minimum infrastructure.

7. **Source of truth**: Having a single source of truth is a cornerstone and an enabler to modern infrastructure management and configuration. Source code control systems such as Git are the standard choice to store and version infrastructure code, where having a single and dedicated source code repository for infrastructure is a recommended practice.

8. **Design for availability**: Kubernetes is a key enabler for the high availability of both the infrastructure and the application layers. Having high availability as a design pillar since day 1 is critical for getting the full power of Kubernetes, so at every design level, you should consider high availability, starting from the cloud and **Infrastructure as a Service (IaaS)** level by choosing multi-zone or region architecture, then going through the Kubernetes layer by designing a multi-master cluster, and finally, the application layer by deploying multiple replicas of each service.

9. **Cloud-agnostic**: Being cloud-agnostic means that you can run your workloads on any cloud with a minimal vendor-lock, but take care of getting obsessed with the idea, and make it as a goal on its own. Docker and Kubernetes are the community's answer to creating and managing cloud-agnostic platforms. This principle also goes further to include other technologies and tool selection (think Terraform versus CloudFormation).

10. **Business continuity**: Public cloud with its elasticity solved one problem that always hindered the business continuity for the online services, especially when it made scaling infrastructure almost instant, which enabled small businesses to have the same infrastructure luxury that was previously only for the giant tech companies.

However, coping with the increased scaling needs and making it real-time remains a challenge, and with introducing containers to deploy and run workload apps become easy to deploy and scale in seconds. This put the pressure back on Kubernetes and the underlying infrastructure layers to support such massive real-time scaling capabilities of the containers. You need to make a scaling decision for the future to support business expansion and continuity. Questions such as whether to use a single large cluster versus smaller multiple clusters, how to manage the infrastructure cost, what the nodes' right sizes are, and what the efficient resource utilization strategy is... all of these questions require specific answers and important decisions to be taken!

11. **Plan for failures**: A lot of distributed systems characteristics apply to Kubernetes containerized apps; specifically, fault tolerance, where we expect failures, and we plan for system components failures. When designing a Kubernetes cluster, you have to design it to survive outages and failures by using high-availability principles. But you also have to intentionally plan for failures. You can achieve this through applying chaos engineering ideas, disaster recovery solutions, infrastructure testing, and infrastructure CI/CD.

12. **Operational efficiency**: Companies usually underestimate the effort required to operate containers in production – what to expect on day 2 and beyond, and how to get prepared for outages, cluster upgrades, backups, performance tuning, resource utilization, and cost control. At this phase, companies need to figure out how to deliver changes continuously to an increasing number of production and non-production environments, and without the proper operations practices, this could create bottlenecks and slow down the business growth, and moreover, lead to unreliable systems that cannot fulfill customers' expectations. We witnessed successful Kubernetes production rollouts, but eventually, things fell apart because of operations teams and the weak practices.

These 12 principles are proven to be a common pattern for successful large scale cloud infrastructure rollouts. We will apply these principles through most of this book's chapters, and we will try to highlight each principle when we make a relevant technical decision based on it.

Applications definition and deployment

Probably, a successful and efficient Kubernetes cluster will not save an application's poor design and implementation. Usually, when an application does not follow containerization best practices and a highly available design, it will end up losing the cloud-native benefits provided by the underlying Kubernetes:

- **Containerization**: This is the de facto standard delivery and deployment form of cloud workloads. For production reliability, containerization best practices play a vital role. You will learn about this principle in detail over the upcoming chapters. Bad practices could lead to production instability and catastrophic outages, such as ignoring containers' graceful shutdown and processes termination signals, and improper application retries to connect to dependent services.

- **Applications' high availability**: This is by deploying two or more app replicas and making use of Kubernetes' advanced placement techniques (node selectors, taints, Affinity, and labeling) to deploy the replicas into different nodes and availability zones, as well as defining pod disruption policies.

- **Application monitoring**: This is done by defining readiness and liveness probes with different checks, deploying **Application Performance Monitoring** (**APM**), and using the famous monitoring approaches, such as RED (Rate, Errors, and Duration), and USE (Utilization, Saturation, and Errors).

- **Deployment strategy**: Kubernetes and cloud-native make deployments easier than ever. These frequent deployments bring benefits to the businesses, such as reducing time to market, faster customer feedback on new features, and increasing product quality overall. However, there are downsides to these as well, as frequent deployments could affect product reliability and uptime if you do not plan and manage properly. This is when defining a deployment and rollback strategy (rolling update, recreate, canary, blue/green, and deployment) comes in place as one of the best practices for application deployments.

The consideration of these four areas will ensure smooth application deployment and operations into the Kubernetes cluster, though further detailed technical decisions should be taken under each of these areas, based on your organization's preferences and Kubernetes use case.

Processes, team, and culture

Cloud transformation came with shocking changes to organizations' culture and processes, and the way they manage and operate infrastructure and applications. DevOps is a reflection of this deep impact of adopting the cloud mentality to organizations' culture, as it affected how companies do dev and ops and how their internal teams are organized.

Day after another, the line between dev and ops is getting thinner, and by introducing Kubernetes and the cloud-native approaches DevOps teams are reshaping into a **Site Reliability Engineering (SRE)** model and also hiring dedicated platform teams, as both approaches consider recommended practices for structuring teams to manage and operate Kubernetes.

Cloud-native approach

The **Cloud Native Computing Foundation (CNCF)** defines cloud-native as scalable applications running in modern dynamic environments that use technologies such as containers, microservices, and declarative APIs. Kubernetes is the first CNCF project, and it is the world's most popular container orchestration platform.

Cloud-native computing uses an open source and modern commercial third-party software stack to build, package, and deploy applications as microservices. Containers and container orchestrators such as Kubernetes are key elements in the cloud-native approach, and both are enabling achieving a cloud-native state and satisfying the 12-factor app methodology requirements. These techniques enable resource utilization, distributed system reliability, scaling, and observability, among others.

> **The 12-factor app methodology**
>
> The 12-factor app methodology defines the characteristics and design aspects for developers and DevOps engineers building and operating software-as-a-service. It is tightly coupled with cloud-native architecture and methods. Find out more about it here: `https://12factor.net/`.

The Cloud Native Computing Foundation

In 2014, Google open sourced Kubernetes, which works much like their internal orchestrator, Borg. Google has been using Borg in their data centers to orchestrate containers and workloads for many years. Later, Google partnered with the Linux Foundation to create CNCF, and Borg implementation was rewritten in Go, renamed to Kubernetes. After that, a lot of technology companies joined CNCF, including Google's cloud rivals: Microsoft and Amazon.

CNCF's purpose is building and managing platforms and solutions for modern application development. It supervises and coordinates the open source technologies and projects that support cloud-native software development, but there are also key projects by commercial providers.

Why we should care about cloud-native

CNCF states the following:

> *"Companies are realizing that they need to be a software company, even if they are not in the software business. For example, Airbnb is revolutionizing the hospitality industry and more traditional hotels are struggling to compete. Cloud native allows IT and software to move faster. Adopting cloud native technologies and practices enables companies to create software in-house, allows business people to closely partner with IT people, keep up with competitors and deliver better services to their customers. CNCF technologies enable cloud portability without vendor lock-in."*

CNCF cloud-native recommendations and software stack are a cornerstone to high-quality up-to-date Kubernetes infrastructure, and this is a critical part of the production-grade infrastructure that we intend to deliver and operate. Following CNCF and keeping track of their solutions landscape is one of the best practices that Kubernetes platform creators and users should keep at the top of their checklists.

Cloud-native landscape and ecosystem

The cloud-native landscape is a combination of open source and commercial software projects supervised and supported by CNCF and its members. CNCF classified these projects according to the cloud-native functionalities and the infrastructure layers. Basically, the landscape has four layers:

- **Provisioning**: This layer has projects for infrastructure automation and configuration management, such as Ansible and Terraform, and container registry, such as Quay and Harbor, then security and appliance, such as Falco, TUF, and Aqua, and finally, key management, such as Vault.

- **Runtime**: This layer has projects for container runtime, such as containerd and CRI-O, cloud-native storage, such as Rook and Ceph, and finally, cloud-native networking plugins, such as CNI, Calico, and Cilium.

- **Orchestration and management**: This is where Kubernetes belongs as a schedular and orchestrator, as well as other key projects, such as CoreDNS, Istio, Envoy, gRPC, and KrakenD.

- **App definition and development**: This layer is mainly about applications and their life cycle, where it covers CI/CD tools, such as Jenkins and Spinnaker, builds and app definition, such as Helm and Packer, and finally, distributed databases, streaming, and messaging.

The CNCF ecosystem provides recommendations that cover every aspect of the cloud-native and Kubernetes needs. Whenever applicable, we will make use of these CNCF projects to fulfill cluster requirements.

Cloud-native trail map

The **cloud native trail map** is CNCF's recommended path through the cloud-native landscape. While this roadmap is meant for cloud-native transformations, it still intersects with our Kubernetes path to production, as deploying Kubernetes as the orchestration manager is a major milestone during this trail map.

We have to admit that most Kubernetes users are starting their cloud transformation journeys or are in the middle of it, so understanding this trail map is a cornerstone for planning and implementing a successful Kubernetes rollout.

CNCF recommends the following stages for any cloud-native transformation that is also supported by different projects through the cloud-native landscape:

1. **Containerization**: Containers are the packaging standard for cloud-native applications, and this is the first stage that you should undergo to cloud-migrate your applications. Docker containers prove to be efficient, lightweight, and portable.

2. **Continuous Integration and Continuous Delivery/Deployment (CI/CD)**: CI/CD is the second natural step after containerizing your applications, where you automate building the containers images whenever there are code changes, which eases testing and application delivery to different environments, including development, test, stage, and even further to production.

3. **Orchestration and application definition**: Once you deploy your applications' containers and automate this process, you will face container life cycle management challenges, and you will end up creating a lot of automation scripts to handle containers' restart, scaling, log management, health checks, and scheduling. This is where orchestrators come onto the scene; they provide these management services out of the box, and with orchestrators such as Kubernetes, you get far more container life cycle management, but also an infrastructure layer to manage cloud underlayers and a base for your cloud-native and microservices above it.

4. **Observability and analysis**: Monitoring and logging are integral parts of cloud-native applications; this information and metrics allow you to operate your systems efficiently, gain feasibility, and maintain healthy applications and **service-level objectives (SLOs)**.

5. **Service proxy, discovery, and mesh**: In this stage, your cloud-native apps and services are getting complex and you will look for providing discovery services, DNS, advanced load balancing and routing, A/B testing, canary testing and deployments, rate limiting, and access control.

6. **Networking and policy**: Kubernetes and distributed containers networking models bring complexity to your infrastructure, and this creates an essential need for having a standard yet flexible networking standard, such as CNCF CNI. Therefore, you need to deploy compliant plugins such as Calico, Cilium, or Weave to support network policies, data filtering, and other networking requirements.

7. **Distributed database and storage**: The cloud-native app model is about scalability, and conventional databases could not match the speed of the cloud-native scaling requirements. This is where CNCF distributed databases fill the gap.

8. **Streaming and messaging**: CNCF proposes using gRPC or NATS, which provide higher performance than JSON-REST. gRPC is a high-performance open source RPC framework. NATS is a simple and secure messaging system that can run anywhere, from large servers and cloud instances to Edge gateways and IoT devices.

9. **Container registry and runtime**: A container registry is a centralized place to store and manage the container images. Choosing the right registry with features that include performance, vulnerability analysis, and access control is an essential stage within the cloud-native journey. Runtime is the software layer that is responsible for running your containers. Usually, when you start the containerization stage you will use a Docker runtime, but eventually, you may consider CNCF-supported runtimes, such as CRI-O or containerd.

10. **Software distribution**: **The Update Framework (TUF)** and its Notary implementation are both projects that are sponsored by CNCF, and they provide modern and cloud-native software distribution.

It is wise to treat the preceding cloud-native transformation stages as a recommended path. It is unlikely that companies will follow this roadmap rigidly; however, it is a great basis to kick off your cloud transformation journey.

Summary

Building a production-grade and reliable Kubernetes infrastructure and clusters is more than just provisioning a cluster and deploying applications to it. It is a continuous journey that combines infrastructure and services planning, design, implementation, CI/CD, operations, and maintenance.

Every aspect comes with its own set of technical decisions to make, best practices to follow, and challenges to overcome.

By now, you have a brief understanding of Kubernetes infrastructure basics, production challenges, and readiness features. Finally, we looked at the industry best practices for building and managing successful Kubernetes productions and learned about the cloud-native approach.

In the next chapter, we will learn the practical details of how to design and architect a successful Kubernetes cluster and the related infrastructure, while exploring the technical and architectural decisions, choices, and alternatives that you need to handle when rolling out your production clusters.

Further reading

You can refer to the following book if you are unfamiliar with basic Kubernetes concepts:

Getting Started with Kubernetes – Third Edition: `https://www.packtpub.com/virtualization-and-cloud/getting-started-kubernetes-third-edition`

2
Architecting Production-Grade Kubernetes Infrastructure

In the previous chapter, you learned about the core components of Kubernetes and the basics of its infrastructure, and why putting Kubernetes in production is a challenging journey. We introduced the production-readiness characteristics for the Kubernetes clusters, along with our recommended checklist for the services and configurations that ensure the production-readiness of your clusters.

We also introduced a group of infrastructure design principles that we learned through building production-grade cloud environments. We use them as our guideline through this book whenever we make architectural and design decisions, and we highly recommend that cloud infrastructure teams consider these when it comes to architecting new infrastructure for Kubernetes and cloud platforms in general.

In this chapter, you will learn about the important architectural decisions that you will need to tackle while designing your Kubernetes infrastructure. We will explore the alternatives and the choices that you have for each of these decisions, along with the possible benefits and drawbacks. In addition to that, you will learn about the cloud architecture considerations, such as scaling, availability, security, and cost. We do not intend to make final decisions but provide the guidance because every organization has different needs and use cases. Our role is to explore them, and guide you through the decision-making process. When possible, we will state our preferred choices, which we will follow through this book for the practical exercises.

In this chapter, we will cover the following topics:

- Understanding Kubernetes infrastructure design considerations
- Exploring Kubernetes deployment strategy alternatives
- Designing an Amazon EKS infrastructure

Understanding Kubernetes infrastructure design considerations

When it comes to Kubernetes infrastructure design, there are a few, albeit important, considerations to take into account. Almost every cloud infrastructure architecture shares the same set of considerations; however, we will discuss these considerations from a Kubernetes perspective, and shed some light on them.

Scaling and elasticity

Public cloud infrastructure, such as AWS, Azure, and GCP, introduced scaling and elasticity capabilities at unprecedented levels. Kubernetes and containerization technologies arrived to build upon these capabilities and extend them further.

When you design a Kubernetes cluster infrastructure, you should ensure that your architecture covers the following two areas:

- Scalable Kubernetes infrastructure
- Scalable workloads deployed to the Kubernetes clusters

To achieve the first requirement, there are parts that depend on the underlying infrastructure, either public cloud or on-premises, and other parts that depend on the Kubernetes cluster itself.

The first part is usually solved when you choose to use a managed Kubernetes service such as EKS, AKS, or GKE, as the cluster's control plane and worker nodes will be scalable and supported by other layers of scalable infrastructure.

However, in some use cases, you may need to deploy a self-managed Kubernetes cluster, either on-premises or in the cloud, and in this case, you need to consider how to support scaling and elasticity to enable your Kubernetes clusters to operate at their full capacity.

In all public cloud infrastructure, there is the concept of compute auto scaling groups, and Kubernetes clusters are built on them. However, because of the nature of the workloads running on Kubernetes, scaling needs should be synchronized with the cluster scheduling actions. This is where Kubernetes cluster autoscaler comes to our aid.

Cluster autoscaler (CAS) is a Kubernetes cluster add-on that you optionally deploy to your cluster, and it automatically scales up and down the size of worker nodes based on the set of conditions and configurations that you specify in the CAS. Basically, it triggers cluster upscaling when there is a pod that cannot schedule due to insufficient compute resources, or it triggers cluster downscaling when there are underutilized nodes, and their pods can be rescheduled and placed in other nodes. You should take into consideration the time a cloud provider takes to execute the launch of a new node, as this could be a problem for time-sensitive apps, and in this case, you may consider CAS configuration that enables node over provisioning.

For more information about CAS, refer to the following link: `https://github.com/kubernetes/autoscaler/tree/master/cluster-autoscaler`.

To achieve the second scaling requirement, Kubernetes provides two solutions to achieve autoscaling of the pods:

- **Horizontal Pod Autoscaler (HPA)**: This works similar to cloud autoscaling groups, but at a pod deployment level. Think of the pod as the VM instance. HPA scales the number of pods based on a specific metrics threshold. This can be CPU or memory utilization metrics, or you can define a custom metric. To understand how HPA works, you can continue reading about it here: `https://kubernetes.io/docs/tasks/run-application/horizontal-pod-autoscale/`.

- **Vertical Pod Autoscaler (VPA):** This scales the pod vertically by increasing its CPU and memory limits according to the pod usage metrics. Think of VPA as upscaling/downscaling the VM instance by changing its type in the public cloud. VPA can affect CAS and triggers upscaling events, so you should revise the CAS and VPA configurations to get them aligned and avoid any unpredictable scaling behavior. To understand how VPA works, you can continue reading about it here: `https://github.com/kubernetes/autoscaler/tree/master/vertical-pod-autoscaler`.

We highly recommend using HPA and VPA for your production deployments (it is not essential for non-production environments). We will give examples on how to use both of them in deploying production-grade apps and services in *Chapter 8, Deploying Seamless and Reliable Applications.*

High availability and reliability

Uptime means reliability and is usually the top metric that the infrastructure teams measure and target for enhancement. Uptime drives the **service-level objectives (SLOs)** for services, and the **service level agreements (SLAs)** with customers, and it also indicates how stable and reliable your systems and **Software as a Service (SaaS)** products are. High availability is the key for increasing uptime, and when it comes to Kubernetes clusters' infrastructure, the same rules still apply. This is why designing a highly available cluster and workload is an essential requirement for a production-grade Kubernetes cluster.

You can architect a highly available Kubernetes infrastructure on different levels of availability as follows:

- A cluster in a single public cloud zone (single data center): This is considered the easiest architecture among the others, but it brings the highest risk. We do not recommend this solution.

- A cluster in multiple zones (multiple data centers) but in a single cloud region: This is still easy to implement, it provides a higher level of availability, and it is a common architecture for Kubernetes clusters. However, when your cloud provider has a full region outage, your cluster will be entirely unavailable. Such full region outages rarely happen, but you still need to be prepared for such a scenario.

- Across multi-region clusters, but within the same cloud provider: In this architecture, you usually run multiple federated Kubernetes clusters to serve your production workloads. This is usually the preferred solution for high availability, but it comes at a cost that makes it hard to implement and operate, especially the possible poor network performance, and shared storage for stateful applications. We do not recommend this architecture since, for the majority of SaaS products, it is enough to deploy Kubernetes in a single region and multiple zones. However, if you have a multi-region as a requirement for a reason other than high availability, you may consider multi-region Kubernetes federated clusters as a solution.

- Multiple clusters across multi-cloud deployment: This architecture is still unpopular due to the incompatibility limitations across cloud providers, inter-cluster network complexity, and the higher cost associated with network traffic across providers, along with implementation and operations. However, it is worth mentioning the increase in the number of multi-cloud management solutions that are endeavoring to tackle and solve these challenges, and you may wish to consider a multi-cluster management solution such as Anthos from Google. You can learn more about it here: `https://cloud.google.com/anthos`.

As you may notice, Kubernetes has different architectural flavors when it comes to high availability setup, and I can say that having different choices makes Kubernetes more powerful for different use cases. Although the second choice is the most common one as of now, as it strikes a balance between the ease of implementation and operation, and the high availability level. We are optimistically searching for a time when we can reach the fourth level, where we can easily deploy Kubernetes clusters across cloud providers and gain all the high availability benefits without the burden of tough operations and increased costs.

As for the cluster availability itself, I believe it goes without saying that Kubernetes components should run in a highly available mode, that is, having three or more nodes for a control plane, or preferably letting the cloud manage the control plane for you, as in EKS, AKE, or GKE. As for workers, you have to run one or more autoscaling groups or node groups/pools, and this ensures high availability.

The other area where you need to consider achieving high availability is for the pods and workloads that you will deploy to your cluster. Although this is beyond the scope of this book, it is still worthwhile mentioning that developing new applications and services, or modernizing your existing ones so that they can run in a high availability mode, is the only way to make use of the raft of capabilities provided by the powerful Kubernetes infrastructure underneath it. Otherwise, you will end up with a very powerful cluster but with monolithic apps that can only run as a single instance!

Security and compliance

Kubernetes infrastructure security is rooted at all levels of your cluster, starting from the network layer, going through the OS level, up to cluster services and workloads. Luckily, Kubernetes has strong support for security, encryption, authentication, and authorization. We will learn about security in *Chapter 6, Securing Kubernetes Effectively*, of this book. However, during the design of the cluster infrastructure, you should give attention to important decisions relating to security, such as securing the Kubernetes API server endpoint, as well as the cluster network design, security groups, firewalls, network policies between the control plane components, workers nodes, and the public internet.

You will also need to plan ahead in terms of the infrastructure components or integrations between your cluster and identity management providers. This usually depends on your organization's security policies, which you need to align with your IT and security teams.

Another aspect to consider is the auditing and compliance of your cluster. Most organizations have cloud governance policies and compliance requirements, which you need to be aware of before you proceed with deploying your production on Kubernetes.

If you decide to use a multi-tenant cluster, the security requirements could be more challenging, and setting clear boundaries among the cluster tenants, as well as cluster users from different internal teams, may result in decisions such as deploying a service mesh, hardening cluster network policies, and implementing a tougher **Role-Based Access Control** (**RBAC**) mechanism. All of this will impact your decisions while architecting the infrastructure of your first production cluster.

The Kubernetes community is keen on compliance and quality, and for that there are multiple tools and tests to ensure that your cluster achieves an acceptable level of security and compliance. We will learn about these tools and tests in *Chapter 6, Securing Kubernetes Effectively*.

Cost management and optimization

Cloud cost management is an important factor for all organizations adopting cloud technology, both for those just starting and those who are already in the cloud. Adding Kubernetes to your cloud infrastructure is expected to bring cost savings, as containerization enables you to highly utilize your computer resources on a scale that was not possible with VMs ever before. Some organizations achieved cost savings up to 90% after moving to containers and Kubernetes.

However, without proper cost control, costs can rise again, and you end up with a lot of wasted infrastructure cost with uncontrolled Kubernetes clusters. There are many tools and best practices to consider in relation to cost management, but we mainly want to focus on the actions and the technical decisions that you need to consider during infrastructure design.

We believe that there are two important aspects that require decisions, and these decisions will definitely affect your cluster infrastructure architecture:

- Running a single, but multi-tenant, cluster versus multi clusters (that is, a single cluster per tenant)
- The cluster capacity: whether to run few large worker nodes or a lot of small workers nodes, or a mix of the two

There are no definitive correct decisions, but we will try to explore the choices in the next section, and how we can reach a decision.

These are other considerations to be made regarding cost optimization where an early decision can be made:

- **Using spot/preemptible instances**: This has proven to achieve huge cost savings; however, it comes at a price! There is the threat of losing your workloads at any time, which affects your product uptime and reliability. Options are available for overcoming this, such as using spot instances for non-production workloads, such as development environments or CI/CD pipelines, or any production workloads that can survive a disruption, such as data batch processing.

  We highly recommend using spot instances for worker nodes, and you can run them in their node group/pool and assign to them the types of workloads where you are not concerned with them being disrupted.

- **Kubernetes cost observability**: Most cloud platforms provide cost visibility and analytics for all cloud resources. However, having cost visibility at the deployment/service level of the cluster is essential, and this needs to be planned ahead, so you use isolated workloads, teams, users, environments, and also using namespaces and assign resource quotas to them. By doing that, you will ensure that using a cost reporting tool will provide you with reports relating the usage to the service or cluster operations. This is essential for further decision making regarding cost reductions.

- **Kubernetes cluster management**: When you run a single-tenant cluster, or one cluster per environment for development, you usually end up with tons of clusters sprawled across your account which could lead to increased cloud cost. The solution to this situation is to set up a cluster management solution from day one. This solution could be as simple as a cluster auto scaler script that reduces the worker nodes during periods of inactivity, or it can be a full automation with dashboards and a master cluster to manage the rest of clusters.

In *Chapter 9*, *Monitoring, Logging, and Observability*, and *Chapter 10*, *Operating and Maintaining Efficient Kubernetes Clusters*, we will learn about cost observability and cluster operations.

Manageability and operational efficiency

Usually, when an organization starts building a Kubernetes infrastructure, they invest most of their time, effort, and focus in urgent and critical demands for infrastructure design and deployment, which we usually call Day 0 and Day 1. It is unlikely that an organization will devote its attention to operational and manageability concerns that we will face in the future (Day 2).

This is justified by the lack of experience in Kubernetes, and the types of operational challenges, or by being driven by gaining the benefits of Kubernetes that mainly relate to development, such as increasing a developer's productivity and agility, and automating releases and deployment.

All of this leads to organizations and teams being less prepared for Day 2. In this book, we try to maintain a balance between design, implementation, and operations, and shed some light on the important aspects of the operation and learn how to plan for it from Day 0, especially in relation to reliability, availability, security, and observability.

Operational challenges with Kubernetes

These are the common operational and manageability challenges that most teams face after deploying Kubernetes in production. This is where you need to rethink and consider solutions beforehand in order to handle these challenges properly:

- **Reliability and scaling**: When your infrastructure scales up, you could end up with tens or hundreds of clusters, or clusters with hundreds or thousands of nodes, and tons of configurations for different environment types. This makes it harder to manage the SLAs/SLOs of your applications, as well as the uptime goals, and even diagnosing a cluster issue could be very problematic. Teams need to develop their Kubernetes knowledge and troubleshooting skills.

- **Observability**: No doubt Kubernetes is complex, and this makes monitoring and logging a must-have service once your cluster is serving production, otherwise you will have a very tough time identifying issues and problems. Deploying monitoring and logging tools, in addition to defining the basic observability metrics and thresholds, are what you need to take care of in this regard.

- **Updateability and cluster management**: Updating Kubernetes components, such as the API server, kubelet, `etcd`, `kube-proxy`, Docker images, and configuration for the cluster add-ons, become challenging to manage during the cluster life cycle. This requires the correct tools to be in place from the outset. Automation and IaC tools, such as Terraform, Ansible, and Helm, are commonly used to help in this regard.

- **Disaster recovery**: What happens when you have a partial or complete cluster failure? What is the recovery plan? How do you mitigate this risk and decrease the mean time to recover your clusters and workloads. This requires deployment of the correct tools, and writing the playbooks for backups, recovery, and crisis management.

- **Security and governance**: You need to ensure that security best practices and governance policies are applied and enforced in relation to production clusters and workloads. This becomes challenging due to the complex nature of Kubernetes and its soft isolation techniques, its agility, and the rapid pace it brings to the development and release life cycles.

There are other operational challenges. However, we found that most of these can be mitigated if we stick to the following infrastructure best practices and standards:

- **Infrastructure as Code (IaC)**: This is the default practice for modern infrastructure and DevOps teams. It is also a recommended approach to use declarative IaC tools and technologies over their imperative counterparts.

- **Automation**: We live in the age of software automation, as we tend to automate everything; it is more efficient and easier to manage and scale, but we need to take automation with Kubernetes to another level. Kubernetes comes with the ability to automate the life cycle of containers, and it also comes with advanced automation concepts, such as operators and GitOps, which are efficient and can literally automate automations.

- **Standardization**: Having a set of standards helps to reduce teams' struggles with aligning and working together, eases the scaling of the processes, improves the overall quality, and increases productivity. This becomes essential for companies and teams that are planning to use Kubernetes in production, as this involves integrating with different infrastructure parts, migrating services from on-premises to the cloud, and many further complexities.

  Defining your set of standards covers processes for operation runbooks and playbooks, as well as technology standardization – using Docker, Kubernetes, and standard tools across teams. These tools should have specific characteristics: open source but battle-tested in production, the ability to support the other principles, such as IaC code, immutability, being cloud-agnostic, and being simple to use and deploy with a minimum of infrastructure.

- **Single source of truth**: Having a source of truth is a cornerstone and enabler to modern infrastructure management and configuration. Source code control systems such as Git are becoming the standard choice to store and version infrastructure code, where having a single and dedicated source code repository for infrastructure is the recommended practice to follow.

Managing Kubernetes infrastructure is about management complexity. Hence, having a solid infrastructure design, applying best practices and standards, increasing the team's Kubernetes-specific skills, and expertise will all result in a smooth operational and manageability journey.

Exploring Kubernetes deployment strategy alternatives

Kubernetes and its ecosystem come with vast choices for everything you can do related to deploying, orchestrating, and operating your workloads. This flexibility is a huge advantage, and enables Kubernetes to suit different use cases, from regular applications on-premises and in the cloud to IoT and edge computing. However, choices come with responsibility, and in this chapter, we learn about the technical decisions that you need to evaluate and take regarding your cluster deployment architecture..

One of the important questions to ask and a decision to make is where to deploy your clusters, and how many of them you may need in order to run your containerized workloads? The answer is usually driven by both business and technical factors; elements such as the existing infrastructure, cloud transformation plan, cloud budget, the team size, and business growth target. All of these aspects could affect this, and this is why the owner of the Kubernetes initiative has to collaborate with organization teams and executives to reach a common understanding of the decision drivers, and agree on the right direction for their business.

We are going to explore some of the common Kubernetes deployment architecture alternatives, with their use cases, benefits, and drawbacks:

- **Multi-availability-zones clusters**: This is the mainstream architecture for deploying a **high availability** (**HA**) cluster in a public cloud. Because running clusters in a multi-availability zones is usually supported by all public cloud providers, and, at the same time, it achieves an acceptable level of HA. This drives the majority of new users of Kubernetes to opt for this choice. However, if you have essential requirements to run your workloads in different regions, this option will not be helpful.

- **Multi-region clusters**: Unless you have a requirement to run your clusters in multiple regions, there is little motivation to opt for it. While a public cloud provider to lose an entire region is a rare thing, but if you have the budget to do a proper design and overcome the operational challenges, then you can opt for a multi-region setup. It will definitely provide you with enhanced HA and reliability levels.

- **Hybrid cloud clusters**: A hybrid cloud is common practice for an organization migrating from on-premise to the public cloud and that is going through a transitional period where they have workloads or data split between their old infrastructure and the new cloud infrastructure. Hybrid could also be a permanent setup, where an organization wants to keep part of its infrastructure on-premise either for security reasons (think about sensitive data), or due to the impossibility of migrating to the cloud. Kubernetes is an enabler of the hybrid cloud model, especially with managed cluster management solutions such as Google Anthos. This nevertheless entails higher costs in terms of provision and operation.

- **Multi-cloud clusters**: Unlike hybrid cloud clusters, I find multi-cloud clusters to be an uncommon pattern, as it usually lacks the strong drivers behind it. You can run multiple different systems in multi-cloud clusters for a variety of reasons, but deploying a single system across two or more clouds over Kubernetes is not common, and you should be cautious before moving in this direction. However, I can understand the motivating factors behind some organizations doing this, such as avoiding cloud lock-in with a particular provider, leveraging pricing models with different providers for cost optimization, minimizing latency, or even achieving ultimate reliability for the workloads.

- **On-premises clusters**: If an organization decides not to move to the cloud, Kubernetes still can manage their infrastructure on-premises, and actually, Kubernetes is a reasonable choice to manage the on-prem workload in a modern fashion, however, the solid on-prem managed Kubernetes solutions still very few.

- **Edge clusters**: Kubernetes is gaining traction in edge computing and the IoT world. It provides an abstraction to the underlying hardware, it is ideal for distributed computing needs, and the massive Kubernetes ecosystem helps to come out with multiple open source and third-party projects that fit edge computing nature, such as KubeEdge and K3s.

- **Local clusters**: You can run Kubernetes on your local machine using tools such as Minikube or Kind (Kubernetes in Docker). The purpose of using a local cluster is for trials, learning, and for use by developers.

We have discussed the various clusters deployments architectures and models available and their use cases. In the next section, we will learn work on designing the Kubernetes infrastructure that we will use in this book, and the technical decisions around it..

Designing an Amazon EKS infrastructure

In this chapter, we have discussed and explored various aspects of Kubernetes clusters design, and the different architectural considerations that you need to take into account. Now, we need to put things together for the design that we will follow during this book. The decisions that we will make here do not mean that they are the only right ones, but this is the preferred design that we will follow in terms of having minimally acceptable production clusters for this book's practical exercise. You can definitely use the same design, but with modifications, such as cluster sizing.

In the following sections, we will explore our choices regarding the cloud provider, provisioning and configuration tools, and the overall infrastructure architecture, and in the chapters to follow, we will build upon these choices and use them to provision production-like clusters as well as deploy the configuration and services above the cluster.

Choosing the infrastructure provider

As we learned in the previous sections, there are different ways in which to deploy Kubernetes. You can deploy it locally, on-premises, or in a public cloud, private cloud, hybrid, multi-cloud, or an edge location. Each of these infrastructure type has use cases, benefits, and drawbacks. However, the most common one is the public cloud, followed by the hybrid model. The remaining choices are still limited to specific use cases.

In a single book like ours, we cannot discuss each of these infrastructure platforms, so we decided to go with the common choice for deploying Kubernetes, by using one of the public clouds (AWS, Azure, or GCP). You still can use another cloud provider, a private cloud, or even an on-premises setup, and most of the concepts and best practices discussed in this book are still applicable.

When it comes to choosing one of the public clouds, we do not advocate one over the others, and we definitely recommend using the cloud provider that you already use for your existing infrastructure, but if you are just embarking on your cloud journey, we advise you to perform a deeper benchmarking analysis between the public clouds to see which one is better for your business.

In the practical exercises in this book, we will use AWS and the **Elastic Kubernetes Service (EKS)**. We explained in the previous chapter regarding the infrastructure design principle that we always prefer a managed service over its self-managed counterpart, and this applies here when it comes to choosing between EKS and building our self-managed clusters over AWS.

Choosing the cluster and node size

When you plan for your cluster, you need to decide both the cluster and node sizes. This decision should be based on the estimated utilization of your workloads, which you may know beforehand based on your old infrastructure, or it can be calculated approximately and then adjusted after going live in production. In either case, you will need to decide on the initial cluster and node sizes, and then keep adjusting them until you reach the correct utilization level to achieve a balance between cost and reliability. You can target a utilization level of between 70 and 80% unless you have a solid justification for using a different level.

These are the common cluster and node size choices that you can consider either individually or in a combination:

- **Few large clusters**: In this setup, you deploy a few large clusters. These can be production and non-production clusters. A cluster could be large in terms of node size, node numbers, or both. Large clusters are usually easier to manage because they are few in number. They are cost efficient because you achieve higher utilization per node and cluster (assuming you are running the correct amount of workloads), and this improved utilization comes from saving the resources required for system management. On the downside, large clusters lack hard isolation for multi-tenants, as you only use namespaces for soft isolation between tenants. They also introduce a single point of failure to your production (especially when you run a single cluster). There is another limitation, as any Kubernetes cluster has an upper limit of 5,000 nodes that it can manage and when you have a single cluster, you can hit this upper limit if you are running a large number of pods.

- **Many small clusters**: In this setup, you deploy a lot of small clusters. These could be small in terms of node size, node numbers, or both. Small clusters are good when it comes to security as they provide hard isolation between resources and tenants and also provide strong access control for organizations with multiple teams and departments. They also reduce the blast radius of failures and avoid having a single point of failure. On the downside, small clusters come with an operational overhead, as you need to manage a fleet of clusters. They are also inefficient in terms of resource usage, as you cannot achieve the utilization levels that you can achieve with large clusters, in addition to increasing costs, as they require more control plane resources to manage a fleet of small clusters that manage the same total number of worker nodes in a large cluster.

- **Large nodes**: This is about the size of the nodes in a cluster. When you deploy large nodes in your cluster, you will have better and higher utilization of the node (assuming you deploy workloads that utilize 70-80% of the node). This is because a large node can handle application spikes, and it can handle applications with high CPU/memory requirements. In addition to that, a well utilized large node usually entails cost savings as it reduces the overall cluster resources required for system management and you can purchase such nodes at discounted prices from your cloud provider. On the downside, large nodes can introduce a high blast radius of failures, thereby affecting the reliability of both the cluster and apps. Also, adding a new large node to the cluster during an upscaling event will add a lot of cost that you may not need, so if your cluster is hit by variable scaling events over a short period, large nodes will be the wrong choice. Added to this is the fact that Kubernetes has an upper limit in terms of the number of pods that can run on a single node regardless of its type and size, and for a large node, this limitation could lead to underutilization.

- **Small nodes**: This is about the size of the nodes per single cluster. When you deploy small nodes in your cluster, you can reduce the blast radius during failures, and also reduce costs during upscaling events. On the downside, small nodes are underutilized, they cannot handle applications with high resource requirements, and the total amount of system resources required to manage these nodes (kubelet, `etcd`, `kube-proxy`, and so on) is higher than managing the same compute power for a larger node, in addition to which small nodes have a lower limit for pods per node.

- **Centralized versus decentralized clusters:** Organizations usually use one of these approaches in managing their Kubernetes clusters.

In a decentralized approach, the teams or individuals within an organization are allowed to create and manage their own Kubernetes clusters. This approach provides flexibility for the teams to get the best out of their clusters, and customize them to fit their use cases; on the other hand, this increases the operational overhead, cloud cost, and makes it difficult to enforce standardization, security, best practices, and tools across the clusters. This approach is more appropriate for organizations that are highly decentralized, or when they are going through cloud transformation, product life cycle transitional periods, or exploring and innovating new technologies and solutions.

In a centralized approach, the teams or individuals share a single cluster or small group of identical clusters that use a similar set of standards, configurations, and services. This approach overcomes and decreases the drawbacks in the decentralized model; however, it can be inflexible, slow down the cloud transformations, and decreases teams' agility. This approach is more suitable for organizations working towards maturity, platform stability, increasing cloud cost reduction, enforcing and promoting standards and best practices, and focusing on products rather than the underlaying platform.

Some organizations can run a hybrid models from the aforementioned alternatives, such as having large, medium, and small nodes to get the best of each type according to their apps needs. However, we recommend that you run experiments to decide which model suits your workload's performance, and meets your cloud cost reduction goal.

Choosing tools for cluster deployment and management

In the early days of Kubernetes, we used to deploy it from scratch, which was commonly called **Kubernetes the Hard Way**. Fast forward and the Kubernetes community got bigger and a lot of tools emerged to automate the deployment. These tools range from simple automation to complete one-click deployment.

In the context of this book, we are not going to explain each of these tools in the market (there are a lot), nor to compare and benchmark them. However, we will propose our choices with a brief reasoning behind the choices.

Infrastructure provisioning

When you deploy Kubernetes for the first time, most likely you will use a command-line tool with a single command to provision the cluster, or you may use a cloud provider web console to do that. In both ways, this approach is suitable for experimental and learning purposes, but when it comes to real implementation across production and development environments a provisioning tool becomes a must.

The majority of organizations that consider deploying Kubernetes already have an existing cloud infrastructure or they are going through a cloud migration process. This makes Kubernetes not the only piece of the cloud infrastructure that they will use. This is why we prefer a provisioning tool that achieves the following:

- It can be used to provision Kubernetes as well as other pieces of infrastructure (databases, file stores, API gateways, serverless, monitoring, logging, and so on).
- It fulfills and empowers the IaC principles.

- It is a cloud-agnostic tool.

- It has been battle-tested in production by other companies and teams.

- It has community support and active development.

We can find these characteristics in Terraform, and this is why we chose to use it in the production clusters that we managed, as well as in this practical exercise in this book. We highly recommend Terraform for you as well, but if you prefer another portioning tool, you can skip this chapter and then continue reading this book and apply the same concepts and best practices.

Configuration management

Kubernetes configuration is declarative by nature, so, after deploying a cluster, we need to manage its configuration. The add-ons deployed provide services for various areas of functionality, including networking, security, monitoring, and logging. This is why a solid and versatile configuration management tool is required in your toolset.

The following are solid choices:

- Regular configuration management tools, such as Ansible, Chef, and Puppet

- Kubernetes-specific tools, such as Helm and Kustomize

- Terraform

Our preferred order of suitable tools is as follows:

1. Ansible

2. Helm

3. Terraform

We can debate this order, and we believe that any of these tools can fulfill the configuration management needs for Kubernetes clusters. However, we prefer to use Ansible for its versatility and flexibility as it can be used for Kubernetes and also for other configuration management needs for your environment, which makes it preferable over Helm. On the other hand, Ansible is preferred over Terraform because it is a provisioning tool at heart, and while it can handle configuration management, it is not the best tool for that.

In the hands-on exercises in this book, we decided to use Ansible with Kubernetes module and Jinja2 templates.

Deciding the cluster architecture

Each organization has its own way of managing cloud accounts. However, we recommend having at least two AWS accounts, one for production and another for non-production. The production Kubernetes cluster resides in the production account, and the non-production Kubernetes cluster resides in the non-production account. This structure is preferred for security, reliability, and operational efficiency.

Based on the technical decisions and choices that we made in the previous sections, we propose the following AWS architecture for the Kubernetes clusters that we will use in this book, which you can also use to deploy your own production and non-production clusters:

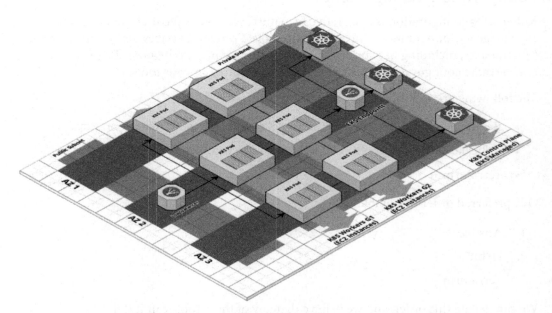

Figure 2.1 – Cluster architecture diagram

In the previous architecture diagram, we decided to do the following:

- Create a separate VPC for the cluster network; we chose the **Classless Inter-Domain Routing** (**CIDR**) range, which has sufficient IPv4 addressing capacity for future scaling. Each Kubernetes node, pod, and service will have its own IP address, and we should keep in mind that the number of services will increase.

- Create public and private subnets. The publicly accessible resources, such as load balancers and bastions, are placed in the public subnets, and the privately accessible resources, such as Kubernetes nodes, databases, and caches, are placed in the private subnets.

- For high availability, we create the resources in three different availability zones. We placed one private and one public subnet in each availability zone.

- For scaling, we run multiple EKS node groups.

We will discuss the details of these design specs in the next chapters, in addition to the remainder of the technical aspects of the cluster's architecture.

Summary

Provisioning a Kubernetes cluster can be a task that takes 5 minutes with modern tools and managed cloud services; however, thus this is far from a production-grade Kubernetes infrastructure and it is only sufficient for education and trials. Building a production-grade Kubernetes cluster requires hard work in designing and architecting the underlying infrastructure, the cluster, and the core services running above it.

By now, you have learned about the different aspects and challenges you have to consider while designing, building, and operating your Kubernetes clusters. We explored the different architecture alternatives to deploy Kubernetes clusters, and the important technical decisions associated with this process. Then, we discussed the proposed cluster design, which we will use during the book for the practical exercises, and we highlighted our selection of infrastructure platform, tools, and architecture.

In the next chapter, we will see how to put everything together and use the design concepts we discussed in this chapter to write IaC and follow industry best practices with Terraform to provision our first Kubernetes cluster.

Further reading

For more information on the topics covered in this chapter, please refer to the following links:

- *Mastering Kubernetes – Third Edition*: https://www.packtpub.com/product/mastering-kubernetes-third-edition/9781839211256

- *Kubernetes on AWS*: https://www.packtpub.com/product/kubernetes-on-aws/9781788390071

3
Provisioning Kubernetes Clusters Using AWS and Terraform

In the previous chapter, we learned about Kubernetes clusters and infrastructure design and how to create a deployment architecture to fulfill best practices and standards. There are multiple alternatives when it comes to designing and building your Kubernetes platform. Choosing the solution that works for your use case and satisfies goals in terms of production readiness is not an easy task. There are still challenges and limitations for Kubernetes, the underlying technologies, and the surrounding ecosystem.

In this chapter, we will go through the detailed implementation of the infrastructure design. Basically, we will learn how to create the Kubernetes infrastructure declaratively with Terraform. While provisioning the infrastructure, we will learn about implementation best practices, such as the encapsulation of infrastructure components into reusable modules, separating Kubernetes clusters per environment without adding an operational overhead and complexity. In addition, you will practice rolling out your first Kubernetes cluster and group of clusters with simple Terraform commands.

In this chapter, we will cover the following topics:

- Implementation principles and best practices
- Cluster deployment and rollout strategy
- Preparing Terraform
- Creating the network infrastructure
- Creating the cluster infrastructure
- Cleaning up and destroying infrastructure resources

Technical requirements

We will need the Terraform tool installed for this chapter as a prerequisite.

In addition to this tool, you will need to have an AWS account and user credentials ready to use. Please ensure the authentication of the AWS CLI with your AWS credentials. You can refer to the AWS documentation for further instructions at `https://docs.aws.amazon.com/cli/latest/userguide/cli-chap-configure.html`.

The code for this chapter is located at `https://github.com/PacktPublishing/Kubernetes-in-Production-Best-Practices/tree/master/Chapter03`.

Check out the following link to see the Code in Action video:

`https://bit.ly/390coyq`

Installing Terraform

Terraform binary is a command-line utility that is used to develop **Infrastructure as Code** (**IaC**), plan, and execute it to create resources, and manage infrastructure providers such as AWS, Azure, GCP, Fastly, OKTA, and more.

You can follow the instructions in the official documentation to download the latest version of Terraform at `https://www.terraform.io/downloads.html`.

After installing Terraform, you are ready to implement the hands-on exercises in the coming sections.

Implementation principles and best practices

In *Chapter 1, Introduction to Kubernetes Infrastructure and Production-Readiness*, you learned about the 12 infrastructure design principles that we will follow during the book. I would like to start this chapter by highlighting the principles that drove us to this implementation of the cluster infrastructure. The following are the three principles that influenced the implementation decisions in this chapter:

1. **Infrastructure as code**: In this chapter, you will write every piece of infrastructure code declaratively. You will achieve this by using Terraform.

2. **Go managed**: There are two fundamental ways in which to create a Kubernetes cluster – either to build and operate Kubernetes control plane and workers on your own (on-prem or on cloud), or to use one of the *managed* Kubernetes services in the cloud, such as **Google Kubernetes Engine (GKE)**, **Azure Kubernetes Service (AKS)**, and AWS **Elastic Kubernetes Service (EKS)**. In this book, I will use EKS as this fulfills the *managed services* principle.

3. **Standardization**: We applied this principle when we selected Terraform as our provisioning and IaC tool. Terraform is not the easiest way to bootstrap a Kubernetes cluster, and there are other tools that could be faster to use and easier to learn. However, we needed to standardize our infrastructure toolset around as few tools as possible. Therefore, Terraform makes sense because in most use cases, your production environment is not Kubernetes on its own. There are databases, caching services, content delivery, load balancers, and so on. These types of infrastructure components are easier to create and manage by Terraform.

Cluster deployment and rollout strategy

In the previous chapter, we explored different infrastructure design alternatives, limitations, and corner cases. We made the architecture decisions that fulfill the infrastructure design principles for the production-grade Kubernetes clusters. And finally, we came up with a full deployment architecture for our Kubernetes infrastructure, which we will build and use over this book. Certainly, while we proceed from one chapter to the next, we will keep enhancing our infrastructure design and implementation, adding more features, and making it better.

In terms of implementation, we should address how we will roll out the clusters and deploy them. Specifically, we are looking for extendibility, simplicity, and operational efficiency. We will follow these principles during the implementation in the next sections:

1. **Developing generic infrastructure modules**: By encapsulating every infrastructure resource in a reusable code module, this will enable us to automate cluster provisioning with minimum to zero code changes. It also promotes code reusability practices essential for simplifying the IaC and increases operational efficiency.

2. **Supporting single and multiple clusters**: In real life, Kubernetes deployment teams require multiple clusters to serve the whole company or a specific product. In this chapter, we will follow a strategy that will enable us to create a group of clusters with the same infrastructure code and configuration. Also, we will create multiple groups of clusters with different configurations. This will help us to serve and automate the provisioning and operation of multiple production and non-production clusters. This implementation is scalable as we can provision many clusters (up to the limit of the underlying IaaS provider) without the need to scale your infrastructure teams.

3. **Separating production and non-production environments with minimal changes**: One of the recommended practices is to have two separate AWS accounts for production and non-production environments, and our implementation also supports this model with minimum code changes and administration work.

4. **Automating infrastructure deployment**: Every single piece of infrastructure is managed by Terraform, and with a limited number of commands, we can provision the entire Kubernetes cluster. We can build automated pipelines for infrastructure deployment and testing with traditional CI/CD such as Jenkins.

In fact, cluster deployment is not a one-time task. It is a continuous process that affects the cluster's quality, stability, operations, and, moreover, the products and services on top of it. So, we are keen to establish a solid infrastructure deployment strategy, which we will follow during implementation in this chapter and also keep improving throughout the book.

Preparing Terraform

Before creating the Terraform configuration and code for the Kubernetes cluster, you need to create a new source code repository for the infrastructure and then create the Terraform directory structure. In addition to that, you will learn how to configure and use Terraform's shared state, which is an essential best practice for managing IaC in production environments.

Terraform directory structure

The Terraform directory is where all the Terraform source code lives in your source code repository. I recommend creating a separate source code repository. This repository should contain all the infrastructure code and configuration. The following is the directory structure of the Terraform source code that we will develop in the forthcoming sections:

```
└── packt-infra-repo
    └── terraform
        ├── modules
        │   ├── cluster
        │   ├── eks-cp
        │   ├── eks-vpc
        │   └── eks-workers
        ├── packtclusters
        ├── packtclusters-vpc
        └── shared-state
```

Figure 3.1 – Terraform directory structure

Persisting the Terraform state

Terraform stores the state of the infrastructure resources under its management to be able to map it to the existing resources in the real world. By default, the state is stored to local files. However, this is not recommended for production-scale infrastructure where preserving consistent state and also sharing it among distributed team members are essential.

As a recommended Terraform best practice, you should configure Terraform to keep the state remote and locked:

- **Remote**: As you already use AWS as an infrastructure provider, you can utilize an S3 bucket to remotely store Terraform state files.

- **Locked**: You can achieve Terraform state lock by using a DynamoDB table. Then, the Terraform state will get locked for the current user until this user finishes up, at which point other users can acquire the lock.

Creating Terraform state configuration

Apply the following steps to create the Terraform directory structure and the directory for the shared state configuration:

1. Create a root directory named `terraform`. This is the root directory for all Terraform source code.

2. Create a subdirectory named `shared-state`. This is the directory that will contain Terraform source code to provision both the S3 bucket and the DynamoDB table. Both of them are used to store the shared state.

In the following steps, you will create the shared state Terraform code under the `shared-state` directory with the following structure:

```
.
├── config.tf
├── terraform.tfvars
├── tf-state-dynamodb.tf
├── tf-state-s3.tf
└── variables.tf
```

Figure 3.2 – Shared state directory structure

> **Important note**
> You can find the complete source code of the shared state Terraform configuration at `https://github.com/PacktPublishing/Kubernetes-in-Production-Best-Practices/tree/master/Chapter03/terraform/shared-state`.

Now, let's create the Terraform files under the `shared-state` directory:

1. Terraform can create and manage infrastructure resources from both cloud and on-prem, and it can achieve this by communicating with the external infrastructure using a provider that is a kind of software plugin that translates Terraform commands into the APIs that the infrastructure provider can understand and execute.

2. In the `config.tf` file, you define the provider's configuration that you will use in this chapter. For each provider, you need to define its name and the version you intend to use. To learn more about defining a "required provider version," visit `https://www.terraform.io/docs/configuration/terraform.html#specifying-required-provider-versions`

    It is important to define the version explicitly, especially when Terraform is used by multiple users or automation tools. This is to avoid the upgrades to newer versions that could break the Terraform state:

    ```
    terraform {
      required_version = "~> 0.14.5"
    }
    ```

This code block defines the AWS provider configuration. You only need to specify both the AWS region and the provider's version:

```
provider "aws" {
  region = var.aws_region
  version = "~> 3.27.0"
}
```

3. In the `terraform.tfvars` file, you define the environment variables that Terraform needs to use during provisioning of the infrastructure resources. Using Terraform `tfvars` files is a good practice to pass environment variables to Terraform. This enables you to keep all of the configuration, including the environment variables, versioned in your source control as your source of truth:

```
aws_region           = "us-east-1"
clusters_name_prefix = "packtclusters"
```

We use `us-east-1` as the default AWS region, but you can use any other region as long as you maintain it for the other exercises.

The second environment variable is the *clusters name prefix*, which you will use for your clusters to identify them as a group of clusters. This name prefix could represent your company's name or the product name. However, you are free to use any appropriate naming convention.

4. In the `variables.tf` file, you define the input variables that Terraform code will use. There are two input variables that you will need for the exercises in this chapter. The first is the AWS region, and the second is the clusters name prefix. Both of them will get their values from the previous `terraform.tfvars` file:

```
variable "aws_region" {
  type = string
}
variable "clusters_name_prefix" {
  type = string
}
```

5. In the `tf-state-s3.tf` file, you define two S3 bucket resources. The first bucket stores the state for the VPC and network resources, while the second bucket stores the state for the Kubernetes cluster resources, such as EKS and workers groups.

The following code snippet uses the Terraform resource called `aws_s3_bucket`, which is a built-in resource in the Terraform AWS provider that can be used to create AWS S3 buckets and set its configuration parameters.

We will use this S3 bucket to persist the Terraform state. And, as you will notice in the following code, this S3 bucket has private access to keep it secure from the public. It also has deletion prevention enabled to protect it from unplanned deletion:

```
resource "aws_s3_bucket" "clusters_tf_state_s3_bucket" {
  bucket = "${var.clusters_name_prefix}-terraform-state"
  acl    = "private"
  versioning {
    enabled = true
  }
  lifecycle {
    prevent_destroy = true
  }
  tags = {
    Name        = "${var.clusters_name_prefix} S3 Remote
Terraform State Store"
    ManagedBy = "terraform"
  }
}
```

The second part of the code is similar to the previous one, but it is used to create the S3 bucket for the networking infrastructure or the **virtual private cloud** (**VPC**) resources state:

```
resource "aws_s3_bucket" "clusters_vpc_tf_state_s3_
bucket" {
  bucket = "${var.clusters_name_prefix}-vpc-terraform-
state"
  acl    = "private"
  versioning {
    enabled = true
  }
  lifecycle {
    prevent_destroy = true
  }
  tags = {
```

```
    Name        = "${var.clusters_name_prefix} VPC S3
Remote Terraform State Store"
    ManagedBy = "terraform"
  }
}
```

Splitting the infrastructure state into two files, as we did in the previous code, is debatable. However, we tend to use a balanced approach as we will not use a separate state for a resource unless it has an independent life cycle from the Kubernetes cluster. This separation facilitates change management of the resources and decouples the critical resources from one another.

6. In the tf-state-dynamodb.tf file, you create two DynamoDB tables, the first for VPC resource state locking, and the second for Kubernetes cluster resources.

The following code snippet uses the Terraform resource called aws_dynamodb_table, which is a built-in resource in the Terraform AWS provider that is used to create an AWS DynamoDB table and set its configuration parameters.

This code creates a DynamoDB table to hold the lock for the shared Terraform state for the Kubernetes cluster resources. This lock will protect parallel runs against the same state file or the same resources, and this prevents users from applying changes to infrastructure at the same time. This could be very dangerous, right?

```
resource "aws_dynamodb_table" "clusters_dynamodb_tf_
state_lock" {
  name          = "${var.clusters_name_prefix}-
terraform-state-lock-dynamodb"
  hash_key      = "LockID"
  read_capacity  = 20
  write_capacity = 20
  attribute {
    name = "LockID"
    type = "S"
  }
}
```

The second part of the `tf-state-dynamodb.tf` file creates a DynamoDB table to hold the locks for the shared Terraform state for the VPC resources:

```
resource "aws_dynamodb_table" "clusters_vpc_dynamodb_tf_
state_lock" {
  name             = "${var.clusters_name_prefix}-vpc-
terraform-state-lock-dynamodb"
  hash_key         = "LockID"
  read_capacity = 20
  write_capacity = 20
  attribute {
    name = "LockID"
    type = "S"
  }
}
```

When you apply the previous Terraform code file, it will create two DynamoDB tables. In the coming sections, we will learn how to configure terraform to use them. Then, Terraform will be able to create locks for its shared state files.

Provisioning the Terraform state

After creating the previous Terraform code files for the shared state resources. You have to perform the following instructions to provision the resources in your AWS account:

1. Initialize the Terraform state:

```
$ cd Chapter03/terraform/shared-state
$ terraform init
Initializing modules...
Initializing the backend...
Initializing provider plugins...
- Checking for available provider plugins...
- Downloading plugin for provider "aws" (hashicorp/aws)
3.27.0...
Terraform has been successfully initialized!
You may now begin working with Terraform. Try running
"terraform plan" to see
any changes that are required for your infrastructure.
All Terraform commands
should now work.
```

> If you ever set or change modules or backend configuration for Terraform,
>
> rerun this command to reinitialize your working directory. If you forget, other
>
> commands will detect it and remind you to do so if necessary.

2. Run the `terraform plan` command to validate the planned changes before applying them:

```
$ terraform plan
```

3. You will get the following output after the `terraform plan` command completes successfully. There are four resources to add – two S3 buckets and two DynamoDB tables:

```
Plan: 4 to add, 0 to change, 0 to destroy.

------------------------------------------------------------------

Note: You didn't specify an "-out" parameter to save this plan, so Terraform
can't guarantee that exactly these actions will be performed if
"terraform apply" is subsequently run.
```

Figure 3.3 – Terraform plan command output

4. Execute the `terraform apply` command. Enter `yes` when you get a prompt to approve execution:

```
$ terraform apply
```

5. You will get the following output after the `terraform apply` command completes successfully. By then, Terraform has successfully created four AWS resources:

```
Plan: 4 to add, 0 to change, 0 to destroy.

Do you want to perform these actions?
  Terraform will perform the actions described above.
  Only 'yes' will be accepted to approve.

  Enter a value: yes

aws_dynamodb_table.clusters_vpc_dynamodb_tf_state_lock: Creating...
aws_dynamodb_table.clusters_dynamodb_tf_state_lock: Creating...
aws_s3_bucket.clusters_tf_state_s3_bucket: Creating...
aws_s3_bucket.clusters_vpc_tf_state_s3_bucket: Creating...
aws_dynamodb_table.clusters_dynamodb_tf_state_lock: Creation complete after 6s [id=packtclusters-terraform-state-lock-dynamodb]
aws_s3_bucket.clusters_vpc_tf_state_s3_bucket: Creation complete after 7s [id=packtclusters-vpc-terraform-state]
aws_s3_bucket.clusters_tf_state_s3_bucket: Creation complete after 7s [id=packtclusters-terraform-state]
aws_dynamodb_table.clusters_vpc_dynamodb_tf_state_lock: Creation complete after 10s [id=packtclusters-vpc-terraform-state-lock-dynamodb]

Apply complete! Resources: 4 added, 0 changed, 0 destroyed.
```

Figure 3.4 – Terraform apply command output

Now you have completed provisioning of the AWS resources to persist and manage the Terraform shared state. In the next section, you will learn how to provision the VPC and the other network resources to run your first Kubernetes cluster.

Utilizing Terraform workspaces

In the previous section, you learned that Terraform configuration has a backend that defines how operations are executed and where the infrastructure state is persisted, such as in S3 buckets. Terraform uses workspaces to organize and isolate multiple states under a single backend.

This concept becomes useful when the user wants to run multiple instances of the same infrastructure without creating multiple backends and state files. Let's assume that you want to use Terraform to provision a Kubernetes cluster, ClusterA, and you want to use the same configuration to provision a second cluster, ClusterB. In this case, workspaces provide an out-of-the-box and scalable solution, as you will be able to use a single backend for all of your clusters (N clusters), but you provision each cluster in its workspace with its own state file.

If you have a Terraform configuration with a backend named `k8s_s3_backend`, and you want to provision N Kubernetes clusters using the same Terraform base code, then you can do the following:

```
$ terraform workspace new cluster1
Created and switched to workspace "cluster1"!

You're now on a new, empty workspace. Workspaces isolate their state,
so if you run "terraform plan" Terraform will not see any existing state
for this configuration.

$ terraform apply
<apply outputs>
```

Then, repeat the same process for every N cluster:

```
$ terraform workspace new clusterN
Created and switched to workspace "clusterN"!

You're now on a new, empty workspace. Workspaces isolate their state,
```

```
so if you run "terraform plan" Terraform will not see any
existing state
for this configuration.


$ terraform apply
<apply outputs>
```

Creating the network infrastructure

In *Chapter 2, Architecting Production-Grade Kubernetes Infrastructure,* you learned in detail about the infrastructure architecture design recommendations and the technical decisions that you should take in relation to the production readiness state for your Kubernetes clusters. In this section, you will use Terraform to provision the network layer of your Kubernetes production infrastructure.

These are the AWS network resources that you will provision with the Terraform code in this section:

- AWS VPC
- Private subnets
- Public subnets
- Route tables
- Internet and NAT gateways

Encapsulating AWS resources into reusable code modules is a recommended IaC practice. In the next subsection, you will create a VPC Terraform module that includes the previous AWS resources. You can then reuse this module with no code changes to provision VPCs for as many Kubernetes clusters as you need.

Developing the VPC Terraform module

Under the `terraform` root directory, create a directory and name it `modules`. Then, create a subdirectory and name it `eks-vpc`. This subdirectory will contain the following Terraform code files:

- `variables.tf`
- `main.tf`
- `outputs.tf`

Input variables

These are the input variables that are accepted by this module. The module's user should provide the values for each of these variables:

- **VPC CIDR block**: The value of the VPC CIDR, such as 10.40.0.0/17.

- **Private subnet prefixes**: The values of private subnet prefixes. This could be 1 or another prefix such as 10.40.64.0/20.

- **Public subnet prefixes**: The values of public subnet prefixes. This could be 1 or another prefix such as 10.40.0.0/20.

- **Cluster name prefix**: The value of the cluster name prefix that is used in naming the VPC resources.

- **Common tags**: Any AWS tags that you want to assign to the VPC resources to help identify and classify them later.

The variables.tf file is defined as follows:

```
variable "eks_vpc_block" {
  type = string
}
variable "eks_private_subnets_prefix_list" {
  type = list(string)
}
variable "eks_public_subnets_prefix_list" {
  type = list(string)
}
variable "clusters_name_prefix" {
  type = string
}
variable "common_tags" {
  type = map(string)
}
```

The previous code snippet defines five Terraform variable blocks and all of the type strings. In the *Creating the cluster VPC* section, you will use this VPC module and learn how to pass the values for each of these variables.

Module main resources

The `main.tf` file defines the network resources that are required to create Kubernetes AWS network components, including the public and private subnets, internet and NAT gateways, and routing tables.

The following code snippet uses the Terraform resource called `aws_vpc`, which is a built-in resource in the Terraform AWS provider that can be used to create AWS VPC and set its configuration parameters.

In the following code block, you define the VPC resource, and a data resource that is used to retrieve the value of the AWS availability zones that you use in the `main.tf` file:

```
resource "aws_vpc" "eks_vpc" {
  cidr_block            = var.eks_vpc_block
  enable_dns_hostnames = true
  tags = merge(
    var.common_tags,
    {
      Name = "${var.clusters_name_prefix}-vpc"
    },
  )
  lifecycle {
    ignore_changes = [
      tags
    ]
  }
}
data "aws_availability_zones" "availability_zones" {
}
```

The following code snippet uses the Terraform resource called `aws_subnet`, which is a built-in resource in the Terraform AWS provider that can be used to create AWS subnets and set their configuration parameters.

This code uses the Terraform built-in `count` construct to create one or more subnets according to the number of private subnet prefixes:

```
resource "aws_subnet" "eks_private_subnets" {
  count                = length(var.eks_private_subnets_prefix_
list)
```

```
  cidr_block              = element(var.eks_private_subnets_prefix_
list, count.index)
  vpc_id                  = aws_vpc.eks_vpc.id
  availability_zone = data.aws_availability_zones.availability_
zones.names[count.index]
  tags = merge(
    var.common_tags,
    {
      Name = "eks-private-${var.clusters_name_prefix}-${data.
aws_availability_zones.availability_zones.names[count.index]}"
    },
  )
  lifecycle {
    ignore_changes = [
      tags
    ]
  }
}
```

In the remaining part of the main.tf file, you define an aws_subnet resource, which
is similar to the private subnet resource, but designed for public subnets. Also, you create
complementary VPC network resources that handle the routing, connect the subnets
together and with the internet, such as NAT and internet gateways, routing tables,
and NAT IPs. You can find the complete source code at https://github.com/
PacktPublishing/Kubernetes-in-Production-Best-Practices/blob/
master/Chapter03/terraform/modules/eks-vpc/main.tf.

Output values

The outputs.tf file defines the output values from the VPC module. Terraform will
need these values to use them as inputs to the Kubernetes cluster module when you
provision it. There are four outputs from the VPC module: the VPC ID; the private subnet
IDs; the public subnet IDs; and the NAT IPs.

The outputs.tf file is defined as follows:

```
output "eks_cluster_vpc_id" {
  value = aws_vpc.eks_vpc.id
}
output "eks_private_subnet_ids" {
```

```
    value = aws_subnet.eks_private_subnets.*.id
}
output "eks_public_subnet_ids" {
  value = aws_subnet.eks_public_subnets.*.id
}
output "eks_nat_ips" {
  value = aws_eip.eks_nat_ips.*.public_ip
}
```

The preceding code snippet defines five Terraform output blocks. In the *Provisioning the cluster* section, you will use these outputs as inputs to the Kubernetes terraform modules.

Developing the cluster VPC

Under the `terraform` root directory, create a directory and name it `packtclusters-vpc`. This directory will contain the following Terraform code files:

- `config.tf`
- `terraform.tfvars`
- `variables.tf`
- `main.tf`
- `outputs.tf`

The previous list of Terraform files comprises your Kubernetes cluster VPC. You will learn about each code and configuration file in the following subsections.

Configuration

`config.tf` has the Terraform shared state configuration and the AWS provider definition:

```
terraform {
  backend "s3" {
    bucket         = "packtclusters-vpc-terraform-state"
    key            = "packtclusters-vpc.tfstate"
    region         = "us-east-1"
    dynamodb_table = "packtclusters-vpc-terraform-state-lock-dynamodb"
  }
```

```
required_version = "~> 0.14.5"
required_providers {
    aws = "~> 3.27"
  }
}
provider "aws" {
  region  = var.aws_region
  version = "~> 3.27"
}
```

The preceding code block tells Terraform which S3 bucket to use to persist the state, and specifies Terraform and AWS provider versions.

Environment variables

The `terraform.tfvars` file defines the values of the input variables. These values are required by the VPC module to set the values of these inputs: the AWS region; the VPC IP CIDR; the private subnet prefix list; and the public subnet prefix list.

The `terraform.tfvars` file is defined as follows:

```
aws_region              = "us-east-1"
clusters_name_prefix = "packtclusters"
vpc_block               = "10.40.0.0/17"
public_subnets_prefix_list = [
    "10.40.0.0/20",
    "10.40.16.0/20",
    "10.40.32.0/20",
]
private_subnets_prefix_list = [
    "10.40.64.0/20",
    "10.40.80.0/20",
    "10.40.96.0/20",
]
```

For the preceding code, you can choose a different CIDR block for the VPC IPs range and different subnet prefixes according to your network topology and applications needs.

> **Important note**
>
> You should make sure that the VPC CIDR is not used by any other VPCs within your own AWS VPC so as to avoid IPs collisions. You should make sure the VPC CIDR has a sufficient number of IPs that exceeds the maximum forecasted number of pods in your Kubernetes cluster.

Input variables

The `variables.tf` file defines the five input variables that Terraform will use during creation of the VPC module resources. It is very similar to the previous `variables.tf` files. You can view its full source code at https://github.com/PacktPublishing/Kubernetes-in-Production-Best-Practices/blob/master/Chapter03/terraform/packtclusters-vpc/variables.tf.

The cluster VPC

The `main.tf` file has two code blocks: the `vpc` module block, which creates an instance of the `eks-vpc` module, and the `locals` code block, which defines `common_tags` to be assigned to VPC resources.

The `main.tf` file is defined as follows:

```
locals {
  common_tags = {
    ManagedBy = "terraform"
  }
}
module "vpc" {
  source                         = "../modules/eks-vpc"
  clusters_name_prefix           = var.clusters_name_prefix
  eks_vpc_block                  = var.vpc_block
  eks_public_subnets_prefix_list = var.public_subnets_prefix_
list
  eks_private_subnets_prefix_list = var.private_subnets_prefix_
list
  common_tags                    = local.common_tags
}
```

Thanks to Terraform modules, this makes the previous code clean and simple, as it hides the complexity of creating the AWS VPC. In the next subsection, you will create the Terraform outputs that you will use while creating the cluster VPC.

Output values

The `outputs.tf` file defines the output values that you need to get after creating the cluster VPC. These outputs are the VPC ID, the private subnet IDs, and the public subnet IDs.

The `outputs.tf` file is defined as follows:

```
output "vpc_id" {
  value = module.vpc.eks_cluster_vpc_id
}
output "private_subnet_ids" {
  value = module.vpc.eks_private_subnet_ids
}
output "public_subnet_ids" {
  value = module.vpc.eks_public_subnet_ids
}
```

The outputs from the previous code block are used as the inputs to the Kubernetes cluster Terraform modules in the next section.

Provisioning the cluster VPC

Once you have completed development of the VPC Terraform files in the previous sections, you can now provision the VPC resources and create them in your AWS account:

1. Initialize the Terraform state:

```
$ cd Chapter03/terraform/packtclusters-vpc
$ terraform init
Initializing modules...
- vpc in ../../modules/eks-vpc
Initializing the backend...
Initializing provider plugins...
- Checking for available provider plugins...
- Downloading plugin for provider "aws" (hashicorp/aws)
3.27.0...
```

```
Terraform has been successfully initialized!

You may now begin working with Terraform. Try running
"terraform plan" to see

any changes that are required for your infrastructure.
All Terraform commands

should now work.

If you ever set or change modules or backend
configuration for Terraform,

rerun this command to reinitialize your working
directory. If you forget, other

commands will detect it and remind you to do so if
necessary.
```

2. Execute the `terraform plan` command to review the planned changes before applying them:

```
$ cd Chapter03/terraform/packtclusters-vpc
$ terraform plan
```

The following is the expected final output after executing the `terraform plan` command. There are 28 resources in the Terraform plan, and when you execute the `terraform apply` command, these 28 resources will be created in your AWS account:

```
Plan: 28 to add, 0 to change, 0 to destroy.

------------------------------------------------------------------

Note: You didn't specify an "-out" parameter to save this plan, so Terraform
can't guarantee that exactly these actions will be performed if
"terraform apply" is subsequently run.
```

Figure 3.5 – The terraform plan command output

3. Execute the `terraform apply` command. Enter `yes` when you get a prompt to approve the execution:

```
$ cd Chapter03/terraform/packtclusters-vpc
$ terraform apply
```

4. You will get the following output once the `terraform apply` command completes successfully, and by then, Terraform has successfully created 28 network resources:

```
Apply complete! Resources: 28 added, 0 changed, 0 destroyed.
Releasing state lock. This may take a few moments...

Outputs:

private_subnet_ids = [
    "subnet-0c37e5cb11722c92b",
    "subnet-04b21723fb8596167",
    "subnet-0dc7a8f4007ff8c43",
]
public_subnet_ids = [
    "subnet-03ddbff373c86c36f",
    "subnet-0c7a7dc7780468137",
    "subnet-0282d86270d3d191a",
]
vpc_id = vpc-02479e3540304f977
```

Figure 3.6 – The terraform apply command output

By completing this section, you should have your Kubernetes cluster VPC and its network components successfully created in your AWS account. It is now ready to provision the cluster above it, as you will learn in the next section.

Creating the cluster infrastructure

In this section, you will develop the following Terraform modules:

- An EKS module
- A Kubernetes worker module
- A Kubernetes cluster module that wraps both the EKS control plan and the workers

After that, you will use these modules to Terraform your first cluster, `Packt cluster`, and then provision it in your AWS account.

Developing the EKS Terraform module

Under the `terraform/modules` directory, create a subdirectory with the name `eks-cp`. This directory will contain the following Terraform source code files for the EKS control plane module:

- `variables.tf`
- `main.tf`
- `security-groups.tf`

- `iam.tf`
- `outputs.tf`

The previous list of files together comprises the EKS Terraform module. You will learn about each of these code and configuration files in the following subsections.

Input variables

The `variables.tf` file defines the input variables that are accepted in the EKS module. The module user should provide the values for each of these variables:

- Full cluster name
- Cluster Kubernetes version
- VPC ID
- Private subnet IDs
- Public subnet IDs
- Common tags

This file is similar to the `variables.tf` file you created in the VPC module. You can view its full source code at `https://github.com/PacktPublishing/Kubernetes-in-Production-Best-Practices/blob/master/Chapter03/terraform/modules/eks-cp/variables.tf`.

Module main resources

The `main.tf` file defines the EKS resources that are required to configure and create it. These include the cluster name, version, and cluster IAM role ARN.

The following code snippet uses the Terraform resource called `aws_eks_cluster`, which is a built-in resource in the Terraform AWS provider that can be used to create an AWS EKS cluster and set its configuration parameters.

The `main.tf` file is defined as follows:

```
resource "aws_eks_cluster" "eks_cluster" {
  name     = var.cluster_full_name
  version  = var.cluster_version
  role_arn = aws_iam_role.eks_cluster_role.arn
  vpc_config {
    security_group_ids = [aws_security_group.eks_cluster_sg.id]
```

```
    subnet_ids           = concat(var.private_subnets, var.
public_subnets)
  }


  depends_on = [
    aws_iam_role_policy_attachment.eks_clusterrole_policy_
attachment,
    aws_iam_role_policy_attachment.eks_servicerole_policy_
attachment,
  ]
}
```

In the previous code, you will notice that the EKS resource references the values of the EKS IAM role and the EKS security group. Both of these are created in the EKS module, but in two separate Terraform files for better code clarity and organization. You will learn about creating EKS security groups and IAM roles in the following subsections.

Security groups

The following code snippet uses the Terraform resource called `aws_security_group`, which is a built-in resource in the Terraform AWS provider that can be used to create an AWS security group and set its configuration parameters.

The following `security-groups.tf` file defines a single security group for the EKS control plane:

```
resource "aws_security_group" "eks_cluster_sg" {
  name        = "${var.cluster_full_name}-cluster"
  description = "EKS cluster Security group"
  vpc_id      = var.vpc_id
  tags = merge(
    var.common_tags,
    {
      Name                                              =
"${var.cluster_full_name}-cluster-sg"
      "kubernetes.io/cluster/${var.cluster_full_name}" =
"owned"
    },
  )
}
```

If you notice, the previous security group does not have ingress/egress rules. These rules will be defined in the cluster workers module.

IAM roles and policies

The `iam.tf` file uses the Terraform resource called `aws_iam_role`, which is a built-in resource in the Terraform AWS provider that can be used to create an AWS IAM role and set its configuration parameters.

There are specific policies that the EKS cluster must acquire in order to operate properly:

- `AmazonEKSClusterPolicy`
- `AmazonEKSServicePolicy`

These policies must be attached to the EKS cluster IAM role that we will create in the next code snippet. To learn more about these policies, you can check the EKS official documentation at `https://docs.aws.amazon.com/eks/latest/userguide/service_IAM_role.html`.

The following `iam.tf` file defines an IAM role and associates two policies with this role:

```
resource "aws_iam_role" "eks_cluster_role" {
  name = "${var.cluster_full_name}-cluster-role"
  assume_role_policy = <<POLICY
{
  "Version": "2012-10-17",
  "Statement": [
    {
      "Effect": "Allow",
      "Principal": {
        "Service": "eks.amazonaws.com"
      },
      "Action": "sts:AssumeRole"
    }
  ]
}
POLICY
  tags = var.common_tags
}
```

The two IAM policies in question are `AmazonEKSClusterPolicy` and
`AmazonEKSServicePolicy`. Both of them are AWS-predefined IAM policies:

```
data "aws_iam_policy" "AmazonEKSClusterPolicy" {
  arn = "arn:aws:iam::aws:policy/AmazonEKSClusterPolicy"
}
data "aws_iam_policy" "AmazonEKSServicePolicy" {
  arn = "arn:aws:iam::aws:policy/AmazonEKSServicePolicy"
}
resource "aws_iam_role_policy_attachment" "eks_clusterrole_
policy_attachment" {
  policy_arn = data.aws_iam_policy.AmazonEKSClusterPolicy.arn
  role       = aws_iam_role.eks_cluster_role.name
  depends_on = [data.aws_iam_policy.AmazonEKSClusterPolicy]
}
resource "aws_iam_role_policy_attachment" "eks_servicerole_
policy_attachment" {
  policy_arn = data.aws_iam_policy.AmazonEKSServicePolicy.arn
  role       = aws_iam_role.eks_cluster_role.name
  depends_on = [data.aws_iam_policy.AmazonEKSServicePolicy]
}
```

You need to attach the IAM role defined in the previous code to the EKS cluster to enable
it to operate within the AWS environment. In the next and final subsection, you will
define the EKS module outputs.

Output values

The `outputs.tf` file defines the output values from the EKS module. There are three
outputs: the security group ID; the cluster **certificate authority** (**CA**); and the cluster API
server endpoint.

The `outputs.tf` file is defined as follows:

```
output "security_group" {
  value = aws_security_group.eks_cluster_sg.id
}
output "kubeconfig" {
  value = local.kubeconfig
}
```

```
output "ca" {
  value = aws_eks_cluster.eks_cluster.certificate_authority[0].
data
}
output "endpoint" {
  value = aws_eks_cluster.eks_cluster.endpoint
}
```

In this section, you learned to develop a Terraform module for the EKS. You will use it with other modules to compose your cluster infrastructure. In the next section, you will learn to develop a Terraform module for the cluster workers.

Developing the workers' Terraform module

Under the `terraform/modules` directory, create a subdirectory and name it `eks-workers`. This directory will contain the following Terraform code files:

- `variables.tf`
- `main.tf`
- `security-groups.tf`
- `iam.tf`
- `user-data.tf`
- `authconfig.tf`
- `outputs.tf`

> **Important note**
>
> AWS recently introduced the managed EKS node group, which is an EKS service to manage workers on your behalf. This is a new service and it lacks important features, such as the ability to provide custom user data, which is essential when it comes to optimizing workers' performance and `kubelet` arguments. This is the reason why the preference is to keep using the self-managed workers until AWS implements this feature.

Input variables

The `variables.tf` file defines the input variables that are required by this module. There are multiple inputs for the workers' module, such as the worker AMI ID, EC2 instance type, user data, and instance storage size.

The `variables.tf` file is defined as follows:

```
variable "workers_ami_id" {
  type = string
}
variable "workers_instance_type" {
  type = string
}
variable "workers_storage_size" {
  type = string
}
```

> **Important note**
>
> AWS periodically releases optimized AMIs for EKS workers. To choose one of them, please check the EKS documentation at `https://docs.aws.amazon.com/eks/latest/userguide/eks-optimized-ami.html`.
>
> You still can build your own AMI for EKS workers, and you can make use of the EKS AMI open source project at `https://github.com/awslabs/amazon-eks-ami`.

Please view the remainder of the variables and the full source code at `https://github.com/PacktPublishing/Kubernetes-in-Production-Best-Practices/blob/master/Chapter03/terraform/modules/eks-workers/variables.tf`.

Module main resources

The `main.tf` file defines the workers' resources and their properties. This module contains two AWS resources:

- Autoscaling group
- Launch template

The autoscaling group uses the launch template to add worker instances according to the launch specs.

The following code snippet uses the Terraform resource called `aws_autoscaling_group`, which is a built-in resource in the Terraform AWS provider that can be used to create an AWS autoscaling group and set its configuration parameters.

The `main.tf` file is defined as follows:

```
resource "aws_autoscaling_group" "workers" {
  name               = "${var.cluster_full_name}-workers-asg-
${var.workers_instance_type}"
  max_size           = var.workers_number_max
  min_size           = var.workers_number_min
  vpc_zone_identifier = var.private_subnet_ids
  launch_template {
    id      = aws_launch_template.workers.id
    version = "$Latest"
  }
}
```

Please view the rest of the `main.tf` source code at `https://github.com/PacktPublishing/Kubernetes-in-Production-Best-Practices/blob/master/Chapter03/terraform/modules/eks-workers/main.tf`.

Security groups

The `security-groups.tf` file defines the workers' security group and the ingress/egress rules that control the flow of traffic between workers, and between the control plane and the workers.

Please refer to *Chapter 2, Architecting Production-Grade Kubernetes Infrastructure*, for more details about the security group ingress/egress rules and the permitted ports.

The `security-groups.tf` file is defined as follows:

```
resource "aws_security_group" "workers" {
  name        = "${var.cluster_full_name}-workers"
  description = "Security group for all nodes in the ${var.
cluster_full_name} cluster"
  vpc_id      = var.vpc_id
  egress {
    from_port   = 0
    to_port     = 0
    protocol    = "-1"
    cidr_blocks = ["0.0.0.0/0"]
  }
}
```

You can view the full source code at `https://github.com/PacktPublishing/ Kubernetes-in-Production-Best-Practices/blob/master/Chapter03/ terraform/modules/eks-workers/security-groups.tf`.

IAM role and policies

The following `iam.tf` file defines an IAM role and associates two policies with this role:

```
resource "aws_iam_role" "workers" {
  name                = "${var.cluster_full_name}-workers"
  assume_role_policy = <<POLICY
{
  "Version": "2012-10-17",
  "Statement": [
    {
      "Effect": "Allow",
      "Principal": {
        "Service": "ec2.amazonaws.com"
      },
      "Action": "sts:AssumeRole"
    }
  ]
}
POLICY
}
```

The IAM policies are `AmazonEKSWorkerNodePolicy`, `AmazonEKS_ CNI_Policy`, `AmazonEC2ContainerRegistryReadOnly`, and `CloudWatchAgentServerPolicy`. All of them are standard predefined IAM policies:

```
resource "aws_iam_role_policy_attachment"
"AmazonEKSWorkerNodePolicy" {
  policy_arn = "arn:aws:iam::aws:policy/
AmazonEKSWorkerNodePolicy"
  role       = aws_iam_role.workers.name
}
resource "aws_iam_role_policy_attachment" "AmazonEKS_CNI_
Policy" {
```

```
   policy_arn = "arn:aws:iam::aws:policy/AmazonEKS_CNI_Policy"
   role       = aws_iam_role.workers.name
}
resource "aws_iam_role_policy_attachment"
"AmazonEC2ContainerRegistryReadOnly" {
   policy_arn = "arn:aws:iam::aws:policy/
AmazonEC2ContainerRegistryReadOnly"
   role       = aws_iam_role.workers.name
}
resource "aws_iam_role_policy_attachment"
"CloudWatchAgentServerPolicy" {
   policy_arn = "arn:aws:iam::aws:policy/
CloudWatchAgentServerPolicy"
   role       = aws_iam_role.workers.name
}
resource "aws_iam_instance_profile" "workers" {
   name = "${var.cluster_full_name}-workers"
   role = aws_iam_role.workers.name
}
```

You need to attach the IAM role defined in the previous code to the workers in order to enable them to operate within the AWS environment.

User data

The user-data.tf file defines the user data script that is executed while the worker instance is booting up.

The following code snippet uses a special Terraform code block called locals, which is used to define a set of key/value configurations. In our solution, we use it to construct the worker user data script.

The user-data.tf file is defined as follows:

```
locals {
  kubelet_extra_args = <<ARGS
--v=3 \
ARGS
  userdata = <<USERDATA
#!/bin/bash
```

```
set -o xtrace
```

```
/etc/eks/bootstrap.sh --b64-cluster-ca "${var.cluster_ca}"
--apiserver-endpoint "${var.cluster_endpoint}" \
USERDATA
```

```
  workers_userdata = "${local.userdata} --kubelet-extra-args
\"${local.kubelet_extra_args}\"  \"${var.cluster_full_name}\""
}
```

Later in the book, we will update the previous code to bootstrap `kubelet` with optimized arguments for worker performance tuning.

Worker authentication

Kubernetes requires workers to be authenticated in order to be able to join the cluster and communicate with `kube-api-server`. EKS provides its own solution to perform this type of authentication, as it requires the cluster admin to create a ConfigMap that contains the workers' IAM role ARN and map it to the Kubernetes system node group. By doing that, workers can join the cluster.

To automate this, the `authconfig.tf` file defines the content of the `authconfig` YAML file, which you will use to register and authenticate the workers with the EKS control plane.

It is worth mentioning that `authconfig` can be applied separately to the cluster using `kubectl`. However, I recommend that you apply it using Terraform to register the nodes immediately after EKS is provisioned, and then you can apply it again later as part of Kubernetes configuration management, and add more users and groups to `authconfig`.

The `authconfig.tf` file is defined as follows:

```
locals {
  authconfig = <<AUTHCONFIG
apiVersion: v1
kind: ConfigMap
metadata:
  name: aws-auth
  namespace: kube-system
data:
```

```
  mapRoles: |
    - rolearn: "${aws_iam_role.workers.arn}"
      username: system:node:{{EC2PrivateDNSName}}
      groups:
        - system:bootstrappers
        - system:nodes
AUTHCONFIG
}
```

In *Chapter 4, Managing Cluster Configuration with Ansible*, we will learn how to extend aws-auth to authenticate other users with the cluster.

Output values

The outputs.tf file defines the output values from the Workers module, such as the worker's instance profile ARN, the IAM role ARN, and other outputs. Please view the full source code of outputs.tf at https://github.com/PacktPublishing/Kubernetes-in-Production-Best-Practices/blob/master/Chapter03/terraform/modules/eks-workers/outputs.tf.

In this section, you learned to develop a Terraform module for the cluster workers. You will use this with other modules to compose your cluster infrastructure. In the next section, you will learn to develop a Terraform module that wraps both EKS and workers in a single module that represents the whole Kubernetes cluster.

Developing the Kubernetes cluster Terraform module

Under the terraform/modules directory, create a subdirectory and name it cluster. This directory will contain the following Terraform code files:

- config.tf
- terraform.tfvars
- variables.tf
- main.tf
- outputs.tf

This cluster module is a wrapper above both the EKS module and the workers' module. You will notice that the inputs and outputs to/from this module are a combination of both EKS and worker modules.

Input variables

The `variables.tf` file defines the input variables that are needed by this module. These inputs are a combination of both EKS and worker modules. Please view the source code with a full list of variables at `https://github.com/PacktPublishing/Kubernetes-in-Production-Best-Practices/blob/master/Chapter03/terraform/modules/cluster/variables.tf`.

EKS control plane

The `eks-cp.tf` file defines an instance of the EKS module. It is defined as follows:

```
module "eks" {
  source            = "../eks-cp"
  vpc_id            = var.vpc_id
  private_subnets   = var.private_subnets
  public_subnets    = var.public_subnets
  cluster_full_name = var.cluster_full_name
  cluster_version   = var.cluster_version
  common_tags       = var.common_tags
}
```

The previous code block creates the EKS control plane by creating an instance from the EKS module and passing to it the required inputs.

EKS workers

The `workers.tf` file defines an instance of the `workers` module:

```
module "workers" {
  source                 = "../eks-workers"
  vpc_id                 = var.vpc_id
  private_subnet_ids     = var.private_subnets
  cluster_full_name      = var.cluster_full_name
  cluster_endpoint       = module.eks.endpoint
  cluster_ca             = module.eks.ca
  cluster_security_group = module.eks.security_group
  workers_ami_id         = var.workers_ami_id
  workers_instance_type  = var.workers_instance_type
```

```
    workers_number_max      = var.workers_number_max
    workers_number_min      = var.workers_number_min
    workers_storage_size    = var.workers_storage_size
    common_tags             = var.common_tags
}
```

The previous code block creates the cluster workers by creating an instance from the `workers` module and passing it to the required inputs. Both of the previous code files comprise the full Kubernetes cluster.

Output values

The `outputs.tf` file contains the output values from the `cluster` module, such as the cluster's full name, the cluster endpoint, `authconfig`, and others. Please view the complete source code at `https://github.com/PacktPublishing/Kubernetes-in-Production-Best-Practices/blob/master/Chapter03/terraform/modules/cluster/outputs.tf`.

In this section, you learned to develop a Terraform module that wraps both EKS and workers in a single module that is used to provision the whole Kubernetes cluster. In the next section, you will use the previous modules to develop your first cluster – the Packt cluster.

Putting all modules together

Now it is time to bring all the modules together by creating your first cluster group, `packtclusters`, and a first cluster, `prod1`.

Under the root `terraform` directory, create a subdirectory and name it `packtclusters`. Then, under this, create the following Terraform code files:

- `config.tf`
- `terraform.tfvars`
- `variables.tf`
- `main.tf`
- `outputs.tf`

In the following subsections, you will create the code files in the previous list and learn all the details about them.

Configuration

The config.tf file contains the Terraform shared state configuration and the AWS provider definition. This file is similar to the config.tf file you created in the *Developing the cluster VPC* section. Please view the complete source code at https://github.com/PacktPublishing/Kubernetes-in-Production-Best-Practices/blob/master/Chapter03/terraform/packtclusters/config.tf.

Environment variables

The terraform.tfvars file defines the input values that are passed to the cluster module. Some of these values are outputs from the VPC module. To retrieve these outputs, you have to execute the following command:

```
$ cd Chapter03/terraform/packtclusters-vpc
$ terraform output
```

Then, copy the following output values:

- VPC ID
- Private subnet IDs
- Public subnet IDs

Then, paste these values into the terraform.tfvars file into their corresponding placeholders.

The terraform.tfvars file is defined as follows:

```
aws_region = "us-east-1"
private_subnet_ids = [
  "subnet-xxxxxxxx",
  "subnet-xxxxxxxx",
  "subnet-xxxxxxxx",
]
public_subnet_ids = [
  "subnet-xxxxxxxx",
  "subnet-xxxxxxxx",
  "subnet-xxxxxxxx",
]
vpc_id                = "vpc-xxxxxxxxx"
clusters_name_prefix  = "packtclusters"
```

```
cluster_version       = "1.16"
workers_instance_type = "t3.medium"
workers_number_min    = 1
workers_number_max    = 3
workers_storage_size  = 10
```

Some of the preceding values can be tuned according to your infrastructure requirements, specifically, the instance type and the worker instance count min/max limits.

For educational purposes, you can use the existing values in the previous code block. However, when you decide to move your cluster to production, please refer to the workers' sizing section in *Chapter 2, Architecting Production-Grade Kubernetes Infrastructure.*

Input variables

The `variables.tf` file defines inputs that Terraform will use while creating the `packtclusters-prod1` cluster. You can view the complete source code at `https://github.com/PacktPublishing/Kubernetes-in-Production-Best-Practices/blob/master/Chapter03/terraform/packtclusters/variables.tf`.

The cluster main resources

The `main.tf` file defines the cluster module. It takes the input variables required to configure EKS and the workers.

The `main.tf` file is defined as follows:

```
module "packtcluster" {
  source                = "../modules/cluster"
  vpc_id                = var.vpc_id
  public_subnets        = var.public_subnet_ids
  private_subnets       = var.private_subnet_ids
  cluster_full_name     = "${var.clusters_name_prefix}-${terraform.workspace}"
  cluster_version       = var.cluster_version
  workers_instance_type = var.workers_instance_type
  workers_ami_id        = data.aws_ssm_parameter.workers_ami_id.value
  workers_number_min    = var.workers_number_min
  workers_number_max    = var.workers_number_max
```

```
    workers_storage_size    = var.workers_storage_size
    common_tags             = local.common_tags
    aws_region              = var.aws_region
}
```

In the previous code block, the `cluster_full_name` input is constructed by concatenating `cluster_name_prefix`, which is `packtclusters`, and the Terraform workspace name, `prod1`. And this is how you can create multiple clusters under one cluster group such as `packtclusters`. All you need is to create a new Terraform workspace and execute your `terraform plan`.

Output values

The `outputs.tf` file defines the outputs from `packtclusters`, primarily `authconfig`, which is used to authenticate the workers with the control plane. You can view the complete source code at `https://github.com/PacktPublishing/Kubernetes-in-Production-Best-Practices/blob/master/Chapter03/terraform/packtclusters/outputs.tf`.

By completing this section, you have a complete Terraform code base that is capable of creating full Kubernetes clusters. In the next section, you will learn the Terraform commands to use this code base to provision your first production cluster.

Provisioning the cluster infrastructure

After you have completed developing the cluster Terraform modules in the previous sections, you can now provision your first Kubernetes cluster and create it in your AWS account:

1. Initialize the Terraform state:

    ```
    $ cd Chapter03/terraform/packtclusters
    $ terraform init
    ```

2. Create a new Terraform workspace for the first cluster and name it `prod1`:

    ```
    $ terraform workspace new prod1
    ```

3. Execute the `terraform plan` command to review the planned changes before applying them:

    ```
    $ terraform plan
    ```

4. This is the `terraform plan` command output that you should get:

```
Plan: 22 to add, 0 to change, 0 to destroy.

------------------------------------------------------------------

Note: You didn't specify an "-out" parameter to save this plan, so Terraform
can't guarantee that exactly these actions will be performed if
"terraform apply" is subsequently run.
```

Figure 3.7 – Terraform plan command output

5. Execute the `terraform apply` command. Enter `yes` when you get a prompt to approve the plan execution:

```
$ terraform apply
```

6. You will get the following output after the `terraform apply` command completes successfully. This means that Terraform has successfully created 22 resources:

```
Apply complete! Resources: 22 added, 0 changed, 0 destroyed.
Releasing state lock. This may take a few moments...

Outputs:

authconfig = apiVersion: v1
kind: ConfigMap
metadata:
  name: aws-auth
  namespace: kube-system
data:
  mapRoles: |
    - rolearn: "arn:aws:iam::698782116220:role/packtclusters-prod1-workers"
      username: system:node:{{EC2PrivateDNSName}}
      groups:
        - system:bootstrappers
        - system:nodes

aws_region = us-east-1
cluster_api = https://76041A413CDC35C70CE83744FE510577.gr7.us-east-1.eks.amazonaws.com
cluster_full_name = packtclusters-prod1
cluster_tag = kubernetes.io/cluster/packtclusters-prod1
cluster_version = 1.15
worker_iam_role_arn = arn:aws:iam::698782116220:role/packtclusters-prod1-workers
```

Figure 3.8 – Terraform apply command output

7. Retrieve the cluster `kubeconfig` file:

```
$ aws eks --region $(terraform output aws_region) update-
kubeconfig --name $(terraform output cluster_full_name)
```

```
Added new context arn:aws:eks:us-east-
1:698782116220:cluster/packtclusters-prod1 to ~/.kube/
config
```

8. Apply `authconfig` to authenticate the workers' nodes with the EKS control plane:

```
$ terraform output authconfig | kubectl -n kube-system
create -f -
configmap/aws-auth created
```

9. Ensure that the cluster worker nodes are up and in the ready state:

```
$ kubectl get nodes
NAME                        STATUS   ROLES    AGE     VERSION
ip-10-40-98-176.ec2.internal Ready   <none>            90s
v1.15.10-eks-bac369
```

After completing the previous instructions, you have a Kubernetes cluster up and running, but it is still not ready to deploy production workloads. In the next chapters, you will deploy more services to the cluster, and optimize their configurations to make it capable of running your production workloads.

Cleaning up and destroying infrastructure resources

After completing the hands-on exercises in this chapter, you can follow the instructions in this section to destroy the Kubernetes cluster and its AWS resources.

You will destroy the resources in reverse order from their creation. First, you will destroy the Kubernetes cluster resources, then the VPC resources, and finally the shared state resources.

Destroying the cluster resources

Follow these Terraform commands to destroy all of the `packtclusters` resources that you created in the previous sections of this chapter:

1. Initialize the Terraform state:

```
$ cd Chapter03/terraform/packtclusters
$ terraform init
```

2. Execute the `terraform destroy` command. Enter `yes` when you get a prompt to approve the destruction:

```
$ terraform destroy
```

3. You will get the following output once the `terraform destroy` command completes successfully. This means that Terraform has successfully destroyed the 22 resources in the cluster:

```
Destroy complete! Resources: 22 destroyed.
Releasing state lock. This may take a few moments...
```

Figure 3.9 – The terraform destroy command output

Having observed the previous instructions, `packtclusters-prod1` is completely destroyed. In the next subsection, you will destroy the VPC resources.

Destroying the VPC resources

Follow these Terraform commands to destroy all of the `packtclusters-vpc` resources that you created in the previous sections of this chapter:

1. Initialize the Terraform state:

```
$ cd Chapter03/terraform/packtclusters-vpc
$ terraform init
```

2. Execute the `terraform destroy` command. Enter `yes` when you get a prompt to approve the destruction:

```
$ terraform destroy
```

3. You will get the following output after the `terraform destroy` command completes successfully. This means that Terraform has successfully destroyed 28 network resources:

```
Destroy complete! Resources: 28 destroyed.
Releasing state lock. This may take a few moments...
```

Figure 3.10 – The terraform destroy command output

Having observed the previous instructions, `packtclusters-vpc` is completely destroyed. In the next subsection, you will destroy the shared state resources.

Destroying the shared state resources

Usually, you do not have to delete the shared state files. However, for educational purposes, you can follow these instructions to destroy these resources.

1. As the shared state S3 buckets have destroy prevention and versioning enabled, you should empty and then destroy Terraform shared state S3 buckets first:

```
$ aws s3 rm s3://packtclusters-terraform-state
--recursive
$ aws s3 rm s3://packtclusters-vpc-terraform-state
--recursive
$ aws s3 rb s3://packtclusters-terraform-state --force
$ aws s3 rb s3://packtclusters-vpc-terraform-state
--force
```

2. Initialize the Terraform state to destroy the shared state DynamoDB tables:

```
$ cd Chapter03/terraform/shared-state
$ terraform init
```

3. Execute the terraform destroy command. Enter yes when you get a prompt to approve the destruction:

```
$ terraform destroy
```

4. You will get the following output after the terraform destroy command completes successfully. By then, Terraform has successfully destroyed both of the DynamoDB tables:

```
Plan: 0 to add, 0 to change, 2 to destroy.

Do you really want to destroy all resources?
  Terraform will destroy all your managed infrastructure, as shown above.
  There is no undo. Only 'yes' will be accepted to confirm.

  Enter a value: yes

aws_dynamodb_table.clusters_dynamodb_tf_state_lock: Destroying... [id=packtclusters-terraform-state-lock-dynamodb]
aws_dynamodb_table.clusters_vpc_dynamodb_tf_state_lock: Destroying... [id=packtclusters-vpc-terraform-state-lock-dynamodb]
aws_dynamodb_table.clusters_dynamodb_tf_state_lock: Destruction complete after 2s
aws_dynamodb_table.clusters_vpc_dynamodb_tf_state_lock: Destruction complete after 4s

Destroy complete! Resources: 2 destroyed.
```

Figure 3.11 – The terraform destroy command output

By now, you have successfully finished destroying your Kubernetes cluster and all of its AWS resources in your AWS account.

I recommend practicing these instructions and repeating them to provision and destroy the cluster, and to create multiple clusters by adding new Terraform workspaces, such as prod2 and prod3.

Summary

In this chapter, you have learned to develop the infrastructure code for Kubernetes clusters using Terraform and AWS. You went through practical steps to implement this code. We started by creating the network components, followed by the cluster's components, using AWS VPC, EKS, autoscaling groups, and other AWS services.

This chapter introduced you to Terraform practical development and its usage in relation to production infrastructure provisioning. It showed you how to follow the best practices of the declarative IaC, and also the best practices of decomposing your IaC into modules and combining them to create Kubernetes clusters.

All of this establishes a foundation for the forthcoming chapters, where we will build on the knowledge introduced here to take the Kubernetes cluster to the next level of its production-readiness journey.

In the next chapter, you will learn in detail about Kubernetes cluster configuration management. You will develop a dynamic templating solution that you can apply to the cluster-level configurations, and you will learn how to make your solution scalable to many clusters without introducing operational overheads and complexity.

Further reading

For more information on the topics covered in this chapter, you can refer to the following books:

- *Getting Started with Terraform – Second Edition*: https://www.packtpub.com/networking-and-servers/getting-started-terraform-second-edition

- *Hands-On Infrastructure Automation with Terraform on AWS*: https://www.packtpub.com/big-data-and-business-intelligence/hands-infrastructure-automation-terraform-aws-video

4
Managing Cluster Configuration with Ansible

In *Chapter 3, Provisioning Kubernetes Clusters Using AWS and Terraform*, you learned how to create a Kubernetes infrastructure with Terraform and AWS, and you also learned how to develop infrastructure as code and provisioned your first production-like cluster.

This was just the first step towards building operational and production-ready Kubernetes clusters. By now, you should have an up-and-running cluster with Terraform infrastructure modules to provision other similar clusters.

These clusters are still plain; they're not configured or optimized to run production workloads. To make these clusters fully operational, we simply need to deploy and configure the required Kubernetes services for them.

In this chapter, you will design and develop a configuration management solution that you can use to manage the configuration of Kubernetes clusters and their supporting services. This solution is automated and scalable, and it requires a minimum effort to maintain and operate.

In this chapter, we will cover the following topics:

- Understanding Kubernetes configuration management challenges
- Designing a configuration management solution for Kubernetes
- Developing a configuration management solution with Ansible
- Applying the solution to configure Kubernetes clusters

Technical requirements

In addition to the tools that you installed in *Chapter 3, Provisioning Kubernetes Clusters Using AWS and Terraform*, you will need to install the following tools:

- `python3`
- `pip3`
- `virtualenv`

I will go into the specifics of these tools' installation and configuration in the next section. If you already know how to do this, you can go ahead and set them up now.

You need to have an up-and-running Kubernetes cluster as per the instructions in *Chapter 3, Provisioning Kubernetes Clusters Using AWS and Terraform*.

The code for this chapter is located at `https://github.com/PacktPublishing/Kubernetes-in-Production-Best-Practices/tree/master/Chapter04`.

Check out the following link to see the Code in Action video:

`https://bit.ly/3cGtqjx`

Installing the required tools

`python3`, `pip3`, and `virtualenv` are the prerequisites to execute the Ansible configuration playbooks that we will develop in this chapter. If you do not have these tools installed on your system, you can follow these instructions:

- Execute the following commands to install `python3`, `pip3`, and `virtualenv` on Ubuntu Linux:

```
$ sudo apt-get update
$ sudo apt-get install python3
$ sudo apt-get install python3-pip
$ sudo pip3 install virtualenv
```

- Execute the following commands to install `python3`, `pip3`, and `virtualenv` on Amazon Linux 2:

```
$ sudo yum update
$ sudo yum install python3
$ sudo python3 -m pip install --upgrade pip
$ sudo python3 -m pip install virtualenv
```

- Execute the following commands to install `python3`, `pip3`, and `virtualenv` on macOS:

```
$ brew install python3
$ curl -O https://bootstrap.pypa.io/get-pip.py
$ sudo python3 get-pip.py
$ sudo -H pip3 install virtualenv
```

- Execute the following commands to install `python3`, `pip3`, and `virtualenv` on Windows:

```
C:\> choco install python3
C:\> pip install virtualenv
```

By installing `python3`, `pip3`, and `virtualenv`, you will be able to execute Ansible playbooks against your Kubernetes clusters. You will learn how to do that later in this chapter, but first, we need to go through the design details of our Kubernetes configuration management solution.

Implementation principles

In *Chapter 1, Introduction to Kubernetes Infrastructure and Production-Readiness*, you learned about the infrastructure design principles that we will follow in this book. I would like to start this chapter by highlighting the notable principles that influenced the configuration management solution and the technical decisions in this chapter:

- **Everything as code**: In this chapter, we will keep our commitment to having everything in the infrastructure as code – cluster configuration is not an exception. You will use Ansible to achieve this goal by creating a configuration management solution for your Kubernetes cluster.

- **Automation**: In the previous chapter, we used Terraform tool to automate infrastructure provisioning. We designed a solution around Terraform that can scale to serve a growing number of clusters without the need to scale up your infrastructure teams. Here, you will create a similar solution to manage the Kubernetes configuration while keeping it automated, scalable, and easy to operate and maintain.

- **Simplicity**: Ansible fulfills this principle in many aspects as it is easy to learn and to use. It has a simple syntax compared to other configuration management tools. It uses YAML, which you do not need to learn a programming language to write. Moreover, it is agentless, which means you do not need a server to run it, as you can run Ansible from your computer. Also, it is modular, which enables separation of concerns and code reusability, which is similar to Terraform. So, they can easily live together and simplify the automation of the infrastructure.

Kubernetes configuration management

The beauty of Kubernetes is that every part of it is abstracted as an object that can be managed and configured declaratively with YAML or JSON through its API server. This makes Kubernetes configuration easier to manage as code. However, it is still challenging to manage this configuration when you have groups of clusters that run hundreds of add-ons and services.

Imagine a scenario where you manage a company's infrastructure with Kubernetes, and you have multiple clusters for development, testing, and production. Add to them the cluster add-ons that run on the Kubernetes services layer as per the following diagram:

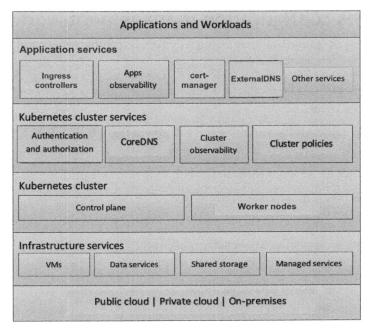

Figure 4.1 – Kubernetes infrastructure layers

This means that you can have *N* clusters with a growing number of add-ons and different environment types, such as development, QA, and production. If we put these together, we end up with a complex and redundant configuration to manage.

The recommended way to manage clusters' configuration is through **Configuration as Code (CaC)**. We will deploy these services and add-ons to the cluster and add their configuration manifests to the source code control. By adopting this pattern, you will be able to redeploy the same configuration in a seamless and automated fashion to your clusters. This solution appears to be easy when you start with a single cluster, but it will be difficult to maintain and scale when provisioning multiple clusters with different configuration values.

This leads us to an enhanced solution, which is configuration templating. Let's assume you have a group of clusters that serve product X, and these clusters have different configurations, such as different users' authentication and authorization, namespaces, resource quotas, and so on.

This solution uses Ansible templating and Jinja2. You write the templates for the Kubernetes manifests once, and then Ansible substitutes the variables in these templates and generates the appropriate manifests for each target cluster. This solution is scalable and easy to maintain, and it fulfills the infrastructure design principles that we introduced in *Chapter 1, Introduction to Kubernetes Infrastructure and Production-Readiness.*

Kubernetes configuration management workflow

After considering the preceding templating solution, our Kubernetes configuration management workflow looks like the following:

1. Create Ansible Jinja2 templates for the Kubernetes cluster services that you want to configure and deploy.

2. Define the values of the variables and categorize them based on the environments and the cluster's group.

3. Provisioning the clusters with Terraform.

4. Pass the Terraform outputs to Ansible.

5. Substitute the variables in the Ansible template with the corresponding values.

6. Use Ansible to apply the Kubernetes manifests to the target clusters.

In the next sections, we will implement this workflow with Ansible and Jinja2 templates, then learn how to use it with a basic example.

Configuration management with Ansible

In this chapter, we will use Ansible as the configuration management tool, and we will build around it our solution for Kubernetes configuration management. In this section, we are going to briefly discuss the reasoning behind this choice, and some Ansible key concepts. If you are willing to learn more about Ansible, you can use its official guide here: `https://www.ansible.com/resources/get-started`.

Why Ansible?

When it comes to templating Kubernetes configuration, we have battle-tested tools. Most notable among them are Ansible and Helm, and both of them have pros and cons. But I am not here to run a full comparison between them. My decision is based on having used both tools in serving production environments, and also our specific use case here. When it comes to pure configuration management and templating, Ansible remains the strongest contender. While Helm supports templating, it remains more like a Kubernetes package manager than a full configuration management tool. This is why we decided to use Ansible to develop a configuration management solution for Kubernetes infrastructure.

What is Ansible?

Ansible is an automation and **configuration management** (CM) tool. It can configure systems, deploy applications and containers, and provision cloud resources. It can orchestrate advanced tasks such as continuous deployments and rolling updates.

In this book, we are not going to dig deep into Ansible's features and use cases. We believe that there are a lot of good books dedicated to this purpose; our main focus is on how to use Ansible to solve Kubernetes' CM problem in a simple and efficient way.

Ansible key concepts

The CM solution that we will implement and use in this book is built with key Ansible concepts. I will not dive deep into these concepts; rather, I will provide brief details about them, as well as highlight how we will utilize each one of them in our CM framework:

- **Inventory**: This is used by Ansible to group similar hosts into groups. This is accomplished by defining the inventory files with the addresses of the hosts.

- **Modules**: This is how Ansible abstracts and groups a specific task to be reused against your host's inventories; modules can even be made public and used by other Ansible users. In our solution, we will use one of the ready-made Kubernetes modules to execute configuration manifests against the clusters.

- **Tasks**: This is where we instruct Ansible about the steps that it should do; it could be installing a piece of software or provisioning a whole system. In our solution, we will create a separate task to configure each Kubernetes component and add-on on its own.

- **Playbooks**: These are the building blocks of Ansible. They are used to gather everything together and provide a sequence of instructions that involves other Ansible blocks, such as tasks, variables, and modules. They then instruct Ansible on how to configure the target system to reach the desired state. In our solution, we will use a playbook to hold the configuration tasks for all of the components and add-ons that are required by all clusters, and we will also have variables and selectors to enable cluster maintainers to switch specific add-ons on/off.

- **Variables**: We will use variables to hold the values for the configuration that is used for each cluster add-on, and we will split these variables into groups that represent different clusters and environments.

- **Templates**: Ansible uses Jinja2 templates to enable dynamic expressions using variables. This enables Ansible to generate new configuration files based on these templates during execution time. In our solution, we will define Kubernetes manifests as Ansible Jinja2 templates, and during configuration execution time, Ansible will be able to generate the correct Kubernetes manifests for each cluster based on the provided or predefined variables.

The previous Ansible concepts are essential to understanding how Ansible works. We will utilize each of them to develop the CM solution in the next section. You will learn about each concept and how to use it as you move forward in this chapter.

Configuring the clusters

Now we put the solution we designed in the previous section into action. We will start by developing the Ansible framework skeleton, which will consist of the following parts:

- `group_vars`: This directory contains the manifest configuration files with variables' default unless a cluster defines its own private variables in its own inventory.

- `inventories`: This directory contains the configuration files with variables' values, which are specific to each cluster or cluster group, meaning that variables defined here override default variables defined under the `groups_vars` directory.

- `tasks`: In this directory, we define a separate task for each cluster service and add-on that we need to deploy and configure; the task definition file is standard across tasks, as we will use Ansible's k8s module and pass to it the YAML templates to deploy against the target cluster.

- `templates`: This directory contains the Kubernetes manifest YAMLs and configuration files for each Kubernetes object we need to manage, and these template files will have the required variables written in Jinja2 expressions format.

- `cluster.yaml`: This is the main playbook that will be passed to Ansible to execute against the target cluster. It contains all the tasks that we need to invoke to configure the cluster objects and add-ons. The playbook also has tags for each task, and this enables the cluster maintainer to switch specific tasks on/off for each target cluster whenever needed.

After creating the Ansible skeleton for Kubernetes cluster configuration management, we will be able to grow it to handle more cluster services and deployments. The development workflow looks as the following:

1. Write Kubernetes manifests in YAML format for the cluster add-ons that you want to deploy, then deploy them to a test cluster to ensure correctness.

2. Convert the Kubernetes manifests from YAML to Jinja2 templates.

3. Create a task file to invoke these templates and add this file under the Ansible `tasks` directory.

4. Create the variable values:

    - For default variable values, under the `group_vars` directory, add the values of
    the variables you created in the template in an appropriate YAML file.

    - For cluster-specific variables, under the `inventories` directory, create a new
    directory with the name of the cluster or cluster group that you want to target, and
    then create its own `group_vars` directory, and create under that a YAML file to
    contain the variable values mapping.

5. Update the playbook file and add a step to invoke the targeted task. Then, associate
    to this task the appropriate tags and properties.

In the hands-on exercise, we will configure `aws-auth` and create a Kubernetes
namespace to illustrate how this Ansible solution works. In the coming chapters, we will
use this solution to deploy more services and add-ons on top of Kubernetes.

The ansible directory's structure

The `ansible` directory is where all the Ansible source code resides in your infrastructure
repository. As a best practice, I recommend having a dedicated infrastructure source
code repository that contains all the infrastructure as code and configuration for your
Kubernetes clusters and the rest of your infrastructure. The following is the proposed
directory structure of the Ansible configuration that we will develop in this chapter:

```
k8s-infra
├── ansible
│   ├── cluster.yaml
│   ├── group_vars
│   │   └── all
│   │       ├── aws-auth.yaml
│   │       └── namespaces.yaml
│   ├── inventories
│   │   └── packtclusters
│   │       ├── group_vars
│   │       │   └── override
│   │       │       ├── aws-auth.yaml
│   │       │       └── namespaces.yaml
│   │       └── hosts
│   ├── tasks
│   │   ├── aws-auth.yaml
│   │   └── namespaces.yaml
│   └── templates
│       ├── auth
│       │   └── aws-auth.yaml
│       └── namespaces
│           └── namespaces.yaml
```

Figure 4.2 – Ansible directory structure

You will learn in detail and with hands-on practices how to develop this solution and all of the configuration code under the `ansible` directory.

Creating Ansible templates

In this section, you will create two templates to learn how you can rewrite Kubernetes manifests into Ansible Jinja2 format.

The second template is for a Kubernetes namespace, which you will use to create new namespaces.

Creating the aws-auth template

The first template is for `aws-auth` ConfigMap, which you will use to define AWS IAM users and roles and then authenticate them to the cluster. You will learn in detail about `aws-auth` and how to use it for cluster access in *Chapter 6, Securing Kubernetes Effectively*.

You will create a Jinja2 template for the `aws-auth` ConfigMap. However, let's first have a look at the default `aws-auth` ConfigMap without templating:

```
apiVersion: v1
kind: ConfigMap
metadata:
  name: aws-auth
  namespace: kube-system
data:
  mapRoles: |
    - rolearn: <ARN of instance role (not instance profile)>
      username: system:node:{{EC2PrivateDNSName}}
      groups:
        - system:bootstrappers
        - system:nodes
```

The previous code block creates an `aws-auth` ConfigMap with one role for the worker EC2. But what if we need to add more roles and users? What if we need to use the same ConfigMap with different clusters and with different worker **Amazon Resource Names (ARNs)**? We either create multiple ConfigMaps with different configurations or create a single template and let Ansible use it to generate the correct `aws-auth` ConfigMap for each cluster.

The next code block for the `aws-auth` template defines a list of specific users and roles who can access the cluster. In the first part of the code, you define the Kubernetes `apiVersion`, the object type as `ConfigMap`, and the metadata:

```
apiVersion: v1
kind: ConfigMap
metadata:
  name: aws-auth
```

In the second part of the code, you define the ConfigMap `data` section that includes the **Identity and Access Management (IAM)** users. First, instead of adding each user's data (name, ARN, and Kubernetes group), you define them inside a Jinja2 `for` loop with Jinja2 variables that can be substituted by Ansible during the execution time. You notice that we use a `for` loop so we can add multiple users:

```
data:
  mapUsers: |
{% for user in map_users.system_masters %}
    - userarn: "{{ user.arn }}"
      username: "{{ user.name }}"
      groups:
        - system:masters
{% endfor %}
```

In the second part of the code, you define another ConfigMap `data` section that includes the IAM roles. First, instead of adding each user's data (name, ARN, and Kubernetes group), you define them inside a Jinja2 `for` loop with Jinja2 variables that can be substituted by Ansible during execution. You notice that we use a `for` loop so we can add multiple roles:

```
  mapRoles: |
{% for role in map_roles.workers_roles %}
    - rolearn: "{{ role }}"
      username: {% raw -%} "system:node:{{ '{{' }}
EC2PrivateDNSName{{ '}}' }}" {%- endraw %}
      groups:
        - system:bootstrappers
        - system:nodes
{% endfor %}
{% for role in map_roles.system_masters %}
```

```
      - rolearn: "{{ role }}"
        username: {% raw -%} "admin:{{ '{{' }}SessionName{{ '}}' 
}}" {%- endraw %}
      groups:
        - system:masters
{% endfor %}
```

The previous template authenticates IAM users and roles to any cluster, and you can even extend it more with different group types according to your needs. But the original concept remains the same, as you have a single template for the aws-auth ConfigMap that can work for any cluster and for any users and roles.

Creating a Kubernetes namespace template

The next code block is for a Jinja2 template that generates a YAML for a Kubernetes namespace manifest. This template defines the basic namespace configuration, such as names, labels, and annotations.

This template can create multiple namespaces as it reads a list of namespaces from the target cluster's Ansible variables and generates the Kubernetes manifest YAMLs for each one of these namespaces:

```
{% for namespace in namespaces_list %}
---
apiVersion: v1
kind: Namespace
metadata:
  name: {{ namespace.name }}
  labels:
    name: {{ namespace.name }}
    owner: {{ namespace.owner }}
{% endfor %}
```

The previous template is an example of how you can create your own templates for Kubernetes objects. I recommend going to the Ansible Jinja2 official documentation when you write these templates to get more ideas about the code blocks and how to use them: https://docs.ansible.com/ansible/latest/user_guide/playbooks_templating.html.

Creating Ansible variables

As you learned earlier in this chapter, the Ansible `group_vars` will contain the global configuration variables that you want to apply to all clusters unless you want to specify a different value for a specific cluster. In this section, you will define default variables for the admin user in the `aws-auth` ConfigMap and define a new namespace.

Defining the aws-auth variables

The following code snippet defines the default variables for a cluster's configuration whenever the cluster does not have its own private variables. The first variable is `worker_iam_role_arn`. Ansible will get the value of `worker_iam_role_arn` from the Terraform outputs. The second variable is the clusters' admin. You also add the ARN or the IAM user that is called `admin`:

```
map_roles:
  workers_roles:
    - "{{ worker_iam_role_arn }}"
  system_masters: []
map_users:
  system_masters:
    - arn: "<ARN of the admin user>"
      name: "admin"
```

You can extend the previous variables and add more roles and users to the cluster according to your needs. You will also learn in *Chapter 6, Securing Kubernetes Effectively*, about the Kubernetes **Role-Based Access Control** (**RBAC**) and access management best practices.

> **Important note**
> In Jinja2 templates, you define the variables between double braces, `{{ }}`. Please refer to Ansible templating documentation: `https://docs.ansible.com/ansible/latest/user_guide/playbooks_templating.html`.

Configuring the default namespace

You will add a single namespace to the `namespaces_list` variable. However, you can add more namespaces according to your needs. This is an illustration to show you how namespace configuration should work with Ansible:

```
namespaces_list:
- name: default-namespace
  owner: admin
```

In this section, you should have learned how to create default configuration variables for your clusters. It is a simple configuration mechanism but is very powerful and efficient.

Creating Ansible inventories

Not all clusters are equal. In the previous section, you learned how to set default variables for your configuration. But what if you need to have different values for one of your clusters? Ansible inventories are the answer. In this section, you will create inventories to define local cluster variables that override the default variables.

Create Ansible's inventory

The way that Ansible configures hosts (servers/VMs) is very simple. Usually, there is a host or group of hosts and you have configuration tasks that you want to apply against these hosts. But our solution is a different use case, as we will use the same concept but not against any remote hosts. This is because, in reality, we do not configure hosts – instead, we configure Kubernetes clusters. Ansible just needs to communicate with the Kubernetes API server.

All you need is to set the Ansible `hosts` to target the `localhost`. Then in turn, `localhost` will use the `kube-server` API endpoint defined in `kubeconfig` to apply the intended configurations:

```
[all]
localhost
[override]
localhost
```

As you will notice in this previous code block, there is only the `localhost` value defined as the target host for Ansible. This `hosts` file should exist for each inventory that Ansible manages.

Overriding the aws-auth variables

To override the aws-auth default variables defined in group_vars, you need to recreate the aws-auth template file under the packtclusters inventory with the new variables' values. The next code block shows you how to override aws-auth. There are two IAM roles defined: the first role for workers and the second for the cluster administrator role. The second part of the code defines a different user other than the default one:

```
map_roles:
  workers_roles:
    - "{{ worker_iam_role_arn }}"
  system_masters:
    - "<ARN of the admin-role user>"
map_users:
  system_masters:
    - arn: "arn:aws:iam::AWS_ACCOUNT_NO:user/packtclusters-admin"
      name: "packtclusters-admin"
```

The previous configuration template will replace the default one for packtclusters. You can do the same for any other template.

Overriding the namespaces variables

To override the namespaces default variables defined in group_vars, you need to recreate the namespaces template file under the packtclusters inventory with the new variables' values. In the next code block, there is a new variable that will override default-namespace with a new one called packtclusters-namespace. So, when you apply this configuration, packtclusters will have the new namespace instead of the default one:

```
namespaces_list:
- name: packtsclusters-namespace
  owner: packtclusters-admin
```

In this section, you have learned how to override Ansible's default variables to use different configuration values based on the cluster.

Creating Ansible tasks

The second step after creating the Ansible templates is creating Ansible tasks. In this section, you will learn how to create Ansible tasks to deploy your configuration templates.

The tasks will use the Ansible k8s module. This module accepts the templated Kubernetes YAMLs and then instructs Ansible to apply these tasks against the target cluster. Ansible can identify the target cluster from the current context in the kubeconfig file.

> **Important note**
>
> You can learn more about Ansible's k8s module from the official documentation: https://docs.ansible.com/ansible/latest/user_guide/modules_intro.html.

Creating the aws-auth task

The following task instructs Ansible on how to generate and apply the aws-auth ConfigMap to the cluster. It takes the path to the template file as an input and applies it to the target cluster.

In the next code block, you define the task specs, with properties such as name, the kubeconfig path, state, and whether to force applying the configuration to the cluster or not. Then, the task defines which Jinja2 template to load and substitutes its variables with the values from the group_vars or inventory directories.

You will notice that there is a loop directive if there are multiple Jinja2 templates to be applied by the k8s module. The other important parameters are retries, which tells Ansible the number of retries until the task succeeds, and delay, which tells Ansible the time in seconds between each of these retries:

```
# ansible/tasks/auth/aws-auth.yaml
- name: deploy aws auth ConfigMap
  k8s:
    definition: "{{ item }}"
    kubeconfig: "{{ k8s_kubeconfig }}"
    state: "{{ k8s_manifests_state }}"
    force: "{{ k8s_force }}"
  loop:
    - "{{ lookup('template', k8s_manifests_base_dir + 'auth/
aws-auth.yaml') | from_yaml_all | list }}"
  register: k8s_result
```

```
until: k8s_result is success
retries: 3
delay: 2
no_log: "{{ k8s_no_log }}"
```

The previous code for the `aws-auth` task will be invoked by an Ansible playbook that you will learn about later in this chapter.

Creating the namespaces task

The following Ansible task file is for creating the cluster namespaces. It takes the path to the namespaces object template file and applies it to the target cluster.

The code structure for the `namespaces` task is very similar to the previous `aws-auth` task, except it has a different name, and it reads a different Jinja2 template file for `namespaces.yaml`:

```
# ansible/tasks/namespaces.yaml
- name: create cluster namespaces
  k8s:
    definition: "{{ item }}"
    kubeconfig: "{{ k8s_kubeconfig }}"
    state: "{{ k8s_manifests_state }}"
    force: "{{ k8s_force }}"
  loop: "{{ lookup('template', k8s_manifests_base_dir +
'namespaces/namespaces.yaml') | from_yaml_all | list }}"
  register: k8s_result
  until: k8s_result is success
  retries: 3
  delay: 2
  no_log: "{{ k8s_no_log }}"
```

The previous code for the `namespaces` task will be invoked by an Ansible playbook that you will learn about later in this chapter.

Creating the cluster's playbook

An Ansible playbook is an Ansible file where you put all tasks in the order that you want Ansible to execute them in. The following cluster playbook is a simple and standard Ansible playbook, and it has three sections: the first section is to define the target hosts, the second section is to define any variables that you want the tasks to use the values of during execution, and the third section is the list of tasks that Ansible will execute.

The following code block defines the hosts and the connection type. In our solution, we will use `localhost` as the target host, as explained before:

```
# ansible/cluster.yaml
---
- name: deploy k8s add-ons
  hosts: localhost
  connection: local
  gather_facts: no
```

The following code block defines the variables that are required during the execution of the tasks. The most notable ones are the physical path to the `kubeconfig` file and the base directory where the Kubernetes templates reside. These variables override any variables with similar names in the `group_vars` and `inventory` directories:

```
vars:
  Ansible_python_interpreter: "{{ Ansible_playbook_python }}"
  k8s_kubeconfig: ~/.kube/config
  k8s_manifests_base_dir: templates/
  k8s_manifests_state: present
  k8s_force: false
  k8s_no_log: false
```

The following code block defines the list of tasks that Ansible executes against the target cluster. You add new tasks to this list and assign meaningful tags to them:

```
tasks:
- import_tasks: tasks/aws-auth.yaml
  tags: aws-auth
- import_tasks: tasks/namespaces.yaml
  tags: namespaces
```

By completing the development of the playbook, tasks, and all the configurations, you are ready to put all the Ansible pieces together apply the playbook and have Ansible configure your cluster. In the next section, you will use the `packtclusters-prod1` cluster, which you created in the previous chapter, to apply the Ansible playbook.

Applying the cluster's Ansible playbook

The next instructions will deploy the Ansible playbook, which will configure your cluster with the intended configuration:

1. Initialize the Terraform state and select the workspace by running the following commands:

```
$ cd terraform/packtclusters
$ terraform init
$ terraform workspace select prod1
```

2. Retrieve and configure the localhost `kubeconfig` with the target cluster:

```
$ aws eks --region $(terraform output aws_region) update-kubeconfig --name $(terraform output cluster_full_name)
```

3. Use Python `virtualenv` to install and execute Ansible:

```
$ virtualenv $HOME/ansible-k8s-workspace
$ source $HOME/ansible-k8s-workspace/bin/activate
```

4. Install Ansible and the prerequisite modules, `openshift`, `pyyaml`, and `requests`:

```
$ pip install ansible==2.9 openshift pyyaml requests
```

5. Execute the Ansible playbook:

```
$ ansible-playbook -i \
../../ansible/inventories/packtclusters/ \
-e "worker_iam_role_arn=$(terraform output worker_iam_role_arn)" \
../../ansible/cluster.yaml
```

You will get the following output after successful execution:

```
(ansible-k8s-workspace)                packtclusters % ansible-playbook -i \
    ../../ansible/inventories/packtclusters/ \
    -e "worker_iam_role_arn=$(terraform output worker_iam_role_arn)" \
    ../../ansible/cluster.yaml

PLAY [deploy k8s add-ons] ******************************************************************************************
**********************************************

TASK [deploy aws auth configmap] *********************************************************************************
**********************************************
changed: [localhost] => (item=[{'apiVersion': 'v1', 'kind': 'ConfigMap', 'metadata': {'name': 'aws-auth', 'namespace': 'kube-system'}, 'data': {'mapUse
rs': "\n- userarn: "arn:aws:iam::917616049678:user/packtclusters-admin"\n  username: "packtclusters.admin"\n  groups:\n    - system:masters\n", 'mapRol
es': "\n- rolearn: "arn:aws:iam::636535661334:role/packtclusters-default-workers"\n  username: "system:node:{{EC2PrivateDNSName}}"\n  groups:\n    - sy
stem:bootstrappers\n    - system:nodes\n\n\n- rolearn: "arn:aws:iam::917616049678:role/admin-role"\n  username: "admin:{{SessionName}}"\n  groups:\n
  - system:masters\n"}}])

TASK [create cluster namespaces] *********************************************************************************
**********************************************
changed: [localhost] => (item={'apiVersion': 'v1', 'kind': 'Namespace', 'metadata': {'name': 'packtsclusters-namespace', 'labels': {'name': 'packtsclus
ters-namespace'}, 'annotations': {'owner': 'packtclusters-admin'}}})

PLAY RECAP *******************************************************************************************************
**********************************************
localhost                  : ok=2    changed=2    unreachable=0    failed=0    skipped=0    rescued=0    ignored=0
```

Figure 4.3 – Ansible execution output

6. Execute the following `kubectl` command to ensure that the cluster configuration is applied successfully:

```
$ kubectl get namespaces
```

You should see an output similar to the following. There is a new namespace called `packtclusters-namespace`:

```
(ansible-k8s-workspace)                    packtclusters % kubectl get namespaces
NAME                      STATUS   AGE
default                   Active   26m
kube-node-lease           Active   26m
kube-public               Active   26m
kube-system               Active   26m
packtsclusters-namespace  Active   11s
```

Figure 4.4 – List of cluster namespaces

You applied the cluster playbook and tasks as per the previous instructions. In the following chapters, you will learn how to use the same configuration management solution to create other tasks to deploy and configure services on top of your clusters.

Destroying the cluster's resources

You can follow the instructions in the *Destroying the network and cluster infrastructure* section of *Chapter 3, Provisioning Kubernetes Clusters Using AWS and Terraform*, to destroy the Kubernetes cluster and its related AWS resources. Please be sure to destroy the resources in the following order:

1. Cluster `packtclusters` resources

2. Cluster VPC resources

3. Terraform shared state resources

After executing the previous steps, all of the cluster AWS resources should be destroyed successfully. You can still log in to the AWS web console and double-check the destruction of the resources to avoid any unwanted AWS charges.

Summary

In this chapter, you learned about Kubernetes configuration management challenges and how to scale your configuration management solution to manage multiple clusters and environments. We designed and developed a solution that is based on Ansible, and we went through practical hands-on examples to deploy this code.

We started by creating Ansible templates for Kubernetes objects and add-ons. Then, we developed the tasks and the playbook to execute the Ansible configuration in sequence against the targeted clusters.

This chapter introduced you to Ansible basic concepts. It showed you how to use the best practices of infrastructure and configuration as code, automation, and Ansible development.

This sets up the base for the coming chapters, where you will use this configuration management solution to configure and deploy clusters' add-ons and services where these add-ons are essential to reach production-readiness.

In the next chapter, you will learn about Kubernetes networking and connectivity. The best practices of deploying and configuring Kubernetes network plugins, cluster DNS, ingresses, network policies, and service mesh will be covered.

Further reading

You can refer to the following links for more information on the topics covered in this chapter:

- *Ansible 2 for Configuration Management [Video]*: https://www.packtpub. com/product/ansible-2-for-configuration-management- video/9781838826475

- *Practical Ansible 2*: https://www.packtpub.com/product/practical- ansible-2/9781789807462

- *Automation with Ansible Playbooks [Video]*: https://www.packtpub. com/product/automation-with-ansible-playbooks- video/9781800206496

5
Configuring and Enhancing Kubernetes Networking Services

In the previous chapter, you learned how to develop a configuration management solution for Kubernetes with Ansible. After completing that solution, you are now ready to build the upper layer of the Kubernetes cluster, and deploy the networking services and add-ons on top of it.

In this chapter, we will learn about enhancing and fine-tuning the essential networking services and add-ons, such as CoreDNS, ExternalDNS, and Ingress Controller. We will not dig into the basic concepts of Kubernetes networking. Topics such as Kubernetes networking models, inter-pod communication, intra-pod communication, cluster services, and basic load balancing will not be covered, as in this book we are more concerned with bringing the cluster to a state of production readiness rather than digging into the basics, which you can learn about in introductory Kubernetes books.

In this chapter, we will focus on bringing the cluster networking closer to the production readiness by reconfiguring the pre-deployed services, and also deploying additional network services that are essential to Kubernetes clusters. You will learn the characteristics of Kubernetes networking best practices, as well as how to create deployment templates for the Kubernetes networking services and fine tune them.

In this chapter, we will cover the following topics:

- Introducing networking production readiness
- Configuring Kube Proxy
- Configuring Amazon CNI plugin
- Configuring CoreDNS
- Configuring ExternalDNS
- Configuring NGINX Ingress Controller
- Deploying the cluster's network services
- Destroying the cluster's resources

Technical requirements

The code for this chapter is located at `https://github.com/PacktPublishing/Kubernetes-in-Production-Best-Practices/tree/master/Chapter05`.

Check out the following link to see the Code in Action video:

`https://bit.ly/3rmhLdX`

Introducing networking production readiness

Since the beginning of Docker and the containerization era, there have been different challenges and complexities associated with handling and managing containers networking. Over the past few years, industry leaders and community contributors have worked on solutions to tackle and solve these challenges, and the efforts are still in progress.

There are multiple container networking models, network plugins, and tools in the Kubernetes ecosystem that support either mainstream use cases or specific corner cases. You can learn more about these projects and tools at the CNCF cloud native network landscape at `https://landscape.cncf.io/category=cloud-native-network&format=card-mode`. In this chapter, we will stick to the services that are essential to the general Kubernetes use cases, and their production readiness, such as CoreDNS, NGINX Ingress Controller, and ExternalDNS.

In the following sections, you will learn how to enhance and configure the pre-deployed network components that are usually shipped with AWS **Elastic Kubernetes Service (EKS)** and how to improve them. This is aside from deploying networking services and add-ons that are essential to networking functionality, operations, and reliability.

These are the network services and add-ons that we will cover:

- `kube-proxy`
- Amazon VPC K8s CNI
- CoreDNS
- ExternalDNS
- NGINX Ingress Controller

For each of these components, we will use the Ansible configuration management solution to deploy and configure them by doing the following:

1. Defining configuration variables under the cluster's Ansible `group_vars` directory, available at `https://github.com/PacktPublishing/Kubernetes-in-Production-Best-Practices/tree/master/Chapter05/ansible/group_vars/all`, and the `inventories` directory, available at `https://github.com/PacktPublishing/Kubernetes-in-Production-Best-Practices/tree/master/Chapter05/ansible/inventories/packtclusters/group_vars/override`

2. Developing a deployment template

3. Creating an Ansible task

4. Adding an entry to the cluster playbook

If there are parts of the code and templates that do not introduce new concepts or change the configuration, we will not include their source code in the chapter text. Instead, you can view them in the book's GitHub source code repository at `https://github.com/PacktPublishing/Kubernetes-in-Production-Best-Practices/tree/master/Chapter05`.

Configuring Kube Proxy

`kube-proxy` is an agent service that runs on each node in the cluster to create, update, and delete network rules on the nodes, usually through the use of Linux iptables. These network rules allow inter-pod and intra-pod communication inside and outside the Kubernetes cluster.

Irrespective of whether you use a self-managed Kubernetes cluster or a hosted one, you need to control the configuration options that you pass to `kube-proxy`. As we are using EKS, `kube-proxy` comes pre-deployed with the cluster, which leaves us without a full control over its configuration, and we need to change this.

During the cluster's lifetime, you need to control the periodic updates of `kube-proxy` and include them within the cluster's updates' pipeline. Also, you need to optimize its performance by controlling the runtime parameters, including `--iptables-sync-period`, `--iptables-min-sync-period`, and `--proxy-mode`.

To learn about the remainder of the configuration options, please check the following link: `https://kubernetes.io/docs/reference/command-line-tools-reference/kube-proxy/#options`.

> **Important note**
>
> You can find the complete source code at `https://github.com/PacktPublishing/Kubernetes-in-Production-Best-Practices/blob/master/Chapter05/ansible/templates/kube-proxy/kube-proxy.yaml`.

Now, let's create the Ansible template and configuration for `kube-proxy`:

1. Define the configuration variables and add them to the `group_vars` directory in this path: `ansible/group_vars/all/kube-proxy.yaml`. The basic configuration contains the image and its tag, which are useful for keeping track of the `kube-proxy` version that is deployed to your cluster, and for controlling its upgrades:

   ```
   kube_proxy:
       image: "602401143452.dkr.ecr.us-west-2.amazonaws.com/
   eks/kube-proxy"
       tag: "v1.15.11"
   ```

2. Create the deployment template for the `kube-proxy` DaemonSet in the following path: `ansible/templates/kube-proxy/kube-proxy.yaml`.

The following code snippet is part of this template, and the only code lines that you need to modify are where the `image` and `command` specs are defined:

```
apiVersion: apps/v1
kind: DaemonSet
metadata:
  labels:
    eks.amazonaws.com/component: kube-proxy
    k8s-app: kube-proxy
  name: kube-proxy
  namespace: kube-system
spec:
  selector:
    matchLabels:
      k8s-app: kube-proxy
  template:
    metadata:
      labels:
        k8s-app: kube-proxy
```

In the following part of the template, you can define and fine-tune the `kube-proxy` runtime options and pass them to the container entry point command:

```
  spec:
    containers:
    - command:
      - kube-proxy
      - --v=2
      - --iptables-sync-period=20s
      - --config=/var/lib/kube-proxy-config/config
      image: {{ kube_proxy.image }}:{{ kube_proxy.tag }}
```

The following are notable configuration options that you need to consider for `kube-proxy`:

- `--proxy-mode`: by default, `kube-proxy` uses the `iptables` mode, as it is hardened on production and is faster for small-sized clusters. On the other hand, the `ipvs` mode is recommended if you have a scaling cluster with services numbering above 5,000, as the `ipvs` implementation ensures superior performance.

- `--kube-api-qps`: this configuration option limits the **queries per second (QPS)** initiated from `kube-proxy` and hit `kube-apiserver`. The default value of this option is 5, but it is recommended to increase it to 10 if you expect your cluster to run above 5,000 services. However, the more QPS that `kube-proxy` sends to `kube-apiserver`, the busier it will become, and this could affect the performance of `kube-apiserver`. You should select the QPS limit based on the cluster size (number of running services) and your control plane capacity, so your cluster can serve all `kube-proxy` requests in a timely manner.

- `--iptables-sync-period`: This option defines the maximum time interval when `iptables` rules are refreshed. By default, it is set to 30s, although it is recommended to decrease this to 20s for small clusters. The cluster admin needs to decide the appropriate time interval and weigh between the conflicting priorities.

  Let's assume you decrease the interval to 1s. This means that `kube-proxy` needs to run the sync process every 1s, which means an increased load on the worker nodes where `kube-proxy` is running, while also rendering `iptables` busy and blocking other operations on them. On the other hand, if you increase the sync period and run the sync process less frequently, this could result in pods being out of iptables sync for a fraction of time, which may lead to loss of transactions.

There are other options available that handle configurations for `ipvs`, `conntrack`, `config`, and `metrics`. However, you should be careful whenever you modify any of these, and if you do decide to modify them, you have to deploy the changes to a non-production cluster to examine the performance prior to promotion to production.

For a complete list of `kube-proxy` configuration options, please refer to the Kubernetes official documentation at `https://kubernetes.io/docs/reference/command-line-tools-reference/kube-proxy/`.

Configuring the Amazon CNI plugin

In Kubernetes, the **Container Network Interface (CNI)** provides a specification and framework for writing container network plugins to manage container networking, including pod communication and **IP Address Management (IPAM)**. In the context of this book, we will not go into the details of the CNI plugins and how they work. What does concern us is how to make the best use of the CNI plugin, and how to configure it properly.

There are multiple CNI plugins that have been battle-tested over the years. Some of these satisfy the needs of general use cases, such as Calico, which is a highly recommended CNI plugin, while there are other CNI plugins that lean toward solving specific use cases.

The list of production tested CNI plugins includes Calico, Cilium, Azure CNI, Contiv, Flannel, Weave Net, and AWS CNI. The list goes on. You can get a comprehensive list of the supported CNI plugins and their features from the Kubernetes official documentation at `https://kubernetes.io/docs/concepts/cluster-administration/networking/`.

For the clusters that we provision in this book, we will use the AWS CNI plugin (**amazon-vpc-cni-k8s**) because it is the default for EKS, and it is developed to cover the general networking uses cases to ensure that Kubernetes works smoothly with AWS.

The AWS CNI plugin comes pre-deployed to the cluster with a default configuration in place. This could be sufficient for simple clusters; however, we need to take full control over the configuration, so we decided to overwrite its DaemonSet and add it to the cluster's Ansible configuration for easier control.

During the lifetime of the cluster, you need to control the periodic updates to `amazon-vpc-cni-k8s` and include them within the cluster's updates' pipeline. Also, you will need to optimize its performance by adjusting the configuration variables that are passed to it, such as `MINIMUM_IP_TARGET`, `WARM_IP_TARGET`, and `AWS_VPC_ENI_MTU`.

To learn more about the other CNI configuration options, please check this link: `https://docs.aws.amazon.com/eks/latest/userguide/cni-env-vars.html`.

> **Important note**
>
> When you redeploy the updated `amazon-vpc-cni-k8s` DaemonSet into your cluster, the CNI pods will get restarted. The updated pods are rolled out one after the other, but this still causes short periods of CNI plugin unavailability, which may be noticeable in the case of a busy cluster.
>
> You can find the complete source code at `https://github.com/PacktPublishing/Kubernetes-in-Production-Best-Practices/blob/master/Chapter05/ansible/templates/cni/amazon-k8s-cni.yaml`.

Now, let's create the Ansible template and configuration for `amazon-vpc-cni-k8s`:

1. Define the configuration variables and add them to the `group_vars` directory in this path: `ansible/group_vars/all/cni.yaml`. The basic configuration contains the image and its tag, which are useful for keeping track of the `amazon-vpc-cni-k8s` version that is deployed to your cluster, and for controlling its upgrades.

There are two important configuration values for cluster performance:

- MINIMUM_IP_TARGET, which is important for pre-scaling as it specifies the number of minimum IP addresses to allocate for pod assignment on the node

- WARM_IP_TARGET, which is important for dynamic scaling as it specifies the number of free IP addresses that the ipamD daemon should attempt to keep available for pod assignment on the node.

Both of these variables together ensure that sufficient IP addresses are available for new pods, which improves the start-up time of pods and enhances cluster uptime and recovery time. You can specify the values of these variables based on the estimated number of pods running in the cluster, and the number during spikes:

```
cni_warm_ip_target: 2
cni_min_ip_target: 10
aws_cni:
   image: "602401143452.dkr.ecr.us-west-2.amazonaws.com/
amazon-k8s-cni"
   tag: "v1.6.2"
```

2. Create the deployment template for the amazon-vpc-cni-k8s DaemonSet in this path: ansible/templates/cni/amazon-k8s-cni.yaml.

The following code snippet is part of this template, and the only code lines that you need to modify are where the image and env specs are defined:

```
---
      containers:
      - image: {{ aws_cni.image }}:{{ aws_cni.tag }}
        imagePullPolicy: Always
        env:
        - name: AWS_VPC_K8S_CNI_LOGLEVEL
          value: DEBUG
        - name: AWS_VPC_K8S_CNI_VETHPREFIX
          value: eni
        - name: AWS_VPC_ENI_MTU
          value: "9001"
        - name: MINIMUM_IP_TARGET
          value: "{{ cni_min_ip_target }}"
        - name: WARM_IP_TARGET
          value: "{{ cni_warm_ip_target }}"
```

```
- name: MY_NODE_NAME
  valueFrom:
    fieldRef:
      fieldPath: spec.nodeName
```

You can configure other options for `amazon-vpc-cni-k8s` by adding them to the container environment variables, as in the previous code snippet for the container section in the DaemonSet template.

Configuring CoreDNS

Kubernetes used to have `kube-dns` as its default cluster DNS service, but starting from version 1.11, it uses CoreDNS. Also, it gets pre-deployed by most of the managed Kubernetes offerings, including EKS, that we use in this book.

For the other Kubernetes managed services that still use `kube-dns`, such as GKE, we recommend referring to the official documentation of `kube-dns`.

CoreDNS is very flexible as it is modular and pluggable. It has a rich set of plugins that can be enabled to enhance DNS functionalities. This is why it is powerful and generally preferred over `kube-dns` and other Kubernetes DNS solutions. To learn more about the supported plugins, please refer to the following list: `https://coredns.io/plugins/`.

During the cluster's lifetime, you need to control CoreDNS configuration as code, its periodic updates, and include all of this within the cluster's deployment pipeline. Also, you will need to optimize your cluster DNS performance and add extra DNS functionalities by enabling CoreDNS plugins.

It is recommended to tune the CoreDNS resource quota for CPU and memory to improve cluster DNS performance, especially in the case of a heavily scaling cluster. For detailed resource configuration and scaling, please check this link: `https://github.com/coredns/deployment/blob/master/kubernetes/Scaling_CoreDNS.md#`.

> **Important note**
>
> You can find this section's complete source code at `https://github.com/PacktPublishing/Kubernetes-in-Production-Best-Practices/blob/master/Chapter05/ansible/templates/core-dns/core-dns.yaml`.

Now, let's create the Ansible template and configuration for `coredns`:

1. Define the configuration variables and add them to the `group_vars` directory in this path: `ansible/group_vars/all/core-dns.yaml`. The basic configuration contains the image and its tag, which are useful for keeping track of the CoreDNS version that is deployed to your cluster, and for controlling its upgrades.

   The default IP of the cluster DNS is usually `172.20.0.10` unless you decide to change it. You can specify the number of CoreDNS pods across the cluster by setting the number of replicas:

   ```
   core_dns_replicas: 2
   dns_cluster_ip: 172.20.0.10
   core_dns:
     image: "602401143452.dkr.ecr.us-east-1.amazonaws.com/
   eks/coredns"
     tag: "v1.6.6"
   ```

2. Create the deployment template for the CoreDNS pods in this path: `ansible/templates/core-dns /core-dns.yaml`.

   The following code snippet is part of this template, and the notable configuration here in this deployment template is the number of CoreDNS replicas and the Docker image:

   ```
   ---
   apiVersion: apps/v1
   kind: Deployment
   metadata:
     name: coredns
     namespace: kube-system
     labels:
       k8s-app: kube-dns
       kubernetes.io/name: "CoreDNS"
       eks.amazonaws.com/component: coredns
   spec:
     replicas: {{ core_dns_replicas }}
   ```

In the following code snippet, you configure the CoreDNS image and tag:

```
containers:
- name: coredns
  image: {{ core_dns.image }}:{{ core_dns.tag }}
```

3. In the following code snippet, you specify the `ConfigMap` CoreDNS, where you can modify `Corefile` to enable additional plugins and fine-tune their configurations:

```
---
apiVersion: v1
kind: ConfigMap
metadata:
  name: coredns
  namespace: kube-system
  labels:
    eks.amazonaws.com/component: coredns
    k8s-app: kube-dns
data:
  Corefile: |
    .:53 {
        errors
        health
        ready
        kubernetes cluster.local {
          pods insecure
          upstream
          fallthrough in-addr.arpa ip6.arpa
        }
        prometheus :9153
        forward . /etc/resolv.conf
        cache 300
        loop
        reload
        loadbalance
        autopath @kubernetes
    }
```

In the previous code for the `ConfigMap`, we added extra plugins that help to improve the cluster's DNS performance as follows:

- `ready`: An HTTP endpoint on port `8181` will return `200 OK`, when all plugins that are able to signal readiness have done so.

- `loop`: This plugin halts the CoreDNS process if a forwarding loop is detected.

- `reload`: This plugin automatically reloads `Corefile` whenever it gets changed.

- `loadbalance`: This plugin randomizes the order of DNS records in the answers and is a round-robin DNS load balancer.

- `autopath @kubernetes`: This plugin follows the chain of search path elements and return the first reply that is not NXDOMAIN.

- `cache`: This plugin enables a frontend cache. It is enabled by default; however, it has `30` seconds as a default caching duration, but we recommend increasing this value to `300` seconds to achieve better performance in the case of large clusters.

I encourage you to use the preceding CoreDNS plugins, and also check the `plugins` directory, which could have other interesting and useful plugins that solve specific problems or provide options for your applications, here: `https://coredns.io/manual/plugins/`.

Configuring ExternalDNS

While CoreDNS serves as the internal DNS server for Kubernetes clusters, ExternalDNS is a Kubernetes add-on that is used to manage your cluster external DNS providers, including Route 53, AzureDNS, and Google Cloud DNS.

It makes Kubernetes deployments and services discoverable through public DNS services, such as Route 53. It queries the Kubernetes API to retrieve a list of services and ingresses, and then it communicates with the public DNS and registers these records.

ExternalDNS allows you to control DNS records (via cloud DNS services such as AWS Route 53 or Google Cloud DNS) dynamically via Kubernetes services and ingresses.

ExternalDNS does not come pre-installed with the cluster, so you need to deploy it and specify its configuration, which includes its Docker image, the number of replicas to run, DNS record syncing and interval updates, the cloud provider type (that is, AWS, Azure, and so on), and the hosted zone ID (in the case of AWS Route 53).

> **Important note**
>
> You can find the complete source code at `https://github.com/PacktPublishing/Kubernetes-in-Production-Best-Practices/blob/master/Chapter05/ansible/templates/external-dns/external-dns.yaml`.

Now, let's create the Ansible template and configuration for ExternalDNS:

1. Define the configuration variables and add them to the `group_vars` directory in this path: `ansible/group_vars/all/external-dns.yaml`. The basic configuration contains the image and its tag, which are useful for keeping track of the ExternalDNS version that is deployed to your cluster, and for controlling its upgrades.

    Also, you specify the values for other configuration variables, including `log_level`, `provider`, `aws_zone_type`, `interval`, `route53_zone_type`, and `external_dns_replicas`:

    ```
    log_level: error
    provider: aws
    aws_zone_type: private
    interval: 1m
    route53_zone_id: Z09817802WZ9HZYSUI2RE
    external_dns_replicas: 2
    external_dns:
      image: "registry.opensource.zalan.do/teapot/external-dns"
      tag: "v0.5.9"
    ```

2. Create the deployment template for the ExternalDNS pods in this path: `ansible/templates/external-dns /external-dns.yaml`.

    In the following code snippet of the template, you configure the number of ExternalDNS replicas:

    ```
    ---
    apiVersion: apps/v1
    kind: Deployment
    metadata:
      name: external-dns
      namespace: kube-system
    ```

```
spec:
  replicas: {{ external_dns_replicas }}
```

3. Then you configure the ExternalDNS image and tag, in addition to the ExternalDNS runtime configuration variables, including `log-level`, `source`, `provider`, `aws-zone-id`, `interval`, `registry`, and `txt-owner-id`:

```
spec:
    serviceAccountName: external-dns
    containers:
    - name: external-dns
      image: {{ external_dns.image }}:{{ external_dns.
tag }}
      args:
      - --log-level={{ log_level }}
      - --source=service
      - --source=ingress
      - --provider={{ provider }}
      - --aws-zone-type={{ aws_zone_type }}
      - --interval={{ interval }}
      - --registry=txt
      - --txt-owner-id={{ route53_zone_id }}-{{
cluster_name }}
```

4. For ExternalDNS to operate properly, it needs to access the Route 53 DNS resources. This is why you need to create the following IAM policy to allow ExternalDNS to list the hosted zones, list the DNS record sets, and change the DNS records:

```
resource "aws_iam_policy" "external_dns_policy" {
  name        = "${var.cluster_full_name}-
ExternalDNSPolicy"
  path        = "/"
  description = "Allows workers nodes to use route53
resources"
  policy = <<EOF
{
  "Version": "2012-10-17",
  "Statement": [
```

```
        {
            "Effect": "Allow",
            "Action": [
              "route53:ChangeResourceRecordSets"
            ],
            "Resource": ["*"]
        },
        {
            "Effect": "Allow",
            "Action": [
              "route53:ListHostedZones",
              "route53:ListResourceRecordSets"
            ],
            "Resource": ["*"]
        }
      ]
    }
EOF
    }
```

If you do not create the preceding IAM policy and attach it to the worker nodes or to the pod, then ExternalDNS will fail to operate.

ExternalDNS can be configured to use the majority of DNS providers, including AzureDNS, Google Cloud DNS, CloudFlare, and DNSimple.

To get more details and detailed code samples on how to use ExternalDNS with your DNS provider and your Kubernetes deployments, please check the official documentation at https://github.com/kubernetes-sigs/external-dns.

Configuring NGINX Ingress Controller

There are three main ways in which to expose Kubernetes services externally: NodePort, load balancers, and Ingress. In this section, we will focus on ingresses, as they fulfill the needs of the majority of the workloads and deployments on Kubernetes clusters.

Ingress exposes TCP/IP L7 services (such as HTTP/HTTPS) and it routes traffic from outside the cluster to services within the cluster. Ingress controls traffic routing through a defined set of rules for each ingress resource and/or a global configuration for all ingress resources.

There are many configurations that an ingress can control, including giving services an external URL, SSL/TLS termination, session validity, and name-based virtual hosting. An ingress controller is the Kubernetes resource that is responsible for fulfilling the ingress.

The most popular and battle-tested ingress is NGINX Ingress Controller. This is an ingress controller for Kubernetes that uses NGINX as a reverse proxy and load balancer.

NGINX Ingress Controller does not come pre-installed with the cluster, so you need to deploy and configure it on your cluster, which includes its Docker image, the number of replicas to run, runtime arguments, and service and cloud load balancer specs.

> **Important note**
>
> You can find the complete source code at `https://github.com/PacktPublishing/Kubernetes-in-Production-Best-Practices/blob/master/Chapter05/ansible/templates/ingress-nginx/ingress-nginx.yaml`.

Now, let's create the Ansible templates and configuration for `ingress-nginx`:

1. Create the configuration variables and add them to the `group_vars` directory in this path: `ansible/group_vars/all/ingress-nginx.yaml`. The basic configuration contains the images for `nginx-ingress-controller` and its webhook. This is useful for keeping track of the `ingress-nginx` version that is deployed to your cluster and for controlling its upgrades:

```
nginx_ingress_controller:
    image: "quay.io/kubernetes-ingress-controller/nginx-ingress-controller"
    tag: "0.32.0"
nginx_ingress_webhook_certgen:
    image: "jettech/kube-webhook-certgen"
    tag: "v1.2.0"
```

2. Create the template for the `ingress-nginx` deployment in this path: `ansible/templates/ingress-nginx/ingress-nginx.yaml`:

```
---
apiVersion: apps/v1
kind: Deployment
```

3. In the following code snippet, the deployment gets the value of the container's image from the `ingress-nginx group_vars` directory:

```
    spec:
      dnsPolicy: ClusterFirst
      containers:
        - name: controller
          image: {{ nginx_ingress_controller.image }}:{{
nginx_ingress_controller.tag }}
```

4. In the following code snippet, you create a `ConfigMap` to configure `nginx-ingress`:

```
---
apiVersion: v1
kind: ConfigMap
metadata:
  labels:
    app.kubernetes.io/name: ingress-nginx
    app.kubernetes.io/instance: ingress-nginx
    app.kubernetes.io/component: controller
  name: ingress-nginx-controller
  namespace: ingress-nginx
data:
```

5. In the following code snippet, you create the service that is used to expose the `nginx-ingress` controller to the public internet. This is achieved by provisioning AWS **Network Load Balancer (NLB)** and assigning it to the `nginx-ingress` service:

```
---
apiVersion: v1
kind: Service
metadata:
  annotations:
    service.beta.kubernetes.io/aws-load-balancer-backend-
protocol: tcp
    service.beta.kubernetes.io/aws-load-balancer-
connection-idle-timeout: '60'
```

```
    service.beta.kubernetes.io/aws-load-balancer-cross-
zone-load-balancing-enabled: 'true'
    service.beta.kubernetes.io/aws-load-balancer-type:
nlb
  labels:
    app.kubernetes.io/name: ingress-nginx
    app.kubernetes.io/instance: ingress-nginx
    app.kubernetes.io/component: controller
  name: ingress-nginx-controller
  namespace: ingress-nginx
spec:
  type: LoadBalancer
  externalTrafficPolicy: Local
```

After completing the creation of the networking services and add-ons with Ansible templates, you are ready to deploy them and apply the Ansible playbook to your cluster. In the next section, you will use the `packtclusters-prod1` cluster, which you created in the previous chapter, to apply all of these changes.

Deploying the cluster's network services

The following instructions will deploy the Ansible playbook and configure your cluster with the networking services and add-ons configuration:

1. Initialize the Terraform state and select the workspace by running the following commands:

```
$ cd terraform/packtclusters
$ terraform init
$ terraform workspace select prod1
```

2. Execute Terraform to apply the infrastructure we added in this chapter – the IAM policy and the policy attachment for ExternalDNS:

```
$ terraform apply -auto-approve
```

Then you should get the following output:

```
Apply complete! Resources: 2 added, 0 changed, 0
destroyed.
Releasing state lock. This may take a few moments...
```

3. Retrieve and configure kubeconfig for the target cluster:

```
$ aws eks --region $(terraform output aws_region) update-
kubeconfig --name $(terraform output cluster_full_name)
```

4. Create virtualenv to install and execute Ansible:

```
$ virtualenv $HOME/Ansible-k8s-workspace
$ source $HOME/Ansible-k8s-workspace/bin/activate
```

5. Install Ansible, along with the prerequisite modules, openshift, pyyaml, and requests:

```
$ pip install Ansible==2.8.10 openshift pyyaml requests
```

6. Execute the Ansible playbook:

```
$ Ansible-playbook -i \
../../Ansible/inventories/packtclusters/ \
-e "worker_iam_role_arn=$(terraform output worker_iam_
role_arn)" \
../../Ansible/cluster.yaml
```

7. You will get the following output following the successful execution of Ansible:

Figure 5.1 – Ansible execution output

8. Execute the following kubectl command to get all the pods running in the cluster. This allows you to verify that the cluster configuration has been applied successfully:

```
$ kubectl get pods --all-namespaces
```

You should get the following output, which lists all the pods running in the cluster, including the new pods for the networking add-ons:

```
NAMESPACE       NAME                                        READY   STATUS      RESTARTS   AGE
ingress-nginx   ingress-nginx-admission-create-7z44v        0/1     Completed   0          51s
ingress-nginx   ingress-nginx-admission-patch-wg7dh         0/1     Completed   1          51s
ingress-nginx   ingress-nginx-controller-5cc4589cc8-77tvx   1/1     Running     0          61s
kube-system     aws-node-gcv2s                              1/1     Running     0          6m10s
kube-system     aws-node-gs2fh                              1/1     Running     0          6m9s
kube-system     aws-node-rjmtl                              0/1     Running     0          42s
kube-system     coredns-84b69cff6f-hb2r6                    1/1     Running     0          68s
kube-system     coredns-84b69cff6f-p2f52                    1/1     Running     0          65s
kube-system     external-dns-558bc6f9bb-f9xp7               1/1     Running     0          65s
kube-system     external-dns-558bc6f9bb-ms7lf               1/1     Running     0          65s
kube-system     kube-proxy-76qwn                            1/1     Running     0          59s
kube-system     kube-proxy-j2mx6                            1/1     Running     0          52s
kube-system     kube-proxy-p6gl4                            1/1     Running     0          45s
```

Figure 5.2 – List of all pods

Now you have completed the application of the cluster configuration as per the previous instructions and your cluster has all of the networking services and add-ons deployed and configured, ready for production workloads.

Destroying the cluster's resources

First, you should delete the ingress-nginx service to instruct AWS to destroy the NLB associated with the ingress controller. This step is required because terraform will fail to destroy this NLB because it has been created by Kubernetes:

```
$ kubectl -n nginx-ingress delete svc nginx-ingress
```

Then, you can follow the rest of the instructions in the *Destroying the network and cluster infrastructure* section in *Chapter 3, Building and Provisioning Kubernetes Clusters*, to destroy the Kubernetes cluster and all related AWS resources. Please ensure that the resources are destroyed in the following order:

1. Kubernetes cluster packtclusters resources

2. Cluster VPC resources

3. Terraform shared state resources

By executing the previous steps, all Kubernetes and AWS infrastructure resources should be destroyed and cleaned up ahead of the hands-on practice in the next chapter.

Summary

In this chapter, you have learned about Kubernetes networking components and services that make a cluster ready for production. You developed the templates and configuration as code for these services with Ansible.

Despite the fact that some of these components come pre-deployed with AWS EKS, you still need to fine-tune their configurations to fulfill your cluster requirements for scaling, availability, security, and performance. You also deployed additional add-ons and services, including ExternalDNS and NGINX Ingress Controller, that proved to be essential for Kubernetes' networking needs.

By using the Ansible configuration management solution that we introduced in the previous chapter, writing the Kubernetes manifests of these services becomes simple, scalable, and maintainable. We follow the same framework and steps to configure each service, and this is repeated for all services and add-on configurations that you will develop during this book.

This chapter covered the network production readiness for Kubernetes clusters, but there are relevant topics that we will cover in the forthcoming chapters, including network security, network policies, service mesh, and network service observability.

In the next chapter, you will learn in detail about Kubernetes security; the security best practices, tools, add-ons, and configuration that you need to deploy and optimize for production-grade clusters.

Further reading

You can refer to the following links for more information on the topics covered in this chapter:

- *Getting Started with Kubernetes – Third Edition* (*Chapter 3, Working with Networking, Load Balancers, and Ingress*): https://www.packtpub.com/virtualization-and-cloud/getting-started-kubernetes-third-edition

- *Mastering Kubernetes – Second Edition* (*Chapter 10, Advanced Kubernetes Networking*): https://www.packtpub.com/application-development/mastering-kubernetes-second-edition

- Hands-On Kubernetes Networking [Video]: https://www.packtpub.com/virtualization-and-cloud/hands-kubernetes-networking-video

6

Securing Kubernetes Effectively

In previous chapters, you learned how to design and provision the infrastructure of Kubernetes clusters, fine-tune their configuration, and deploy extra add-ons and services on top of the clusters, such as networking, security, monitoring, and scaling.

In this chapter, you will learn about the different aspects of Kubernetes security, focusing on qualifying the cluster to have a production-grade security. We will follow an end-to-end security approach to cover all of the essential areas that every production cluster should have. We will know how to bring the cluster security closer to the production readiness state by fine-tuning the security configuration of the cluster and its infrastructure and deploying new security add-ons and tools, and finally ensure cluster security compliance and conformance to security standards and checks.

In this chapter, we will cover the following topics:

- Securing Kubernetes infrastructure
- Managing cluster access
- Managing secrets and certificates
- Securing workloads and apps
- Ensuring cluster security and compliance

- Bonus security tips
- Deploying the security configurations
- Destroying the cluster

Technical requirements

You should have the following tools installed from the previous chapters:

- AWS CLI V2
- AWS IAM Authenticator
- `kubectl`
- Terraform
- Python3
- PIP 3
- virtualenv
- You need to have an up-and-running Kubernetes cluster

The code for this chapter is available at `https://github.com/PacktPublishing/Kubernetes-in-Production-Best-Practices/tree/master/Chapter06`.

Check out the following link to see the Code in Action video:

`https://bit.ly/2MBwZNk`

Securing Kubernetes infrastructure

In *Chapter 2, Architecting Production-Grade Kubernetes Infrastructure*, we discussed the best practices for the network infrastructure for Kubernetes clusters and we proposed design guidelines that are essential for the infrastructure security of clusters. While these guidelines are essential for you to consider and follow, you still need to evaluate the entire network security requirements of your infrastructure to be sure that you have a complete and appropriate security solution for your environment and product.

Most of these security recommendations and best practices are implemented within the Terraform and Ansible configurations that we did in the previous chapters:

- Use multiple availability zones (three or more) to deploy your Kubernetes cluster for high availability.

- Deploy the control plane and worker nodes in private subnets only. Use the public subnets for internet-facing load balancers.

- Do not allow public access to worker nodes. Expose services externally through load balancers or ingress controllers, and not through node ports.

- Serve all the traffic between the API server and other control plane components or workers over TLS.

- Limit network access to the Kubernetes API endpoint.

- Block access to `kubelet`.

- Use security groups to block access to workers and control plane ports, except secure ones.

- Disable SSH access to worker nodes. You can use AWS Systems Manager Session Manager instead of running SSHD to connect to nodes.

- Restrict access to the EC2 instance profile credentials. By default, the containers in a pod use the same IAM permissions assigned to the node instance profile. This is considered an insecure behavior, because it gives the containers full control over the node and the underlying AWS services. To avoid this behavior, you must disable the pod's access to the node's instance profile by executing the following `iptables` commands inside the node:

```
$ yum install -y iptables-services
$ iptables --insert FORWARD 1 --in-interface eni+
--destination 169.254.169.254/32 --jump DROP
$ iptables-save | tee /etc/sysconfig/iptables
$ systemctl enable --now iptables
```

We will achieve the same by using the `kube2iam` add-on. It manages the pod's IAM access, and it will block the containers from accessing the instance profile credentials. You will learn about `kube2iam` in detail later in this chapter.

- As we are using EKS, it is highly recommended to use a regular **Auto Scaling Group (ASG)** instead of the EKS node group. This is because we cannot modify the user data of the EC2 instances in the EKS node group, which prevents us from customizing the deployed services to EC2, including the `kubelet` agent. Another reason for avoiding EKS node groups is that it enforces the attachment of public IPs to the worker nodes, which can represent security threats.

The preceding list covers the essential production infrastructure security guidelines for your Kubernetes clusters. All of these guidelines are covered by cluster provisioning and configuration management, which we implemented in the previous chapters. It is worth mentioning that your cluster infrastructure may have extra security requirements that you should consider during infrastructure design and provisioning.

Managing cluster access

Requests from a cluster's users, either humans or service accounts, need to go through authentication and authorization stages before hitting the API server and manipulating the required Kubernetes objects. A typical request goes through three access stages before it gets either allowed or rejected:

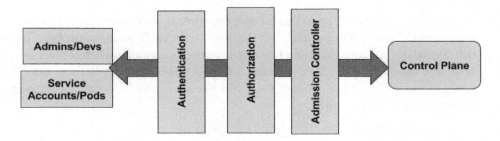

Figure 6.1 – Kubernetes access stages

The request has to go through the authentication stage to verify the client's identity by any of the mechanisms supported by Kubernetes, then it goes through the authorization stage to verify which actions are allowed for this user, and finally it goes through the admission controller stage to decide whether any modifications need to be made. You will learn about each of these in the following subsections.

Cluster authentication

Kubernetes cluster users need to successfully authenticate into the cluster to access its objects. However, normal cluster users, such as developers and administrators, are not supposed to be managed by Kubernetes, but by an external service outside the cluster, such as **Lightweight Directory Access Protocol (LDAP)**, **OpenID Connect (OIDC)**, AWS **Identity and Access Management (IAM)**, or even a file with users and password pairs. On the other hand, service accounts are managed by Kubernetes, and you can add or delete them using Kubernetes API calls.

As a cluster owner, you need to decide how you will manage the cluster's normal users, in other words, which external service to use. To authenticate users in the case of production clusters, we recommend using AWS IAM as the authentication service. However, it is also possible to use an OIDC identity provider, such as Azure Active Directory, or GitHub.

It's worth mentioning that Kubernetes has different authentication modules for different means of authentication, such as client TLS certificates, passwords, and tokens. And the cluster administrator can configure some or all of them during cluster provisioning.

Authenticating users with AWS IAM

EKS supports the webhook token authentication and service account tokens. The webhook authentication verifies the bearer tokens. These bearer tokens are generated by the `aws-iam-authenticator` client when you execute `kubectl` commands. Then, the token is passed to `kube-apiserver` before being forwarded to the authentication webhook, which returns the user's account and ARN to `kube-apiserver`.

Once the user's identity has been authenticated by the AWS IAM service, `kube-apiserver` reads the `aws-auth` ConfigMap in the `kube-system` namespace to determine the **Role-Based Access Control (RBAC)** group to associate with the user. The `aws-auth` ConfigMap is used to create a mapping between the IAM users and roles, and Kubernetes RBAC groups for authorization purposes. These RBAC groups can be referenced in Kubernetes ClusterRoleBindings or RoleBindings.

We already learned how to create a custom `aws-auth` ConfigMap in *Chapter 4, Managing Cluster Configuration with Ansible*, where we can add IAM users and IAM roles that users can assume to access the cluster. Please check the `aws-auth` ConfigMap's full configuration code here: `https://github.com/PacktPublishing/ Kubernetes-in-Production-Best-Practices/blob/master/Chapter06/ ansible/templates/auth/aws-auth.yaml`.

We recommend using IAM roles to manage production cluster access, and you can assign these IAM roles to IAM groups and users, which makes Kubernetes authentication easier to operate and scale.

Modifying the EKS cluster creator

It is worth noting that EKS gives the IAM user or whatever IAM role that creates the cluster a permanent administrator authentication on the cluster's Kubernetes API service. AWS does not provide any way to change this or to move it to a different IAM user or role. To minimize the security drawbacks of this limitation, we suggest doing the following:

1. Use a dedicated but temporary IAM role to provision each new cluster.

2. After provisioning the cluster, remove all IAM permissions from this role.

3. Update the `aws-auth` ConfigMap in the `kube-system` namespace and add more IAM users and roles to be able to manage and use the cluster.

4. Add these groups as subjects of `RoleBindings` and `ClusterRoleBindings` in the cluster RBAC as needed.

You already learned in *Chapter 4*, *Managing Cluster Configuration with Ansible*, how to handle this drawback in the Ansible cluster configuration as we created a custom `aws-auth` ConfigMap and `ClusterRoleBindings`.

Cluster authorization

The second stage of cluster access is authorization. This determines whether the operation requested is allowed. In order for Kubernetes to authorize a request, it considers three inputs; first, the user who initiated the request, then the requested action, and finally the Kubernetes resource to be modified by the action, such as pods and services.

When you create a cluster, you configure the authorization mode by passing its value to the API server. However, in EKS, all of the authorization modes (RBAC, attribute-based access control, and webhooks) are enabled by default, and Kubernetes will check each of them to authorize the requests.

Admission controller

The final stage of cluster access is passing through the admission controller. In this step, requests are validated based on the rules defined in the admission controller and the requested object. There is also another type of admission controller, called a mutating controller, which can modify the request, such as injecting side car containers or modifying pod specs before sending the request to `kube-api-server`.

An admission controller is a powerful authorization mechanism, and it can be extended by cluster users or third parties to enforce special validations and rules on cluster users.

Managing secrets and certificates

Secrets and TLS certificates are essential security needs for modern applications, and while Kubernetes provides a native solution to create and consume secrets and sensitive data, it remains in need of additional hardening. On the other hand, Kubernetes has no native answer to certificate issuing and management, which is why we will deploy one of the popular add-ons and use it for this purpose.

Creating and managing secrets

Kubernetes has a secret resource type that can be used to store sensitive data, such as passwords, tokens, certificates, and SSH keys. Pods can consume these secrets by mounting them as volumes or environment variables. However, we do not recommend environment variables because they can leak out and get compromised.

Another challenge here arises when users decide to store the secrets that YAML manifests in Git repositories. In such a case, the sensitive data can be easily compromised because secrets do not use encryption, but Base64 encoding, which can simply be decoded.

Sealed Secrets solves this problem by providing a mechanism to encrypt the secret sensitive data and make it safe to store in Git repositories.

Sealed Secrets consists of two parts:

1. A command-line tool, `kubeseal`, to transform **Custom Resource Definition (CRD)** secrets into sealed secrets.
2. A Sealed Secrets controller that is used to generate the encryption key, and decrypt sealed secrets into secrets to be used by the pods.

To learn more about Sealed Secrets and the `kubeseal` client, please review these here: `https://github.com/bitnami-labs/sealed-secrets`.

This is how it works. `kubeseal` communicates with the Sealed Secrets controller to retrieve the encryption public key, and then it uses this key to encrypt the secret CRD into a sealed secret CRD. And when a pod requires use of the sealed secret, the controller uses the encryption private key to decrypt the sealed secret CRD and convert it to a regular secret CRD.

It is worthwhile mentioning that Sealed Secrets mitigates the security risks associated with secrets in a multi-tenant cluster by introducing the concept of scopes to limit secret use and manipulation within a namespace, or cluster-wide, and with the possibility to restrict or change the secret name and namespace. The details of the reasoning behind this can be found here in the official documentation: `https://github.com/bitnami-labs/sealed-secrets#scopes`.

Now, let's create the Ansible template and configuration to deploy the Sealed Secrets controller to the cluster:

1. Define the required configuration variables and add them to the `group_vars` directory in this path – `ansible/group_vars/all/sealed-secrets.yaml`. The basic configuration contains the number of deployment replicas and the image tag, which is useful for keeping track of the deployed version and controlling its upgrades:

    ```
    sealed_secrets_replicas: 1
    seald_secrets:
      image: "quay.io/bitnami/sealed-secrets-controller"
      tag: "v0.12.4"
    ```

    > **Important note**
    >
    > You can find the complete source code of the Sealed Secrets deployment template at `https://github.com/PacktPublishing/Kubernetes-in-Production-Best-Practices/blob/master/Chapter06/ansible/templates/sealed-secrets`.

2. Create the deployment template for the Sealed Secrets controller in this path – `ansible/templates/sealed-secrets/sealed-secrets.yaml`. In this controller, we will only set variables for the deployment replicas and image tags. You can check the complete manifest YAML file at `https://github.com/PacktPublishing/Kubernetes-in-Production-Best-Practices/blob/master/Chapter06/ansible/templates/sealed-secrets/sealed-secrets.yaml`.

3. Install the `kubeseal` CLI for macOS as follows:

    ```
    $ brew install kubeseal
    ```

    Install it for Linux using the following command:

    ```
    $ wget https://github.com/bitnami-labs/sealed-secrets/
    releases/download/v0.12.4/kubeseal-linux-amd64 -O
    kubeseal
    $ sudo install -m 755 kubeseal /usr/local/bin/kubeseal
    ```

To deploy the Sealed Secrets controller, please apply the deployment steps covered at the end of this chapter under the *Deploying the security configurations* section.

Managing TLS certificates with Cert-Manager

Cert-Manager is a Kubernetes add-on and controller that allows certificates to be issued from different sources, such as SelfSigned, CA, Vault, and ACME/Let's Encrypt, and external issuers, such as AWS Private Certificate Authority and AWS Key Management Service. It also ensures the validity of certificates and auto-renews and rotates them. You can learn more about the project here: `https://cert-manager.io/docs/`.

Cert-Manager will make TLS certificates available out of the box for Kubernetes workloads, and it will make issuing and managing these certificates a native feature within the Kubernetes cluster, which is easy to manage and operate.

Cert-Manager does not come pre-installed with the cluster, so you need to deploy it and specify its configuration, which includes its Docker image, the number of replicas to run, certificate issuers, DNS Route 53 zones, and so on.

To deploy Cert-Manager, we will create three Kubernetes manifest files: namespace, controller, and certificate issuers.

There are various issuers supported by Cert-Manager. Please check here: `https://cert-manager.io/docs/configuration/`. In this chapter, we decided to use Let's Encrypt as it is free and commonly used, but you can use Cert-Manager documentation and the same deployment here with any of the other issuers.

Now, let's create the Ansible template and the configuration for it:

> **Important note**
>
> You can find the complete source code of the Cert-Manager deployment template at `https://github.com/PacktPublishing/Kubernetes-in-Production-Best-Practices/tree/master/Chapter06/ansible/templates/cert-manager`.

1. Define the required configuration variables and add them to the `group_vars` directory in this path – `ansible/group_vars/all/cert-manager.yaml`. The basic configuration contains the number of deployment replicas and the image tags for controller, webhook, and `cainjector`, which is useful for keeping track of the version deployed and for controlling its upgrades. Also, there is the configuration of Let's Encrypt issuers for both `prod` and `nonprod` ACME URLs:

```
log_level: error
letsencrypt_email: security@packt.com
letsencrypt_prod_url: https://acme-v02.api.letsencrypt.
org/directory
```

```
letsencrypt_nonprod_url: https://acme-staging-v02.api.
letsencrypt.org/directory
cert_manager_replicas: 1
cert_manager_controller:
  image: "quay.io/jetstack/cert-manager-controller"
  tag: "v0.15.2"
cert_manager_cainjector:
  image: "quay.io/jetstack/cert-manager-cainjector"
  tag: "v0.15.2"
cert_manager_webhook:
  image: "quay.io/jetstack/cert-manager-webhook"
  tag: "v0.15.2"
```

2. Create the namespace for Cert-Manager in this path – `ansible/templates/cert-manager/namespace.yaml`:

```
---
apiVersion: v1
kind: Namespace
metadata:
  name: cert-manager
  labels:
    certmanager.k8s.io/disable-validation: "true"
```

3. Create the deployment template for the Cert-Manager controller resources in this path – `ansible/templates/cert-manager/cert-manager.yaml`. In this controller, we will only set variables for the deployment replicas and image tags. You can check the complete manifest YAML file here: `https://github.com/PacktPublishing/Kubernetes-in-Production-Best-Practices/blob/master/Chapter06/ansible/templates/cert-manager/cert-manager.yaml`.

4. Create the issuer configuration for Let's Encrypt in this path – `ansible/templates/cert-manager/letsencrypt-clusterissuer.yaml`. In this file, there are two configurations, the first for the certificates used for production workloads, and the other for non-production workloads. The main difference is that Let's Encrypt will allow you to issue as many certificates as you want for non-production, but only limited numbers per week for production ones:

```yaml
---
apiVersion: certmanager.k8s.io/v1alpha1
kind: ClusterIssuer
metadata:
  name: letsencrypt-prod
spec:
  acme:
    email: {{ letsencrypt_email }}
    server: {{ letsencrypt_prod_url }}
    privateKeySecretRef:
      name: letsencrypt-prod
    solvers:
    - http01:
        ingress:
          class: nginx
    - selector:
        matchLabels:
          use-dns01-solver: "true"
      dns01:
        route53:
          region: {{ aws_default_region }}
          hostedZoneID: {{ route53_zone_id }}
```

The second part of the previous issuer configuration is very similar to the production issuer, but with a different Let's Encrypt server.

To deploy the Cert-Manager add-on, please apply the deployment steps at the end of this chapter under the *Deploying the security configurations* section.

Here is an example of how to use Cert-Manager and Let's Encrypt and associate it with an ingress controller and a domain:

```
apiVersion: extensions/v1beta1
kind: Ingress
metadata:
  annotations:
    cert-manager.io/cluster-issuer: letsencrypt-prod
  name: test-ingress
  namespace: test-ingress
spec:
  rules:
  - host: example.com
    http:
      paths:
      - backend:
          serviceName: myservice
          servicePort: 80
        path: /
  tls:
  - hosts:
    - example.com
    secretName: example-cert
```

The previous `Ingress` resource uses the Cert-Manager annotation to connect to the Let's Encrypt TLS production certificate issuer, and it defines a host with a sample DNS `example.com` and `secretName` as `example-cert`, where Cert-Manager will store the TLS certificates retrieved from Let's Encrypt, and to be used by this `Ingress` resource. You can use the same `Ingress` resource, but with a domain name that you own.

To get an idea of how to use Cert-Manager in other use cases, please check the official documentation at `https://cert-manager.io/docs/usage/`.

Securing workloads and apps

Kubernetes provides different built-in and third-party solutions to ensure that your production workloads are running securely. We will explore what we regard as a must-have for your cluster before going to production, such as workload isolation techniques, pod security policies, network policies, and monitoring workload runtime security.

Isolating critical workloads

Kubernetes, by design, has a single control plane for each cluster, which makes sharing a single cluster among tenants and workloads challenging, and requires the cluster owners to have a clear strategy about cluster multi-tenancy and resource sharing.

There are different use cases where it is critical to address tenant and workload isolation:

- In many organizations, there are multiple teams, products, or environments that share a cluster.
- There are cases where you provide Kubernetes as a service for your own organization or external organizations.
- Also, there is a common case when your Kubernetes infrastructure serves a **Software as a Service (SaaS)** product.

For the preceding use cases, we need to ensure that the cluster has the required configuration for workload isolation, where we can approach soft multi-tenancy using various Kubernetes objects, such as namespaces, RBAC, quotas, and limit ranges. This is what you will learn in this section and across this chapter.

Now, we need to explore the different techniques for implementing tenants' isolation, while decreasing the risks associated with Kubernetes' single-tenancy design.

Using namespaces

Namespaces are the first layer of isolation that Kubernetes provides. They provide a soft-tenancy mechanism to create boundaries for Kubernetes resources. A lot of Kubernetes security controls, such as network policies, access control, secrets, certificates, and other important security controls can be scoped on the namespace level. By separating tenant workloads into their own namespaces, you will be able to limit the impact of security attacks, as well as intentional and non-intentional mistakes by cluster users.

Creating separate node groups

We usually avoid privileged containers, but in some cases, such as system pods or product-specific technical requirements, they are unavoidable. To reduce the impact of a security break, we isolate these pods on dedicated nodes and node groups where other tenants' workloads cannot get scheduled. The same can be applied to the pods with sensitive data. This approach decreases the risk of sensitive data being accessed by a less-secure application that shares the worker node. However, it does come with a drawback as it could increase the infrastructure cost, and when you take this design decision, you should weigh security versus cost.

Implementing hard multi-tenancy

In specific use cases, hard multi-tenancy is a must, which is usually due to laws and regulatory requirements. In this situation, multi-tenancy can be achieved by provisioning separate clusters for each tenant, and this is what we call hard multi-tenancy. On the flip side, however, there are drawbacks, such as the challenges associated with managing these clusters when they grow in number, the increased total cost, and also the decreased compute utilization per cluster.

Hardening the default pod security policy

Pod security policy (PSP) is a Kubernetes resource that is used to ensure that a pod has to meet specific requirements before getting created.

PSPs have different security settings that you can configure either by increasing or decreasing pod privileges, aspects such as Linux capabilities allowed to the containers, host network access, and filesystem access.

It is still worthwhile mentioning that PSP is still in beta, and it would be unwelcome to deploy a beta feature for companies with strict production policies.

You can define multiple PSPs in your cluster and assign them to different types of pods and namespaces to ensure that every workload and tenant has the correct access rights. EKS clusters come with a default PSP called `eks.privileged`, which is automatically created when you provision the cluster. You can view the specs of the `eks.privileged` PSP by describing it as follows:

```
$ kubectl describe psp eks.privileged
Name:   eks.privileged
Settings:
  Allow Privileged:                      true
  Allow Privilege Escalation:            0xc0004ce5f8
```

Default Add Capabilities:	<none>
Required Drop Capabilities:	<none>
Allowed Capabilities:	*
Allowed Volume Types:	*
Allow Host Network:	true
Allow Host Ports:	0-65535
Allow Host PID:	true
Allow Host IPC:	true
Read Only Root Filesystem:	false
SELinux Context Strategy: RunAsAny	
User:	<none>
Role:	<none>
Type:	<none>
Level:	<none>
Run As User Strategy: RunAsAny	
Ranges:	<none>
FSGroup Strategy: RunAsAny	
Ranges:	<none>
Supplemental Groups Strategy: RunAsAny	
Ranges:	<none>

This default `eks.privileged` PSP allows any authenticated user to run privileged containers across all namespaces. This behavior is intended to allow system pods such as the AWS VPC CNI and `kube-proxy` to run as privileged because they are responsible for configuring the host's network settings. However, you have to limit this behavior for other types of pods and namespaces.

As a best practice, we recommend that you limit privileged pods to service accounts within the `kube-system` namespace or any other namespace that you use to isolate system pods. For all other namespaces that host other types of pods, we recommend assigning a restrictive default PSP. The following manifest defines a PSP to restrict privileged pods, and accessing the host network. We will add this manifest to our Ansible template's automation at the following path: `ansible/templates/psp/default-psp.yaml`:

```
---
apiVersion: extensions/v1beta1
kind: PodSecurityPolicy
metadata:
```

```
name: default-psp
annotations:
    seccomp.security.alpha.kubernetes.io/allowedProfileNames:
'docker/default,runtime/default'
    apparmor.security.beta.kubernetes.io/allowedProfileNames:
'runtime/default'
    seccomp.security.alpha.kubernetes.io/defaultProfileName:
'runtime/default'
    apparmor.security.beta.kubernetes.io/defaultProfileName:
'runtime/default'
```

The following code snippet defines specs of the default PSP. It will not allow privileged containers, disables container privilege escalation, and drops all Linux capabilities:

```
spec:
  privileged: false
  defaultAllowPrivilegeEscalation: false
  allowedCapabilities: []
  requiredDropCapabilities:
    - ALL
```

 You can check the complete source code of the previous PSP resource here: `https://github.com/PacktPublishing/Kubernetes-in-Production-Best-Practices/tree/master/Chapter06/ansible/templates/psp`.

The following `ClusterRole` definition allows all roles that are bound to it to use the previous `default-psp` PSP:

```
---
apiVersion: rbac.authorization.k8s.io/v1
kind: ClusterRole
metadata:
  name: default-psp-user
rules:
- apiGroups:
  - extensions
  resources:
  - podsecuritypolicies
  resourceNames:
  - default-psp
```

```
  verbs:
  - use
```

The following `ClusterRoleBinding` definition binds the `default-psp-user` `ClusterRole` to the `system:authenticated` RBAC group of users, which means that any user who is added to the cluster RBAC group, `system:authenticated`, has to create pods that comply with the `default-psp` PSP:

```
---
apiVersion: rbac.authorization.k8s.io/v1
kind: ClusterRoleBinding
metadata:
  name: default-psp-users
subjects:
- kind: Group
  name: system:authenticated
roleRef:
    apiGroup: rbac.authorization.k8s.io
    kind: ClusterRole
    name: default-psp-user
```

You can create additional pod security policies according to your security requirements, but basically, your cluster needs to have two pod security policies; the first is `eks.privileged` for the pods in the `kube-system` namespace, and the second is `default-psp` for any other namespaces.

Limiting pod access

Usually, pods require access to the underlying cloud services, such as object stores, databases, and the DNS. Ideally, you do not want the production pods to access all services, or to access a service that they are not intended to use. This is why we need to limit pod access to just the services they use.

In the AWS world, this can be achieved by utilizing the IAM roles and attaching this role and an access policy to the pod. `kube2iam` is one of Kubernetes' add-ons that can do this job efficiently. It is an open source project that is battle-tested in production. It is easy to deploy, configure, and use. You can learn more about it here: `https://github.com/jtblin/kube2iam`.

`kube2iam` does not come pre-installed with the cluster, so you need to deploy it and specify its configuration, which includes its Docker image, iptables control, and the host network interface.

Now, let's create the Ansible template and configuration for them:

> **Important note**
>
> You can find the complete source code at `https://github.com/PacktPublishing/Kubernetes-in-Production-Best-Practices/tree/master/Chapter06/ansible/templates/kube2iam`.

1. Define the required configuration variables and add them to the `group_vars` directory in this path – `ansible/group_vars/all/kube2iam.yaml`. The basic configuration contains the image tag for the `kube2iam` DaemonSet, which is useful for keeping track of the deployed version and for controlling its upgrades:

    ```
    kube2iam:
        image: "jtblin/kube2iam"
        tag: "0.10.9"
    ```

2. Create the deployment template for the Cert-Manager controller resources in this path – `ansible/templates/cert-manager/cert-manager.yaml`. In this controller, we will only set variables for the deployment replicas and image tags:

    ```
    ---
    apiVersion: apps/v1
    kind: DaemonSet
    metadata:
      name: kube2iam
      namespace: kube-system
      labels:
        app: kube2iam
    ```

    The following code snippet is the specification of the `kube2iam` DaemonSet. The most important part of the spec is the container runtime arguments' section:

    ```
    spec:
    ---
          containers:
            - image: {{ kube2iam.image }}:{{ kube2iam.tag }}
    ```

```
            name: kube2iam
            args:
                - "--auto-discover-base-arn"
                - "--auto-discover-default-role=true"
                - "--iptables=true"
                - "--host-ip=$(HOST_IP)"
                - "--node=$(NODE_NAME)"
                - "--host-interface=eni+"
                - "--use-regional-sts-endpoint"
```

The most notable configuration parameter in the previous YAML file is
`"--iptables=true"`, which allows kube2iam to add iptables rules to block the
pods from accessing the underlying worker node instance profile.

To deploy kube2iam, please apply the deployment steps at the end of this chapter under
the *Deploying the cluster's security configuration* section.

To use kube2iam with a pod, you have to add the iam.amazonaws.com/role
annotation to the pod annotations section, and add the IAM role to be used by the
pod. Here is an example to illustrate how to use kube2iam with your pods:

```
apiVersion: v1
kind: Pod
metadata:
  name: aws-cli
  labels:
    name: aws-cli
  annotations:
    iam.amazonaws.com/role: <add-role-arn-here>
spec:
  containers:
  - image: fstab/aws-cli
    command:
        - "/home/aws/aws/env/bin/aws"
        - "s3"
        - "ls"
        - "add-any-bucket-name-here"
    name: aws-cli
```

The preceding pod will run an `aws-cli` container that executes the S3 list command for a bucket. Please make sure to replace the placeholders with a valid IAM role ARN to the annotation section, and a valid S3 bucket name in the container command section.

Creating network policies with Calico

Communication between all pods within the cluster is allowed by default. This behavior is unsecure, especially in multi-tenant clusters. Earlier, you learned about the cluster network infrastructure and how to use security groups to control the network traffic among a cluster's nodes. However, security groups are not effective when it comes to controlling the traffic between pods. This is why Kubernetes provides the **Network Policy API**. These network policies allow the cluster's users to enforce ingress and egress rules to allow or deny network traffic among the pods.

Kubernetes defines the Network Policy API specification, but it does not provide a built-in capability to enforce these network policies. So, to enforce them, you have to use a network plugin, such as Calico network policy.

You can check your cluster to see whether there are any network policies in effect by using the following `kubectl` command:

```
$ kubectl get networkpolicies --all-namespaces
No resources found.
```

Calico is a network policy engine that can be deployed to Kubernetes, and it works smoothly with EKS as well. Calico implements all of Kubernetes' network policy features, but it also supports an additional richer set of features, including policy ordering, priority, deny rules, and flexible match rules. Calico network policy can be applied to different types of endpoints, including pods, VMs, and host interfaces. Unlike Kubernetes' network policies, Calico policies can be applied to namespaces, pods, service accounts, or globally across the cluster.

Creating a default deny policy

As a security best practice, network policies should allow least privileged access. You start by creating a deny all policy that globally restricts all inbound and outbound traffic using Calico.

The following Calico global network policy implements a default, deny-all ingress and egress policy across the cluster:

```
apiVersion: crd.projectcalico.org/v1
kind: GlobalNetworkPolicy
metadata:
  name: default-deny
spec:
  selector: all()
  types:
  - Ingress
  - Egress
```

Once you have the default network policy to deny all traffic, you can add allow rules whenever needed by your pods. One of these policies is to add a global rule to allow pods to query CoreDNS for DNS resolution:

```
apiVersion: crd.projectcalico.org/v1
kind: GlobalNetworkPolicy
metadata:
  name: allow-dns-egress
spec:
  selector: all()
  types:
  - Egress
  egress:
  - action: Allow
    protocol: UDP
    destination:
      namespaceSelector: name == "kube-system"
      ports:
      - 53
```

The preceding policy will allow egress network traffic from pods at any namespaces to query the CoreDNS in the `kube-system` namespace.

EKS does not come with Calico installed by default. So, we will include it in our Ansible configuration. You can view the full source code here: `https://github.com/PacktPublishing/Kubernetes-in-Production-Best-Practices/tree/master/Chapter06/ansible/templates/calico-np`.

Monitoring runtime with Falco

There is an essential need to monitor workloads and containers for security violations at runtime. Falco enables the cluster's users to react in a timely manner for serious security threats and violations, or to catch security issues that bypassed cluster security scanning and testing.

Falco is an open source project originally developed by Sysdig with a core functionality of threat detection in Kubernetes. It can detect violations and abnormally behaving applications and send alerts pertaining to them. You can learn more about the Falco project here: `https://github.com/falcosecurity/falco`.

Falco runs as a daemon on top of Kubernetes' worker nodes, and it has the violation rules defined in configuration files that you can customize according to your security requirements.

Execute the following commands at the worker nodes that you want to monitor. This will install and deploy Falco:

```
curl -o install_falco -s https://falco.org/script/install
sudo bash install_falco
```

To automate Falco's deployment, we will include the previous commands in the worker node bootstrap user data using Terraform in this file: `terraform/modules/eks-workers/user-data.tf`.

One example of the security runtime violations that Falco can detect is detecting whenever a shell is started inside a container. The Falco rule for this violation appears as follows:

```
- macro: container
  condition: container.id != host
- macro: spawned_process
  condition: evt.type = execve and evt.dir=<
- rule: run_shell_in_container
```

```
    desc: a shell was spawned by a non-shell program in a
container. Container entrypoints are excluded.

    condition: container and proc.name = bash and spawned_process
and proc.pname exists and not proc.pname in (bash, docker)

    output: "Shell spawned in a container other than entrypoint
(user=%user.name container_id=%container.id container_
name=%container.name shell=%proc.name parent=%proc.pname
cmdline=%proc.cmdline)"

    priority: WARNING
```

There are enormous rules that you can use and define in your Falco configuration. To learn more about them, refer to the Falco documentation and examples here: `https://falco.org/docs/examples/`.

Ensuring cluster security and compliance

There are lots of moving parts and configurations that affect Kubernetes cluster security. And after deploying the security add-ons and adding more configurations, we need to make sure of the following:

- The cluster security configuration is valid and intact
- The cluster is compliant with the standard security guidelines according to the **Center of Internet Security** (**CIS**) benchmark
- The cluster passes the conformance tests defined by the CNCF and its partners and community

In this section, you will learn how to validate and guarantee each of the previous points through using the relevant tools.

Executing Kubernetes conformance tests

The Kubernetes community and CNCF have defined a set of tests that you can run against any Kubernetes cluster to ensure that this cluster passes tests in terms of specific storage features, performance tests, scaling tests, provider tests, and other types of validation that are defined by CNCF and the Kubernetes community. This gives the cluster operators the confidence to use it to serve in production.

Sonobuoy is a tool that you can use to run these conformance tests, and we recommend doing that for the new clusters, and periodically whenever you update your cluster. Sonobuoy makes it easier for you to ensure the state of your cluster without harming its operations or causing any downtime.

Installing Sonobuoy

Apply the following instructions to install Sonobuoy on your local host:

1. Download the latest Sonobuoy release that matches your operating system: `https://github.com/vmware-tanzu/sonobuoy/releases`.

2. Extract the Sonobuoy binary archive:

    ```
    $ tar -xvf <RELEASE_TARBALL_NAME>.tar.gz
    ```

3. Move the Sonobuoy binary archive to your `bin` folder or to any directory on the `PATH` system.

Running Sonobuoy

Apply the following instructions to run Sonobuoy and then view the conformance test results:

1. Execute the following command to let Sonobuoy run the conformance tests and wait until it finishes:

    ```
    $ sonobuoy run --wait --mode quick
    ```

2. To get the test results, execute the following commands:

    ```
    $ sonobuoy_results=$(sonobuoy retrieve)
    $ sonobuoy results $sonobuoy_results
    ```

3. After you finish, you can delete Sonobuoy and it will remove its namespace and any resources that it created for testing purposes:

    ```
    $ sonobuoy delete --wait
    ```

To ensure that your Kubernetes cluster is in a conformance state, we recommend automating execution of the Sonobuoy tests to run periodically on a daily basis or following the deployment of infrastructure and Kubernetes system-level changes. We do not recommend more frequent and continuous runs of Sonobuoy tests to avoid the excessive load this could bring to the cluster.

Scanning cluster security configuration

After completing the cluster conformance testing, you need to scan the configurations and security settings and ensure that there are no insecure or high-risk configurations. To achieve this, we will use kube-scan, which is a security scanning tool that scans cluster workloads and the runtime settings and assigns each one a rating from 0 (no risk) to 10 (high risk). kube-scan utilizes a scoring formula based on the Kubernetes Common Configuration Scoring System framework.

Installing kube-scan

kube-scan is installed as a Kubernetes deployment in your cluster by using the following kubectl command:

```
$ kubectl apply -f https://raw.githubusercontent.com/
octarinesec/kube-scan/master/kube-scan.yaml
```

kube-scan scans the cluster when it starts, and will periodically scan it once every day. This way, you can enforce rescanning by restarting the kube-scan pod.

Running kube-scan

Apply the following instructions to run kube-scan and view the scanning results:

1. To access the kube-scan results, you need to port forward the kube-scan service to port 8080 on your local machine:

    ```
    $ kubectl port-forward --namespace kube-scan svc/kube-
    scan-ui 8080:80
    ```

2. Then, open http://localhost:8080 in your browser to view the scan results.

3. Once you finish, you can delete kube-scan and its resources by using the following kubectl command:

    ```
    $ kubectl delete -f https://raw.githubusercontent.com/
    octarinesec/kube-scan/master/kube-scan.yaml
    ```

We recommend deploying kube-scan to your cluster and automating the scan result validation to run periodically on a daily basis or after deploying infrastructure and Kubernetes system-level changes. We do not recommend more frequent and continuous runs of Sonobuoy tests to avoid the excessive load this could bring to the cluster.

Executing the CIS Kubernetes benchmark

In the final security validation stage of the cluster, you should test whether the cluster is deployed and configured according to the Kubernetes benchmark developed by the CIS.

To execute this test, you will use `kube-bench`, which is a tool that is used to run CIS Kubernetes benchmark checks.

> **Important note**
>
> For managed Kubernetes services such as EKS, you cannot use `kube-bench` to inspect the master nodes as you do not have access to them. However, it is still possible to use `kube-bench` to inspect the worker nodes.

Installing kube-bench

There are multiple ways to install `kube-bench`, one of them is to use a Docker container to copy the binary and the configurations to the host machine. The following command will install it:

```
$ docker run --rm -v `pwd`:/host aquasec/kube-bench:latest
install
```

Running kube-bench

Execute `kube-bench` against a Kubernetes node, and specify the Kubernetes version, such as 1.14 or any other supported version:

```
$ kube-bench node --version 1.14
```

Instead of specifying a Kubernetes version, you can use a CIS Benchmark version, such as the following:

```
$ kube-bench node --benchmark cis-1.5
```

And for EKS, you are allowed to run these specific targets: `master`, `node`, `etcd`, and `policies`:

```
$ kube-bench --benchmark cis-1.5 run --targets
master,node,etcd,policies
```

The outputs are either PASS; FAIL, which indicate that the test is completed; WARN, which means the test requires manual intervention; INFO is an informational output that requires no action.

> **Important note**
>
> We recommend automating the execution of Sonobuoy, kube-scan, and kube-bench on a daily basis to verify security and compliance for your clusters.

Enabling audit logging

Ensure that you enabled the cluster audit logs, and also that they are monitored for anomalous or unwanted API calls, especially any authorization failures. For EKS, you need to opt-in to enable these logs and have them streamed to CloudWatch.

To enable this, you need to update the Terraform EKS resource in this file, `terraform/modules/eks-cp/main.tf`, and add the following line of code:

```
enabled_cluster_log_types = var.cluster_log_types
```

After applying this Terraform change to the EKS configuration, the cluster audit logs will be streamed to CloudWatch, and you can take it from there and create alerts.

Bonus security tips

These are some general security best practices and tips that did not fit under any of the previous sections. However, I find them to be useful:

1. Always keep Kubernetes updated to the latest version.

2. Update worker AMIs to the latest version. You have to be cautious because this change could introduce some downtime, especially if you are not using a managed node group.

3. Do not run Docker in Docker or mount the socket in a container.

4. Restrict the use of `hostPath` or, if `hostPath` is necessary, restrict which prefixes can be used and configure the volume as read-only.

5. Set requests and limits for each container to avoid resource contention and **Denial of Service (DoS)** attacks.

6. Whenever possible, use an optimized operating system for running containers.

7. Use immutable infrastructure, and automate the rotation of the cluster worker nodes.

8. You should not enable the Kubernetes dashboard.

9. Enable AWS VPC Flow Logs to capture metadata about the traffic flowing through a VPC, and then analyze it further for suspicious activities.

Kubernetes security is a fast-growing domain, and you should keep following the latest guidelines and best practices, and integrate them into your processes and DevSecOps automations.

Deploying the security configurations

The following instructions will deploy the cluster's Ansible playbook, and it will deploy the security add-ons and configuration to the cluster:

1. Initialize the Terraform state and select the workspace by running the following commands:

```
$ cd terraform/packtclusters
$ terraform workspace select prod1
```

2. Retrieve and configure kubeconfig for the target cluster:

```
$ aws eks --region $(terraform output aws_region) update-kubeconfig --name $(terraform output cluster_full_name)
```

3. Execute the Ansible playbook:

```
$ source ~/ansible/bin/activate
$ ansible-playbook -i \
../../ansible/inventories/packtclusters/ \
-e "worker_iam_role_arn=$(terraform output worker_iam_role_arn) \
cluster_name=$(terraform output cluster_full_name) \
aws_default_region=$(terraform output aws_region)" \
../../ansible/cluster.yaml
```

4. You will get the following output following successful Ansible execution:

```
PLAY RECAP ********************************************************************
localhost           : ok=10   changed=6   unreachable=0   failed=0   skipped=0   rescued=0   ignored=0
```

Figure 6.2 – Ansible execution output

5. Execute the following `kubectl` command to get all the pods running in the cluster. This will ensure that the cluster configuration is applied successfully:

```
$ kubectl get pods --all-namespaces
```

You should get the following output, which lists all the pods running in the cluster including the new pods for the security add-ons:

```
NAMESPACE       NAME                                            READY   STATUS      RESTARTS   AGE
ingress-nginx   ingress-nginx-admission-create-c4sk2            0/1    Completed   0          2m29s
ingress-nginx   ingress-nginx-admission-patch-d7ps7            0/1    Completed   0          2m28s
ingress-nginx   ingress-nginx-controller-866488c6d4-x5545      1/1    Running     0          2m39s
kube-system     aws-node-75kq7                                  1/1    Running     0          15m
kube-system     aws-node-rb9rp                                  1/1    Running     0          15m
kube-system     aws-node-vpzhv                                  1/1    Running     0          15m
kube-system     coredns-76dc8ddb47-mm9dd                        1/1    Running     0          88m
kube-system     coredns-76dc8ddb47-whfmb                        1/1    Running     0          12m
kube-system     external-dns-786699d876-r24fs                   1/1    Running     0          2m57s
kube-system     external-dns-786699d876-r5clm                   1/1    Running     0          2m57s
kube-system     kube-proxy-g9ngd                                1/1    Running     0          15m
kube-system     kube-proxy-lnssz                                1/1    Running     0          15m
kube-system     kube-proxy-rhtnk                                1/1    Running     0          15m
kube-system     kube2iam-88mwj                                  1/1    Running     0          2m3s
kube-system     kube2iam-pzxkd                                  1/1    Running     0          2m3s
kube-system     kube2iam-rmb6c                                  1/1    Running     0          2m3s
kube-system     sealed-secrets-controller-699854fbd9-zhvh8     1/1    Running     0          20s
```

Figure 6.3 – List of all pods

Now you have completed applying the cluster configuration as per the previous instructions. And your cluster has all of the security add-ons and configuration deployed and ready for serving production.

Destroying the cluster

First, you should delete the `ingress-nginx` service to instruct AWS to destroy the NLB associated with the ingress controller. We need this step because Terraform will fail to destroy this NLB because it is created by Kubernetes:

```
$ kubectl -n nginx-ingress destroy svc nginx-ingress
```

Then, you can follow the rest of the instructions in the *Destroying the network and cluster infrastructure* section in *Chapter 3, Provisioning Kubernetes Clusters Using AWS and Terraform*, to destroy the Kubernetes cluster and all related AWS resources. Please ensure that the resources are destroyed in the following order:

1. Kubernetes cluster `packtclusters` resources

2. Cluster VPC resources

3. Terraform shared state resources

By executing the previous steps, you should have all Kubernetes and AWS infrastructure resources destroyed and cleaned up, ready for the hands-on practice in the next chapter.

Summary

In this chapter, you have learned about Kubernetes security best practices, and learned how to apply an end-to-end security approach to the cluster's infrastructure, network, containers, apps, secrets, apps, and the workload's runtime. You also learned how to apply and validate security compliance checks and tests. You developed all of the required templates and configuration as code for these best practices, controllers, and add-ons with Ansible and Terraform.

You deployed Kubernetes add-ons and controllers to provide essential services such as `kube2iam`, Cert-Manager, Sealed Secrets, and Falco, in addition to tuning Kubernetes-native security features such as pod security policies, network policies, and RBAC.

You acquired a solid knowledge of Kubernetes security in this chapter, but you should do a detailed evaluation of your cluster security requirements and take further action to deploy any extra tools and configurations that may be required.

In the next chapter, you will learn in detail about Kubernetes observability, and the monitoring and logging of best practices, tools, add-ons, and configurations that you need to deploy and optimize for production-grade clusters.

Further reading

You can refer to the following links for more information on the topics covered in this chapter:

- *Getting Started with Kubernetes – Third Edition* (*Chapter 14, Hardening Kubernetes*): `https://www.packtpub.com/virtualization-and-cloud/getting-started-kubernetes-third-edition`

- *Mastering Kubernetes – Second Edition* (*Chapter 5, Configuring Kubernetes Security, Limits, and Accounts*): `https://www.packtpub.com/application-development/mastering-kubernetes-second-edition`

- *Learn Kubernetes Security*: `https://www.packtpub.com/security/learn-kubernetes-security`

7
Managing Storage and Stateful Applications

In the previous chapters, we learned how to provision and prepare our Kubernetes clusters for production workloads. It is part of the critical production readiness requirement to configure and fine-tune day zero tasks, including networking, security, monitoring, logging, observability, and scaling, before we bring our applications and data to Kubernetes. Kubernetes was originally designed for mainly stateless applications in order to keep containers portable. Therefore, data management and running stateful applications are still among the top challenges in the cloud native space. There are a number of ways and a variety of solutions to address storage needs. New solutions emerge in the Kubernetes and cloud-native ecosystem every day; therefore, we will start with popular in-production solutions and also learn the approach and criteria to look for when evaluating future solutions.

In this chapter, we will learn the technical challenges associated with stateful applications on Kubernetes. We will follow the cloud-native approach completely to fine-tune Kubernetes clusters for persistent storage. We will learn the different storage solutions and their shortcomings, and how to use and configure them with our Kubernetes cluster.

In this chapter, we will cover the following main topics:

- Understanding the challenges with stateful applications
- Tuning Kubernetes storage
- Choosing a persistent storage solution
- Deploying stateful applications

Technical requirements

You should have the following tools installed from the previous chapters:

- AWS CLI V2
- AWS IAM Authenticator
- `kubectl`

We will also need to install the following tools:

- Helm
- CSI driver

You need to have an up and running Kubernetes cluster as per the instructions in *Chapter 3, Provisioning Kubernetes Clusters Using AWS and Terraform.*

The code for this chapter is located at `https://github.com/PacktPublishing/Kubernetes-Infrastructure-Best-Practices/tree/master/Chapter07`.

Check out the following link to see the Code in Action video:

`https://bit.ly/3jemcot`

Installing the required tools

In this section, we will install the tools that we will use to provision applications using Helm charts and provide dynamically provisioned volumes to the stateful applications in your Kubernetes infrastructure during this chapter and the upcoming ones. As a cloud and Kubernetes learner, you may be familiar with these tools from before.

Installing Helm

Helm is a package manager for Kubernetes. Helm is also a great way to find and deploy vendor and community published applications on Kubernetes. We will use Helm to deploy applications on our Kubernetes cluster. If you do not have Helm installed in your cluster, you can follow these instructions to do that.

Execute the following commands to install Helm 3 in your Kubernetes cluster:

```
$ curl -fsSL -o get_helm.sh https://raw.githubusercontent.com/
helm/helm/master/scripts/get-helm-3
$ chmod 700 get_helm.sh
$ ./get_helm.sh
```

Next, we will install the CSI drivers.

Installing CSI drivers

Container Storage Interface (**CSI**) is the standardized APIs to extend Kubernetes with third-party storage provider solutions. CSI drivers are vendor specific and, of course, you only need an AWS EBS CSI driver if you are running on AWS infrastructure, including EC2 or EKS-based clusters. To install the latest AWS EBS CSI drivers, refer to the Amazon EKS official documentation at https://docs.aws.amazon.com/eks/latest/userguide/ebs-csi.htm.

If you are running on a self-managed Kubernetes solution, bare metal/on-premises, or virtualized environment, you may need to use another vendor's CSI driver or **Container Attached Storage** (**CAS**) solutions. To install other CSI vendor drivers, you can refer the links to specific driver instructions on the official CSI documentation at https://kubernetes-csi.github.io/docs/drivers.html.

Now that we have installed the prerequisites required in the chapter to deploy Helm Charts and consume AWS EBS volumes using the CSI driver, let's go over the implementation principles we will be following, making storage provider decisions with a view to solving our stateful application challenges.

Implementation principles

In *Chapter 1, Introduction to Kubernetes Infrastructure and Production-Readiness*, we learned about the infrastructure design principles that we will follow during the book. I would like to start this chapter by highlighting the notable principles that influenced the cloud-native data management suggestions and the technical decisions in this chapter:

- **Simplication**: In this chapter, we will retain our commitment to the simplification principle. Unless you are operating in a multi-cloud environment, it is not necessary to introduce new tools and complicate operations. On public clouds, we will use the native storage data management technology stack provided, and which is supported by your managed service vendor. Many stateful applications today are designed to fail and provide built-in, high-availability functionality. We will identify different types of stateful applications and learn how to simply data paths and fine-tune for performance. We will also learn the additional design principles to achieve higher availability across availability zones, as well as unifying data management in on-premises and hybrid cloud environments.

- **Cloud agnostic**: Data has gravity. When running stateless applications, cloud vendor lock-in may not be as important since container images can be brought up almost instantly on any infrastructure, but when dealing with stateful workloads, it is easy to get into this situation. We will use cloud-native solutions to abstract storage layers and eliminate dependencies. The solutions we will implement will work exactly the same way on any cloud provider, managed Kubernetes service, and even on a self-managed on-premise environment.

- **Design for availability**: CSI is great, but, at the same time, it is nothing more than standardized APIs. Your data still needs to be stored on a highly available media somewhere. It is important to consider the blast radius of your storage solution. It doesn't make sense to store your loosely coupled applications in a single scale-out storage solution, or on a legacy storage appliance. Doing so would create scale bottlenecks and will slow you down along the way. We will learn the benefits of cloud-native storage solutions. We will also learn how to use snapshots, clones, and backups for increased service availability and quick service recovery.

- **Automation**: You can't automate your CI/CD pipelines unless everything can be dynamically provisioned. We will learn about Kubernetes storage primitives and the use of dynamic provisioners.

In this section, we have covered the implementation principles we will be following when making storage provider decisions. Let's now take a look at some of the common stateful application challenges we will need to address.

Understanding the challenges with stateful applications

Kubernetes was initially built for stateless applications in order to keep containers portable. Even when we run stateful applications, the applications themselves are actually very often stateless containers where the state is stored separately and mounted from a resource called **Persistent Volume** (**PV**). We will learn the different resource types used to maintain state and also keep some form of flexibility later in the *Understanding storage primitives in Kubernetes* section.

I would like to highlight the six notable stateful application challenges that we will try to address in this chapter:

- **Deployment challenges**: Especially when running a mission-critical service in production, finding the ideal deployment method of a certain stateful application can be challenging to start with. Should we use a YAML file we found in a blog article, open source repository examples, Helm charts, or an operator? Your choice will have an impact on future scalability, manageability, upgrades, and service recoverability. We will learn the best practices to follow for deploying a stateful application later in this chapter in the *Deploying stateful applications* section.

- **Persistency challenges**: Storing the actual persistent data that makes the application stateful needs to be carefully picked. You should never store the state inside the application container itself since the container images and pods can be restarted and updated, which would result in losing the data. Similarly, if you are running your cluster across multiple availability zones on top of EBS volumes when a node is restarted, your application may come up in a node located on a separate availability zone with no access to previous EBS volumes. In that case, you should consider a container-attached storage solution with across **availability zone** (**AZ**) replication functionality.

On the other hand, if your application is a distributed database with built-in high availability, adding an additional layer of high availability from a storage provider would have a negative impact on capacity, cost, and performance. Persistency decisions need to carefully consider an application's requirements.

- **Scalability challenges**: One of the main reasons behind the popularity of the Kubernetes orchestration platform is the flexibility of scaling up services. Kubernetes platforms allow you to start on a single worker node and dynamically scale up to thousands of nodes according to demand and increasing loads. Not every storage solution is designed for scale. We will learn the best practices to follow and the differences between the storage options to consider when deploying a scalable stateful application later in this chapter in the *Choosing a persistent storage solution* section.

- **Mobility challenges**: Data mobility means being able to get data where and when you need it. Especially in an infrastructure where hybrid or multi-cloud are requirements, your choice of storage provider becomes a key factor. This requirement is also aligned with the cloud-agnostic design principles that we introduced in *Chapter 1, Introduction to Kubernetes Infrastructure and Production-Readiness*. If needed, your stateful applications should be able to migrate to different zones and even different storage and cloud vendors.

- **Life cycle manageability challenges**: The real challenge starts after you deploy your stateful applications. Day two operations need to be planned in advance before you go to production with your services. This sometimes creates a dependency and requirement on your deployment method as well. You need to pick the deployment method that will support rollover upgrades, monitoring, observability, and troubleshooting.

- **Disaster recovery (DR) and backup challenges**: You need to plan for service availability in case of application and or infrastructure failures. Your data needs to be backed up on a regular basis. Some applications may require application-consistent backups, and some might be good with just crash-consistent backups. CSI-operated snapshots and copying that data to object storage needs to be scheduled. Taking a backup is one side of the problem, but being able to recover from your backup in a timely fashion is another challenge. When there is a service outage, end user service impact is measured using mainly two data points; the **Recovery Time Objective (RTO)** and the **Recovery Point Objective (RPO)**. RTO measures the time required to bring a service back, while RPO measures the backup frequency. Data created by your application may grow quickly when you go to production with your services. Recovering a large amount of data from S3-like object storage will take time. In that case, stream backup solutions need to be considered. This requirement is also aligned with the *design for availability* design principles that I introduced in *Chapter 1, Introduction to Kubernetes Infrastructure and Production-Readiness*. If needed, your application needs to be able to switch to its DR copy as quickly as possible with minimal downtime.

These six core challenges contribute to the architectural design decisions we need to make in order to run stateful applications in production. We will consider these challenges later in this chapter when we evaluate our storage options and make a relevant technical decision based on it.

Tuning Kubernetes storage

At some point, we have all experienced and been frustrated by storage performance and the technical limitations of it. In this chapter, we will learn the fundamentals of Kubernetes storage, including storage primitives, creating static **persistent volumes** (**PVs**), and using storage classes to provision dynamic PVs to simplify management.

Understanding containerized stateful applications requires us to get into the cloud-native mindset. Although referred to as stateful, data used by pods is either accessed remotely or orchestrated and stored in Kubernetes as separate resources. Therefore, some flexibility is maintained to schedule applications across worker nodes and update when needed without losing the data. Before we get into the tuning, let's understand some of the basic storage primitives in Kubernetes.

Understanding storage primitives in Kubernetes

The beauty of Kubernetes is that every part of it is abstracted as an object that can be managed and configured declaratively with YAML or JSON through the `kube-api` server. This makes Kubernetes configuration easier to manage as code. Storage is also handled as abstracted objects. To be able to understand the reasoning behind the best practices, I highly recommend that you learn the separation of the storage object. In this section, we will learn the following core storage primitives to request persistent storage from Kubernetes and orchestrate the provisioning through storage providers associated with it:

- Volume
- **Persistent Volume (PV)**
- **Persistent Volume Claim (PVC)**
- **Storage Class (SC)**

Let's discuss each of these in the following sections.

Volumes

Kubernetes volumes are basically just a directory accessible to the applications running in containers in a pod. How this directory is created and protected, and where it is stored really depends on the type of volume used, which makes this a critical decision when running stateful applications in production. Kubernetes supports many types of volumes. For a detailed list of support volume types, refer to the official Kubernetes documentation at `https://kubernetes.io/docs/concepts/storage/volumes/`. Some of the volume types are ephemeral, in other words, their lifespan is limited to its pod. Therefore, they should only be used for stateless applications where the persistency of data is not necessary across restarts. In the context of stateful applications, our focus is PV types, including remote PVs and local PVs. Let's now learn about the use of PV objects.

PVs

PVs are volumes that can retain the data during pod restarts or other resource failures. PVs can be created either statically in advance or dynamically when requested by the user application. I will explain the use of static or dynamic PV objects with a practical example while we deploy a Percona server.

> **Important note**
> You can find the complete source code at `https://github.com/PacktPublishing/Kubernetes-in-Production-Best-Practices/blob/master/Chapter07/stateful/percona/pv-percona.yaml`.

Let's start with a static volume to understand its limitations, in other words, the value and logic behind the dynamic provisioning:

1. Create an AWS Elastic Block Store volume with a size of 100 GB using the volume type gp2. Make sure that the EBS volume is in the same availability zone as your Kubernetes worker nodes:

   ```
   $ aws ec2 create-volume --size=10 --availability-zone=us-east-1a --volume-type=gp2
   ```

2. Repeat the previous step to create one volume per worker node available in your cluster. If you have three nodes available, then create a total of three volumes. Execute the following command to get the list of `InstanceId` strings for the nodes:

   ```
   $ aws ec2 describe-instances | grep InstanceId
   ```

3. Execute the following command to attach each volume you have created to one worker node in your cluster at a time using the AWS CLI. Replace WORKER_NODE_ ID and VOLUME_ID from the output of step 1:

```
$ aws ec2 attach-volume --device /dev/sdf --instance-id
<WORKER_NODE_ID> --volume-id <YOUR_VOLUME_ID>
```

4. Create a Kubernetes PV named percona-pv1 with a size of 5Gi in the following path – stateful/percona/pv-percona.yaml. Make sure to replace volumeID with a valid volume ID of your EBS volume:

```
apiVersion: v1
kind: PersistentVolume
metadata:
  name : percona-pv1
spec:
  accessModes:
  - ReadWriteOnce
  capacity:
    storage: 5Gi
  persistentVolumeReclaimPolicy: Retain
  awsElasticBlockStore:
    volumeID: <YOUR EBS VOLUME ID HERE>
    fsType: xfs
```

5. Execute the following kubectl command to create a static PV in the cluster:

```
$ kubectl apply -f pv-percona.yaml
```

Now you have created a PV that can bind to your stateful application. As you can see, if you have a dynamically scaling environment, creating volumes manually in advance will not provide a scalable option.

PV claims

A **PV claim** (**PVC**) is a request for storage. PVC requests can be fulfilled either by static or dynamic PVs.

Here, we will create a PVC manifest to request the static PV we created earlier:

1. Create a PVC named `percona-pv1` with a size of `5Gi` in the following path –
   `stateful/percona/pvc-percona.yaml`:

```
kind: PersistentVolumeClaim
apiVersion: v1
metadata:
  name: percona-pvc
spec:
  accessModes:
    - ReadWriteOnce
  resources:
    requests:
      storage: 5Gi
```

2. In the following part of the template, we will set `storageClassName` to blank.
   Otherwise, the default storage class will be used and a PV is created dynamically
   using the default storage provisioner. This time, we are specifically requesting a PV
   with no storage class specified, so it can only be bound to our existing PV:

```
storageClassName: ""
```

3. Execute the following `kubectl` command to create a PVC object in the cluster:

```
$ kubectl apply -f pv-percona.yaml
```

In the following code snippet, you create the `percona` deployment that will use the PVC to request the PV we created earlier:

1. Create a Kubernetes secret to keep the Percona root password by executing the following command. This will be used in the deployment later. You can read more about the detailed usage of Kubernetes secrets at `https://kubernetes.io/docs/concepts/configuration/secret/`:

```
$ kubectl create secret generic mysql-root \
    --from-literal=mysql-root-passwd=MyP@ssW0rc1 \
    --dry-run -o yaml | kubectl apply -f -
```

2. Create the template for the `percona` deployment in the following path – `stateful/percona/deployment-percona.yaml`:

```yaml
---
apiVersion: apps/v1
kind: Deployment
metadata:
  name: percona
spec:
  selector:
    matchLabels:
      app: percona
  template:
    metadata:
      labels:
        app: percona
    spec:
      containers:
      - image: percona
        name: percona
        env:
        - name: MYSQL_ROOT_PASSWORD
          valueFrom:
            secretKeyRef:
              name: mysql-root
              key: mysql-root-passwd
```

```
        ports:
        - containerPort: 3306
          name: percona
```

3. In the following part of the template, we will define the `volumeMounts` using the name `percona-volume`, with the `mountPath` parameter configured as the path `/var/lib/mysql`, where your PV will be mounted inside the container:

```
        volumeMounts:
        - name: percona-volume
          mountPath: /var/lib/mysql
```

4. Finally, in the following part of the template, we will define where your request will be directed. In our case, as defined before in the case of `claimName`, this should be `percona-pvc`:

```
      volumes:
      - name: percona-volume
        persistentVolumeClaim:
          claimName: percona-pvc
```

5. Execute the following `kubectl` command to create `percona` deployment in the cluster:

```
$ kubectl apply -f deployment-percona.yaml
```

Now you have created a stateful application deployment with a binding to a static PV. Although it can be useful to know how to clone an existing volume and mount it to a new pod, this is not a scalable solution. Therefore, we will now learn about the dynamic provisioning of PVs using `StorageClass`.

Storage class

The `StorageClass` object allows dynamic provisioning requests through a PVC. You can maintain multiple classes that map to different availability and QoS levels using internal or external third-party provisioners. The `StorageClass` concept is similar to tiers or profiles in traditional storage solutions.

Let's review a `StorageClass` template used for provisioning EBS volumes on AWS:

```
apiVersion: storage.k8s.io/v1
kind: StorageClass
metadata:
  name: gp2
```

In the following part of the template, we set `StorageClass` as the default storage class. It is highly recommended good practice to set a default storage class, so PVCs missing the `storageClassName` field are automatically assigned to your default class:

```
  annotations:
    storageclass.kubernetes.io/is-default-class: "true"
```

In the following part of the template, we set the EBS volume type to `gp2`, with AWS EBS volumes of `io1`, `gp2`, `sc1`, or `st1`. You can read about the differences in the official AWS documentation at `https://docs.aws.amazon.com/AWSEC2/latest/UserGuide/ebs-volume-types.html`. We also set `fsType` to `ext4`:

```
parameters:
  type: gp2
  fsType: ext4
```

In the following part of the template, we set the `provisioner` type to `kubernetes.io/aws-ebs`. This field can be internal or an external provisioner. In our following template, it is set to Kubernetes' internal `aws-ebs` provisioner, `kubernetes.io/aws-ebs`. We will review the available storage options later in this chapter in the *Choosing a persistent storage solution* section:

```
provisioner: kubernetes.io/aws-ebs
reclaimPolicy: Retain
allowVolumeExpansion: true
volumeBindingMode: Immediate
```

`reclaimPolicy` can be set to `Delete`, `Recycle`, or `Retain` and it defines the action when a corresponding PVC is deleted. When `Retain` is selected, after the PVC is removed, the PV is moved to the `Released` state. Hence, `Retain` is the suggested option to avoid accidents.

The `allowVolumeExpansion` field is used if you need to request a larger size PVC later and you want the same volume to be resized instead of getting a new volume. You can only expand a PVC if its storage class has the `allowVolumeExpansion` parameter set to `true`.

> **Note**
>
> AWS EBS volume expansions can take time and one modification is allowed every 6 hours.

`volumeBindingMode` can be set to `Immediate` or `WaitForFirstConsumer`. This parameter stipulates when the volume binding should occur.

To learn about the remainder of the `StorageClass` parameters, please check the official Kubernetes documentation here: `https://kubernetes.io/docs/concepts/storage/storage-classes/`.

> **Important note**
>
> You can find the complete source code at `https://github.com/PacktPublishing/Kubernetes-in-Production-Best-Practices/blob/master/Chapter07/stateful/percona/deployment-percona-sc.yaml`.

Now, we will modify the `pvc-percona.yaml` and `deployment-percona.yaml` manifest files. We will adjust the `percona` deployment to use a storage class to dynamically request a PV through a PVC:

1. Edit the template for the `percona-pvc` PVC in this path, `stateful/percona/pvc-percona.yaml`, using your preferred text editor. Adjust the name and `storageClassName` fields as follows:

```
kind: PersistentVolumeClaim
apiVersion: v1
metadata:
  name: percona-pvc-gp2
spec:
```

```
accessModes:
  - ReadWriteOnce
resources:
  requests:
    storage: 5Gi
storageClassName: gp2
```

2. Edit the template for the `percona` deployment in this path, `stateful/percona/deployment-percona.yaml`, using your preferred text editor. Adjust the last line, `claimName`, as follows:

```
claimName: percona-pvc-gp2
```

3. Execute the following `kubectl` commands to create a `percona` deployment in the cluster using a dynamically provisioned PV:

```
$ kubectl apply -f pv-percona.yaml
$ kubectl apply -f deployment-percona.yaml
```

Now you have created a stateful application deployment with a binding to a dynamically provisioned PV using `StorageClass`. This step completely eliminated the need for manual EBS volume creation. Therefore, we will use this method later in this chapter when creating new stateful applications.

Choosing a persistent storage solution

Two of the biggest stateful application challenges in Kubernetes are storage orchestration and data management. There are an infinite number of solutions out there. First, we will explain the main storage attributes and topologies we need to consider when evaluating storage alternatives. Let's review the topologies used by the most common storage systems:

- **Centralized**: Traditional, or also referred to as monolithic, storage systems are most often tightly coupled with a proprietary hardware and internal communication protocols. They are usually associated with scale-up models since it is difficult to scale-out tightly coupled components of the storage nodes.

- **Distributed**: Distributed storage systems are more likely to be a software-defined solution and they may be architected to favor availability, consistency, durability, performance, or scalability. Usually, distributed systems scale out better than others to support many storage server nodes in parallel.

- **Hyperconverged**: Hyperconverged storage solutions are designed to take advantage of the same network and compute resources where the applications run. They are largely designed to run as software and are orchestrated by the same platform used to manage applications, VMs, or containers, such as a hypervisor or container orchestrators.

- **Sharded**: Sharded storage solutions partition the data into datasets and store them across multiple nodes. Sharded storage solutions can be complex to manage and rebalance and performance is limited to the performance of a single node where the dataset is located.

The category of storage solutions available for the cloud-native application is known as cloud-native storage by the **Cloud Native Computing Foundation** (**CNCF**). Currently, there are 17 open source and 32 proprietary solutions, hence a total of 49 solutions, listed in the category.

For the most up-to-date list of solutions, you can refer to the official CNCF cloud-native interactive landscape documentation at `https://landscape.cncf.io/`:

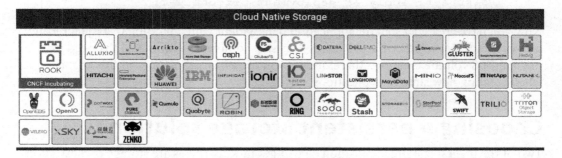

Figure 7.1 – CNCF cloud-native landscape with cloud-native storage providers

When the challenges mentioned in the *Understanding the challenges with stateful applications* section are considered for the simplicity of the deployment and life cycle management of block storage, **Container Attached Storage (CAS)** and **Cloud Storage** are preferred over the centralized topology. To satisfy persistence across different infrastructure and data mobility requirements, **CAS** and **Distributed** solutions should be preferred over the solutions on the right. When we talk about Kubernetes-grade scalability, again **Cloud Storage** and **CAS** solutions offer significant advantages over the centralized topology. Overall, **CAS** and **Cloud Storage** providers satisfy all the architectural concerns. That said, on many occasions, we will have to utilize your company's existing investment. Cloud storage is only available on the cloud vendor provided infrastructure, and if you are running on-premises/private clouds, you may need to utilize your existing hardware solutions. In that case, you can still leverage **CAS** solutions to unify data management, add the advantages of cloud-native storage, including data mobility and scalability, and simplify the life cycle management of PVs on top of your investment.

Now that you have learned the storage topologies used by the most common storage solutions, let's focus on how we can use a CAS solution to deploy a stateful application.

Deploying stateful applications

Kubernetes provides a number of controller APIs to manage the deployment of pods within a Kubernetes cluster. Initially designed for stateless applications, these controllers are used to group pods based on need. In this section, we will briefly learn the differences between the following Kubernetes objects – pods, ReplicaSets, deployments, and StatefulSets. In the event of a node failure, individual Pods will not be rescheduled on other nodes. Therefore, they should be avoided when running stateful workloads.

Deployments are used when managing pods, and **ReplicaSets** when we need to roll out changes to replica Pods. Both ReplicaSets and Deployments are used when provisioning stateless applications. To learn about Deployments, please check the official Kubernetes documentation here: `https://kubernetes.io/docs/concepts/workloads/controllers/deployment/`.

StatefulSets are another controller that reached a **General Availability (GA)** milestone with the release of Kubernetes 1.9. The real adoption of stateful applications started following the introduction of the StatefulSets object. With StatefulSets, every pod replica has its own state, in other words, its own volume, and therefore retains its state and identity across restarts. When deploying stateful applications, and when we need storage to be stateful, we will use StatefulSets. The following diagram shows the components of an application deployed using StatefulSets:

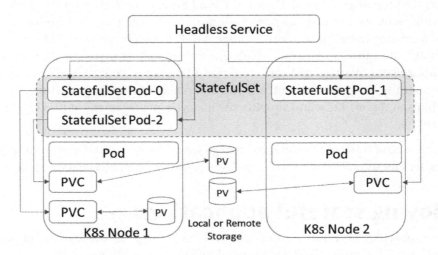

Figure 7.2 – Kubernetes StatefulSet deployment diagram

StatefulSets require a headless service for handling the network identity of the related pods. When a StatefulSet requests volumes to be created, it uses the StorageClass to call the PV provisioner. Earlier in this chapter, you learned to use StorageClass to dynamically provision PVs.

Before we deploy a stateful application, we will learn how to install one of the popular open source storage provisioner options, OpenEBS, which we mentioned in the *Choosing a persistent storage solution* section.

Installing OpenEBS

OpenEBS is an open source CNCF project for Kubernetes designed to enable stateful applications to easily access dynamic local PVs, or replicated and highly available PVs. OpenEBS is an example of the new category of cloud-native storage solutions known as CAS. CAS solutions are easy to maintain, are portable, can run on any platform, are scalable, and fulfil the infrastructure design principles that I introduced in *Chapter 1, Introduction to Kubernetes Infrastructure and Production-Readiness*.

To learn more about its prerequisites and the detailed usage of OpenEBS, please refer to the following link: `https://docs.openebs.io/`.

Now, let's install OpenEBS on your Kubernetes cluster and prepare your cluster to provide dynamically provisioned PVs:

1. Create a namespace called `openebs`:

    ```
    $ kubectl create ns openebs
    ```

2. Add the OpenEBS Helm chart repository to your local repository list:

    ```
    $ helm repo add openebs https://openebs.github.io/charts
    ```

3. Update the Helm chart repositories:

    ```
    $ helm repo update
    ```

4. Install `openebs` from its Helm repository:

    ```
    $ helm install --namespace openebs openebs openebs/
    openebs
    ```

5. Verify successful installation by executing the following command:

    ```
    $ kubectl get pods -n openebs
    ```

6. The output of the preceding command should look as follows:

    ```
    NAME                                                READY  STATUS   RESTARTS  AGE
    openebs-admission-server-59cb5d6f64-jtkpd           1/1    Running  0         96s
    openebs-apiserver-76549b589b-mvxjw                  1/1    Running  0         96s
    openebs-localpv-provisioner-75d886744d-mb6g8        1/1    Running  0         96s
    openebs-ndm-6ns5l                                   1/1    Running  0         96s
    openebs-ndm-787fh                                   1/1    Running  0         96s
    openebs-ndm-f6txb                                   1/1    Running  0         96s
    openebs-ndm-operator-75fccb9cfb-l8kb9               1/1    Running  0         96s
    openebs-provisioner-6d987f8b79-xw8b9                1/1    Running  0         96s
    openebs-snapshot-operator-68fdb8d49d-8zjqs          2/2    Running  0         96s
    ```

Figure 7.3 – List of the OpenEBS pods running following successful installation

Now that you can use OpenEBS for dynamically creating PVs, you can either create a new SC or use one of the default storage classes provided by OpenEBS.

OpenEBS provides various types of block storage options, including storage engines called `Jiva`, `cStor`, and `Mayastor`, for persistent workloads that require highly available volumes during node failures and `Dynamic Local PV` (device, host path, ZFS) alternatives for distributed applications, such as Cassandra, Elastic, Kafka, or MinIO.

Execute the following command to get the list of default storage classes in your cluster:

```
$ kubectl get sc
```

You will notice the new storage classes, `openebs-device`, `openebs-hostpath`, `openebs-jiva-default`, and `openebs-snapshot-promoter`, added to your list.

Here is an example of a YAML manifest to create a PVC using the default `openebs-jiva-default` storage class:

```
---
kind: PersistentVolumeClaim
apiVersion: v1
metadata:
  name: openebs-pvc
spec:
  storageClassName: openebs-jiva-default
  accessModes:
    - ReadWriteOnce
  resources:
    requests:
      storage: 5G
---
```

Now you have learned who to create a PV for with your stateful applications using an open source CAS alternative – OpenEBS.

From now on, if running on an AWS infrastructure, you can continue to consume your existing EBS volumes using the `gp2` storage class or the `ebs-sc` storage class created earlier using `Amazon_EBS_CSI_Driver`, or take advantage of OpenEBS to abstract data management. OpenEBS, in the same way as CAS solutions, helps to reduce many of the challenges we described in the *Understanding the challenges with stateful applications* section earlier in this chapter.

Now that we have learned how to use storage provisioners to dynamically provision a PV, let's use it, along with a stateful application, to simplify the life cycle of data management.

Deploying a stateful application on OpenEBS volumes

OpenEBS provides a flexible data plane with a few storage engines options that are optimized for different application and performance expectations. You can read about the differences between storage engines on the official OpenEBS documentation site at `https://docs.openebs.io/docs/next/casengines.html`. Here, we will dive into one of the defaults, the low-footprint storage engine option, `Jiva`.

Now, we will modify the `pvc-percona.yaml` and `deployment-percona.yaml` manifest files. We will adjust the `percona` deployment to use a StorageClass to dynamically request a PV through a PVC:

1. Create a `StorageClass` named `openebs-jiva-3r` with a `ReplicaCount` of 3 in the following path – `stateful/percona/sc-openebs-jiva.yaml`. This will create three copies of the volume and make it highly available in the event of node failure:

    ```
    apiVersion: storage.k8s.io/v1
    kind: StorageClass
    metadata:
      name: openebs-jiva-3r
      annotations:
        openebs.io/cas-type: jiva
        cas.openebs.io/config: |
          - name: ReplicaCount
            value: "3"
          - name: StoragePool
            value: default
    provisioner: openebs.io/provisioner-iscsi
    ```

2. Execute the following `kubectl` command to create the StorageClass:

    ```
    $ kubectl apply -f sc-openebs-jiva.yaml
    ```

3. Edit the template for the `percona-pvc` PVC in this path, `stateful/percona/pvc-percona.yaml`, using your preferred text editor. Adjust the name and `storageClassName` fields as follows:

    ```
    storageClassName: openebs-jiva-3r
    ```

4. Edit the template for the `percona` deployment in this path, `stateful/`
    `percona/deployment-percona.yaml`, using your preferred text editor.
    Adjust the last line, `claimName`, as follows:

    ```
    claimName: percona-pvc-openebs
    ```

5. Execute the following `kubectl` commands to create the `percona` deployment in
    the cluster using a dynamically provisioned PV:

    ```
    $ kubectl apply -f pvc-percona.yaml
    $ kubectl apply -f deployment-percona.yaml
    ```

Now you have created a stateful application deployment backed by dynamically created
OpenEBS PVs. This step helped us to abstract data management on cloud and bare-metal
or VM-based Kubernetes clusters.

Summary

In this chapter, we learned the stateful application challenges and best practices to
consider when choosing the best storage management solutions, both open source and
commercial, and finally, the stateful application considerations when deploying them in
production using Kubernetes' StatefulSet and deployment objects.

We deployed the AWS EBS CSI driver and OpenEBS. We also created a highly available
replicated storage using OpenEBS and deployed our application on OpenEBS volumes.

We gained a solid understanding of Kubernetes storage in this chapter, but you should
perform a detailed evaluation of your cluster storage requirements and take further action
to deploy any extra tools and configurations that may be required, including your storage
provider's CSI driver.

In the next chapter, we will learn in detail about seamless and reliable applications. We
will also get to grips with containerization best practices to easily scale our applications.

Further reading

You can refer to the following links for more information on the topics covered in this chapter:

- *Kubernetes – A Complete DevOps Cookbook* (*Chapter 5, Preparing for Stateful Workloads*): `https://www.packtpub.com/product/kubernetes-a-complete-devops-cookbook/9781838828042`.

- *Kubernetes Container Storage Interface (CSI) Documentation*: `https://kubernetes-csi.github.io/docs/introduction.html`

- *QuickStart Guide to OpenEBS*: `https://docs.openebs.io/docs/next/quickstart.html`

8
Deploying Seamless and Reliable Applications

In previous chapters, we learned how to prepare our platform and infrastructure components for production usage. We also learned Kubernetes data management considerations and storage best practices to deploy our first stateful application using the Operator Framework. One of the most underestimated topics in container orchestration is container image management. Although developing applications in Kubernetes is out of the scope of this book, we need to understand the critical components of our images. There are multiple sources, public container registries, and vendors where we can find ready-to-consume application images. Mishandling container images can not only cause overutilization of our cluster resources but, more importantly, can also impact the reliability and security of our services.

In this chapter, we will discuss topics such as containers and image management. We will learn about the technical challenges when selecting or creating our application images that affect the Kubernetes cluster's stability and security. We will focus on application rollout best practices when deploying and creating our production services before hosting on our cluster to avoid creating instability or misuse of the cluster. This will help us to get the full benefits of using Kubernetes to orchestrate our services securely.

In this chapter, we're going to cover the following main topics:

- Understanding the challenges with container images
- Learning application deployment strategies
- Scaling applications and achieving higher availability

Technical requirements

You should have the following tools installed from previous chapters:

- `kubectl`
- `metrics-server`

You need to have an up-and-running Kubernetes cluster as per the instructions in *Chapter 3, Provisioning Kubernetes Clusters Using AWS and Terraform.*

The code for this chapter is located at `https://github.com/PacktPublishing/Kubernetes-in-Production-Best-Practices/tree/master/Chapter08`.

Check out the following link to see the Code in Action video:

`https://bit.ly/3rpWeRN`

Understanding the challenges with container images

In this section, we will learn about the considerations and best practices followed by industry experts when building or selecting the right container images. Before we discuss the challenges and get into our options, let's learn what goes into a container image.

Exploring the components of container images

To understand the behavior of a container image, we need to have basic knowledge of the **Operating System (OS)** and hierarchical protection domains. For security segregation purposes, the OS handles virtual memory in two layers called **kernel space** and **user space**. Basically, the kernel runs in the most privileged protection ring, called **Ring 0**, and interacts directly with critical resources such as CPU and memory. The kernel needs to be stable since any problem or instability would cause instability in the overall system and bring everything to a panic state. As we can see in *Figure 8.1*, drivers, low-level system components, and all user applications run in the least privileged protection rings and in user space:

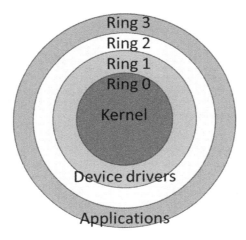

Figure 8.1 – Privilege rings, also called hierarchical protection domains

To learn about the user space, please check out the detailed explanation here: `https://debian-handbook.info/browse/stable/sect.user-space.html`.

Linux containers take the segregation of security one step further and allow us to manage application and OS dependencies separately in what is called the **container host** and **container image**.

The container host is where the OS runs along with the **container runtime** (some of the popular container runtimes include **containerd**, **CRI-O**, **Firecracker**, and **Kata**) and **container engine** (some of the popular container engines include Docker and the **Linux Container Daemon (LXD)**). In this book, we will not discuss the differences between container runtimes and engines, since most of the time they are part of the platform, which is outside of our scope. In traditional monolithic architectures, we run applications on top of the OS along with OS dependencies and other applications, whereas in cloud-native microservices architectures, we run applications and their dependencies inside a container image (see *Figure 8.2*):

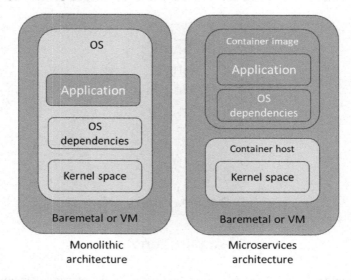

Figure 8.2 – Comparison of monolithic and microservices architecture

When we run an application in Kubernetes, such as NGINX, Cassandra, Kafka, MongoDB, and so on, our container engine pulls the container image from its container registry to the local registry, then it wraps one or more containers into an object called a **pod** and **schedules** it on an available worker node.

The container image (most of the time, this term is misused instead of *base image*) used in this process is a layered image consisting of the user application and the container base image.

The container base image contains the interchangeable user space components of the OS. The container image is packaged following the Docker image or **Open Container Initiative (OCI)** industry standards. This is where our options and challenges come in. Most container base images contain a root filesystem with the minimal user space applications of an OS distribution, some other external libraries, utilities, and files. Container images are typically used for software development and provide a functional application written in common programming languages. Programming languages, including both compiled and interpreted ones, depend on external drivers and libraries. These dependencies make the container base image selection critically important.

Before we build our application or run an application based on an existing image in production, we need to understand the critical differences between the popular container base images. Now that you've learned what goes into container images, let's learn the differences between the common container base images and some of the best practices for choosing the right image type.

Choosing the right container base image

Choosing a container base image is not much different than choosing your container hosts' Linux distribution. Similar criteria such as security, performance, dependencies, core utilities, package managers, the size of its community and ecosystem, and the security response and support must be considered.

I would like to highlight the five notable container image challenges that we will try to address in this chapter:

- **Image size**: One of the important benefits of container images is portability. A smaller container image size reduces the build and rollout times since pulling the image itself will be faster. Smaller images are achieved by limiting extra binaries, which also bring a minimized attack surface and increased security benefits.

- **Stability**: Updating base images is not fun, but updating every container image is the worst. Container images that only include your application and its runtime dependencies, such as distroless images, may sound attractive. Still, when it comes to patching **Common Vulnerabilities and Exposures (CVEs)**, you will need to update all your containers that can introduce stability issues.

> **Important note**
>
> Distroless images are container images that don't contain package managers or any other application. You can read more about distroless Docker images and watch a presentation here: `https://github.com/GoogleContainerTools/distroless`.

- **Security**: Every binary that is added to our container images adds unpredictable risks to the overall platform security. When choosing base images, their update frequency, ecosystem and community size, and vulnerability tracking methods such as a CVE database and **Open Vulnerability and Assessment Language (OVAL)** data are important factors to consider. Check the properties of executables such as the **Position Independent Executable (PIE)**, **Relocation Read-Only (RELRO)**, **Patches for the Linux Kernel (PaX)**, canaries, **Address Space Layout Randomization (ASLR)**, FORTIFY_SOURCE, and the RPATH and RUNPATH runtime search paths.

> **Important note**
>
> You can find the Bash script to check the properties of the binary hardening tools at `https://github.com/slimm609/checksec.sh`.

- **Speed/performance**: Popular container base images may not always be the fastest. Although Alpine is famous for its size and is recommended in some cases, it may cause serious build performance issues. Alpine might be acceptable if you are using the Go language. If you are using Python instead, you will quickly notice that Alpine images will sometimes get two to three times larger, are more than 10 times slower to build, and might even cause build problems.

> **Important note**
>
> You can find the Kubernetes-related performance test tools here: `https://github.com/kubernetes/perf-tests`.

- **Dependencies**: The C library used in the container image should not be underestimated. While most base images use `glibc`, Alpine includes `muslc` and can show implementation differences. Also, utilities included in the image for troubleshooting and support need to be considered.

The following are some of the common container base image options compared by their size, security, and support options:

- **Alpine (alpine:3.12)**: A very popular lightweight container base image mainly used to reduce image size. Technically, it is `busybox` with a package manager. `glibc/musl` library differences are known to cause problems and performance issues that are hard to track down:

  - **Size**: 2.6 MB.

  - **Security**: Community-updated; Alpine Linux bug tracker available at `https://bugs.alpinelinux.org/projects/alpine/issues`.

  - **Support**: Support via community. 386, AMD64, ARMv6, ARMv7, ARM64v8, ppc64le, and S390x architectures supported.

- **Amazon Linux 2 (amazonlinux:2)**: A Linux image maintained by **Amazon Web Services (AWS)** to be used on Amazon EC2 instances. It is binary-compatible with RHEL and CentOS:

  - **Size**: 59.14 MB.

  - **Security**: Vendor-updated; Amazon Linux Security Center available at `https://alas.aws.amazon.com/alas2.html`.

  - **Support**: LTS support included with AWS EC2; AMD64 and ARM64v8 architectures supported.

- **CentOS (centos:8)**: Community-driven container base image of the popular Linux distribution. Due to the rollout of CentOS Stream, its future is unknown. At this point, it is better to wait for the replacement Rocky Linux base images or use Amazon Linux 2:

  - **Size**: 71.7 MB.

  - **Security**: Community-updated; CentOS security alerts can be found here: `https://lwn.net/Alerts/CentOS/`.

  - **Support**: Support via community only. AMD64, ARM64v8, and ppc64le architectures supported.

- **Debian (debian:buster-slim)**: A large community-driven container base image of the popular Debian Linux distribution. Debian is preferred over Alpine due to a more compatible C library (`libc`) included in Debian images:

  - **Size**: 26.47 MB

  - **Security**: Community-updated; Security Bug Tracker (`https://security-tracker.debian.org/tracker/`) and OVAL at `https://www.debian.org/security/oval/`

  - **Support**: Support via community only. 386, AMD64, and ARM64v5 architectures supported

- **Ubuntu (ubuntu:21.04)**: A Debian-based larger community and enterprise-supported Linux distribution base image:

  - **Size**: 29.94 MB

  - **Security**: Ubuntu CVE Tracker at `https://people.canonical.com/~ubuntu-security/cve/` and cloud image bug tracker at `https://bugs.launchpad.net/cloud-images`

  - **Support**: Community and commercial support. AMD64, ARMv7, and ARM64v8 architectures supported

- **Red Hat Universal Base Image (UBI) (registry.redhat.io/ubi8/ubi-minimal:8.3)**: A **Red Hat Enterprise Linux** (**RHEL**)-based stripped-down image that uses `microdnf` as a package manager. It is preferred when running applications on the **Red Hat OpenShift** platform. Red Hat UBI provides three base images, minimal (`ubi-minimal`), standard (`ubi`), and multi-service (`ubi-init`), for different use cases:

  - **Size**: 37.6 MB.

  - **Security**: The best container base image in terms of completeness of vulnerability checks. Errata provided at `https://access.redhat.com/errata` and OVAL data provided at `https://www.redhat.com/security/data/oval/`.

  - **Support**: Community and commercial support. AMD64, ARM64v8, ppc64le, and S390x architectures supported.

- **Distroless (gcr.io/distroless/base-debian10)**: Builds on the Debian distribution by Google. They don't contain package managers or shells. Preferred for security and size. Additional builds can be found at `https://console.cloud.google.com/gcr/images/distroless/GLOBAL`:

  - **Size**: 75.1 MB

  - **Security**: Avoids image vulnerabilities, but introduces another challenge where dependent library updates need to be carefully tracked for every container image

  - **Support**: Support via community only. AMD64, ARM, ARM64, ppc64le, and S390x architectures supported

Now you have learned about the challenges we deal with when choosing the right container base image and how the most common popular base images compare. Let's find out some of the best practices for reducing your final image size and scanning your container images for vulnerabilities.

Reducing container image size

An excellent way to achieve smaller container images would be by starting with small base images such as Alpine, `ubi-minimal`, or distroless base images.

> **Note**
>
> For reproducible builds and deployment, you can also use the Nix package manager and create slim builds. There is a lot of enthusiasm around Nix, but since there is a steep learning curve and custom expression language is involved, we will not discuss Nix in this book. You can learn about building container images using Nix here at the official NixOS documentation page: `https://nixos.org/guides/building-and-running-docker-images.html`.

Excluding some of the unnecessary files, using a `.dockerignore` file can help us to reduce our image size. Here is an example of a `.dockerignore` file:

```
# ignoring git folder
.git
#ignoring visual studio code related temp data
.vs
.vscode
# other files and CI manifests
.DS_Store
```

```
.dockerignore
.editorconfig
.gitignore
.gitlab-ci.yml
.travis.yml
# ignore all files and directories starting with temp
# in any subdirectory
*/temp*
# ignore all files and directories starting with temp
# in any subdirectory two levels below root
*/*/temp*
# ignore all files and directories starting with temp
# followed by any character
temp?
```

Size-optimized images can be achieved by utilizing multistage builds and avoiding extra layers. Multistage builds add a couple of new syntaxes and allow us to use a FROM section in our Dockerfile multiple times to start a new stage of the build and copy only the artifacts we want to take from previous stages. You can learn more about the multistage build on the official Docker documentation website at https://docs.docker.com/develop/develop-images/multistage-build/.

Here is an example of a Dockerfile with two stages:

```
FROM node:14.15 AS base
ADD . /app
WORKDIR /app
RUN npm install

FROM gcr.io/distroless/nodejs AS stage2
COPY --from=base /app /app
WORKDIR /app
EXPOSE 8080
CMD ["server.js"]
```

In our preceding example, the first stage, base, starts with the node:14.15 Node.js base image. We copy our application code to the /app directory and execute the npm install command.

We move to the second stage, called `stage2`, this time using a `distroless/nodejs` base image. Then, we copy our application code and our `node_modules` from the first stage using the `COPY --from=base /app /app` syntax. This way, we are reducing our container image size as well as the attack surface since distroless images do not contain `bash` or other tools that can be maliciously executed.

You can read about the best practices for writing Dockerfiles at `https://docs.docker.com/develop/develop-images/dockerfile_best-practices/`.

Now we have learned a few techniques for reducing our container image size. Let's look at how we can proactively scan our images against security vulnerabilities and patch them in a timely manner before running them in production.

Scanning container images for vulnerabilities

We've built our container images or pulled some of the vendor-provided images to our local registry and now we are ready to run in our production environment. How do we know they are safe to run? How do we know they have the latest security vulnerabilities patched? Most **Continuous Integration and Continuous Delivery (CI/CD)** solutions today have additional security scanning tools. It is one of the golden rules not to roll out any service into production before going through a quick image validation during our pipeline. For this purpose, we will now learn about a popular open source solution called **Trivy**.

Trivy is a comprehensive vulnerability scanner for container images. Trivy is capable of detecting vulnerabilities in most images based on popular base images, including Alpine, CentOS, and Red Hat UBI, and application package dependencies such as npm, yarn, bundler, and composer.

Here, we will manually install the `trivy` binaries and run a vulnerability analysis:

1. Let's get the latest release version tag of `trivy` and keep it in a variable called TRIVYVERSION:

```
$ TRIVYVERSION=$(curl -silent "https://api.github.com/
repos/aquasecurity/trivy/releases/latest" | grep '"tag_
name":' | \
sed -E 's/.*"v([^"]+)".*/\1/')
```

2. Now, download the latest `trivy` binary and install it:

```
$ curl --silent --location "https://github.com/
aquasecurity/trivy/releases/download/v${TRIVYVERSION}/
trivy_${TRIVYVERSION}_Linux-64bit.tar.gz" | tar xz -C /
tmp
```

```
$ sudo mv /tmp/trivy /usr/local/bin
```

3. Confirm that the installation is successfully completed by executing the following command:

```
$ trivy --version
```
```
Version: 0.14.0
```

4. Run `trivy` checks with a target image location and its tag. In our example, we scanned the `alpine:3.12` base image from its official Docker Hub repository:

```
$ trivy alpine:3.12
```

The output of the preceding command should look as follows since no issues are found in the particular container image:

```
2020-12-20T15:53:30.380-0800    INFO    Need to update DB
2020-12-20T15:53:30.380-0800    INFO    Downloading DB...
19.55 MiB / 19.55 MiB [----------------------------------------
2020-12-20T15:53:34.412-0800    INFO    Detecting Alpine vulnerabilities.
2020-12-20T15:53:34.413-0800    INFO    Trivy skips scanning programming

alpine:3.12 (alpine 3.12.3)
===================================
Total: 0 (UNKNOWN: 0, LOW: 0, MEDIUM: 0, HIGH: 0, CRITICAL: 0)
```

Figure 8.3 – Trivy results of a container image with no known vulnerabilities

5. Now, let's scan a publicly available version of the popular MongoDB database container image. MongoDB is used by many modern cloud-native applications and services:

```
$ trivy mongo:4.4
```

6. You will notice that Trivy returned `93` known vulnerabilities, including `2` high and `28` medium severity issues:

```
2020-12-20T16:00:20.720-0800    INFO    Detecting Ubuntu vulnerabilities...
2020-12-20T16:00:20.722-0800    INFO    Trivy skips scanning programming language libraries because no supported f
ile was detected
mongo:4.4 (ubuntu 18.04)
========================
Total: 93 (UNKNOWN: 0, LOW: 63, MEDIUM: 28, HIGH: 2, CRITICAL: 0)

+------------------------+--------------------+----------+--------------------+-----------------------+-------+
|        LIBRARY         |  VULNERABILITY ID  | SEVERITY |  INSTALLED VERSION |     FIXED VERSION     |       |
|         TITLE          |                    |    URL   |                    |                       |       |
+------------------------+--------------------+----------+--------------------+-----------------------+-------+
| apt                    | CVE-2020-27350     | MEDIUM   | 1.6.12ubuntu0.1    | 1.6.12ubuntu0.2       | APT h |
| ad several integer     |                    | avd.aquasec.com/nvd/cve-2020-27350 |      |                       | overf |
| lows and underflows while |                 |          |                    |                       | parsi |
| ng .deb packages, aka... |                  |          |                    |                       |       |
+------------------------+--------------------+----------+--------------------+-----------------------+-------+
```

Figure 8.4 – Trivy results showing vulnerabilities

In the long analysis returned by the Trivy scanner, you can find vulnerability IDs and severity URLs to learn more about the issues. You can also see that some issues come from the Ubuntu 18.04 base image used in the container image and can be resolved by just updating the base image of the container.

Trivy supports most CI tools, including Travis CI, CircleCI, Jenkins, and GitLab CI. To learn more about Trivy and integration details, you can read the official documentation at `https://github.com/aquasecurity/trivy`.

Now we have learned how to test container images against known vulnerabilities. It is highly recommended to have test conditions in your build pipelines. Let's look into how we can test the impact of container image downloads from public repositories.

Testing the download speed of a container image

CI is a key component of automation, and the reduction of every second spent in the pipeline execution will be important. Download time also impacts the speed of the new container image rollout to the production environment. Therefore, we need to consider the download speeds of the container images used.

Here, we will use the `time` command in Linux to execute `docker run` in a specified container base image and compare the summary of the real-time user CPU time and system CPU time spent during the process:

1. Install the `curl` utility in the `debian:buster-slim` Debian base image:

```
$ time docker run --rm debian:buster-slim sh -c "apt-get
update && apt-get install curl -y"
real    0m43.837s
user    0m0.024s
sys     0m0.043s
```

2. For comparison, let's now run the same command in the `alpine:3.12` image:

```
$ time docker run --rm alpine:3.12 sh -c "apk update &&
apk add --update curl"
real    0m2.644s
user    0m0.034s
sys     0m0.021s
```

Note that both images were not available in the local registry and were pulled for the first time from the public Docker Hub location. As you can see, the Alpine image completed the task in close to 2 seconds, whereas the same request took more than 40 seconds longer to finish using the Debian image.

Now we have learned about measuring the command execution speed in containers based on different base images. Let's summarize everything we have learned in this section into a short list of simple container image best practices.

Applying container base images best practices

Technically, most applications will run in containers layered on top of all the common and popular container base images. This may be acceptable for development and test purposes, but before rolling out any container images into production, there are a few common-sense best practices we should consider:

- The size of the container image is important as long as the container base image does not introduce a performance tax and vulnerabilities. Using a stable, compatible, and supported base image is preferred over saving a few megabytes.

- Never use the `latest` tag to pull base images when building your container images.

- Make sure to use container images with the exact tested and validated version of the image. You can also specify its digest by replacing `<image-name>:<tag>` with `<image-name>@<digest>` to generate stable reproducible builds.

- Check `imagePullPolicy` in your application manifests. Unless required otherwise, it is suggested to use `IfNotPresent`.

- When possible, use the same base OS in your container host and container images.

- Integrate image vulnerability scanners into your CI pipelines and make sure to clear at least high and critical severity vulnerabilities before rolling your images into production.

- Monitor container image size changes over time and notify maintainers of sudden large size changes.

- When using public container registries, store your container images in multiple registries. Some public registries include Docker Hub, GitLab Container Registry, Red Hat Quay, Amazon ECR, Azure Container Registry, and Google Cloud Container Registry.

- For increased security, use a private container registry and monitor public container registry pulls into the production environment.

Now we have learned about the challenges of choosing container images and production best practices. Let's look at different deployment strategies and their use cases.

Learning application deployment strategies

Organizations without the expertise to design an application deployment strategy before getting their services to production users can face great operational complexity when managing their application life cycle. Many users still face container and microservices adoption issues later in their digital transformation journey and end up going back to the more expensive **Database as a Service** (**DbaaS**) model or even using traditional deployment methods in VMs. To avoid common mistakes and production anti-patterns, we need to be aware of some of the common strategies that will ensure our success in deploying and managing applications on Kubernetes.

We learned about the differences between different Kubernetes controllers such as Deployments, ReplicaSets, and StatefulSets in the *Deploying stateful applications* section in *Chapter 7, Managing Storage and Stateful Applications*.

In this section, we will learn about the following containerized application deployment best practices:

- Choosing the deployment model
- Monitoring deployments
- Using readiness and liveness probes

Let's discuss each of them in the following sections.

Choosing the deployment model

In Kubernetes, applications can be rolled out following various deployment procedures. Choosing the right strategy is not always easy since it really depends on your services and how your applications are accessed by users. Now, we will review the most common models:

- A/B testing
- Blue/green
- Canary release
- Clean deployment
- Incremental deployment

Let's learn about the advantages of each of them in the following sections.

A/B testing

A/B testing deployments allow routing groups of users to a new deployment based on conditions such as HTTP headers, location, browser cookies, or other user metadata. A/B testing deployments are preferred when a specific feature of the application needs to be tested on a certain group of users and rollout needs to continue based on the conversation rate. Price and UX testing are also done using A/B testing. Other than the complexity of the parameters that need to be managed, it is the most flexible model with low cloud cost, minimum impact on users, and quick rollback times.

Blue/green

In the blue/green deployment model, an equal amount of instances of each application is deployed on your cluster. This model can be executed either by traffic switching or by traffic mirroring when a service mesh such as Istio is used. It is preferred when service changes need to be tested for load and compliance with no impact on actual users. When the metrics return successful data, a new deployment (green) gets promoted. This model cannot be used to target a specific group of users and can be expensive in terms of cloud resource consumption cost due to its full deployment model.

Canary release

Canary deployments gradually shift traffic from one deployment to another based on percentage, sometimes triggered by metrics such as success rate or health. Canary releases are preferred when confidence in the new releases is not high or when deploying releases on a completely new platform. Groups of users cannot be targeted. This method doesn't increase public cloud costs and rollback times can be rather quick.

Clean deployment

In this method, one version of the application is destroyed and a new version is deployed. It is preferred in deployment since it is the simplest method, although this method should not be used in production unless the service is not in use. If the deployment fails compared to the other methods, the rollback time would be the highest, and the service downtime would be the longest.

Incremental deployment

In this method, a new version of the application is deployed in a rolling update fashion and slowly migrated. The only advantage of this model compared to a clean deployment is that incremental deployment does not introduce downtime.

Some of the methods can only be implemented with the help of **service mesh** solutions, such as Istio, Linkerd, or AWS App Mesh, and ingress controllers, including Contour, Gloo, NGINX, or Traefik.

Orchestration of multiple deployment strategies can turn into a complex configuration puzzle. In this case, the usage of an application delivery operator can be very useful. **Flagger** is one of the most complete progressive delivery Kubernetes operators in the Kubernetes ecosystem. Flagger can automate complex rollover scenarios using Istio, Linkerd, App Mesh, NGINX, Skipper, Contour, Gloo, or Traefik based on the metrics analysis from the metrics collected by Prometheus. To learn more about Flagger operators and a tutorial covering the models discussed here, you can read the official documentation at `https://docs.flagger.app/`.

Monitoring deployments

Smooth, production-ready application deployment and canary analysis cannot be achieved without monitoring the application usage metrics. We can monitor our applications using tools such as Prometheus, Datadog, or Splunk.

We will cover monitoring, visualizations, logging, tracing solutions, and how to make visualization dashboards relevant to serve our production needs in *Chapter 9, Monitoring, Logging, and Observability*.

Using readiness and liveness container probes

When a new pod is scheduled in our Kubernetes cluster, its phase is represented by the `PodStatus` object. These phases reported as `Pending`, `Running`, `Succeeded`, `Failed`, or `Unknown` do not represent or guarantee our application's intended function. You can read more about the pod life cycle and its phases on the official Kubernetes documentation site at `https://kubernetes.io/docs/concepts/workloads/pods/pod-lifecycle/`.

To monitor our application's real health status inside the container, a regular diagnostic task can be executed. These diagnostic tests performed periodically are called **container probes**. `kubelet` can perform three types of container probes, as follows:

- `livenessProbe`
- `readinessProbe`
- `startupProbe`

It is highly recommended to use at minimum the readiness and liveness probes to control your application's health when starting and periodically after it is scheduled in your Kubernetes cluster. When enabled, `kubelet` can call three different handlers, `ExecAction`, `TCPSocketAction`, and `HTTPGetAction`, inside or against the pod's IP and validate your application's health.

> **Important note**
> You can find the complete source code at `https://github.com/PacktPublishing/Kubernetes-in-Production-Best-Practices/blob/master/Chapter08/probes/liveness/busybox.yaml`.

In the next code snippet, we will create a `busybox` pod example that will use `livenessProbe` to execute a command inside the container image to check our pod's liveness.

Create the template for the `busybox` pod in this `probes/liveness/busybox.yaml` path:

```yaml
apiVersion: v1
kind: Pod
metadata:
  labels:
    test: liveness
  name: liveness-execaction
spec:
  containers:
  - name: liveness
    image: k8s.gcr.io/busybox
    args:
    - /bin/sh
    - -c
    - touch /tmp/alive; sleep 30; rm -rf /tmp/alive; sleep 300
    livenessProbe:
      exec:
        command:
        - cat
        - /tmp/alive
      initialDelaySeconds: 10
      periodSeconds: 10
```

When the container starts, it executes the command specified under the `args` section. This command first creates a file under `/tmp/alive`, and then waits 30 seconds and removes it. `livenessProbe`, as specified in the same file, first waits 10 seconds, as defined by the `initialDelaySeconds` parameter, and then periodically, every 10 seconds, as defined by the `periodSeconds` parameter, executes the `cat /tmp/alive` command. In the first 30 seconds, our command will be successful and once the file is removed, `livenessProbe` will fail, and our pod will be restarted for losing its liveness state. Make sure you allow enough time for the pod to start by setting a reasonable `initialDelaySeconds` value.

Similarly, we can add `readinessProbe` by replacing the `livenessProbe` field with `readinessProbe`.

Now we have learned about the production deployment best practices on Kubernetes. We have also learned about common deployment strategies for rolling production applications and using container probes for verifying the health of our application. Next, we will learn how to scale our applications.

Scaling applications and achieving higher availability

The Kubernetes container orchestration platform provides a wide range of functionality to help us deploy our applications in a scalable and highly available way. When designing architecture that will support horizontally scalable services and applications, we need to be aware of some common strategies that will help to successfully scale our applications on Kubernetes clusters.

In the previous section, *Learning application deployment strategies*, we covered some strategies that would help us to scale our applications, including deployment strategies and implementing health checks using container probes. In this section, we will learn about scaling applications using the **Horizontal Pod Autoscaler (HPA)**.

When we first deploy our application on Kubernetes clusters, applications will very likely not get accessed immediately and usage will gradually increase over time. In that case, rolling out a deployment with many replicas would result in wasting our infrastructure resources. HPA in Kubernetes helps us increase the necessary resources in different scenarios.

> **Important note**
>
> You can find the complete source code at `https://github.com/PacktPublishing/Kubernetes-in-Production-Best-Practices/blob/master/Chapter08/hpa/deployment-nginx.yaml`.

Now, we will learn about configuring a basic HPA based on CPU utilization metrics. You can read more about HPA on the official Kubernetes documentation site at `https://kubernetes.io/docs/tasks/run-application/horizontal-pod-autoscale/`:

1. If you haven't installed it before, make sure to install **Metrics Server** by executing the following command:

    ```
    $ kubectl apply -f https://github.com/kubernetes-sigs/
    metrics-server/releases/download/v0.4.1/components.yaml
    ```

2. Create a deployment named `nginx-hpa` with a `replicas` count of `1` in the `hpa/deployment-nginx.yaml` path. Make sure to have `resources.request.cpu` set, otherwise HPA cannot function. In our example, we used an NGINX deployment. You can instead use any deployment you would like to apply HPA to:

```
apiVersion: apps/v1
kind: Deployment
metadata:
  name: nginx-hpa
  namespace: default
spec:
  replicas: 1
  selector:
    matchLabels:
      app: nginx-hpa
  template:
    metadata:
      labels:
        app: nginx-hpa
    spec:
      containers:
      - name: nginx-hpa
        image: nginx:1.19.6
        ports:
        - containerPort: 80
        resources:
          requests:
            cpu: "200m"
```

3. Execute the following command to create the deployment:

```
$ kubectl apply -f deployment-nginx.yaml
```

4. Confirm that your deployment is successful by checking its state:

```
$ kubectl get deployments
NAME        READY   UP-TO-DATE   AVAILABLE   AGE
nginx-hpa   1/1     1            1           11s
```

5. Now create an HPA named `nginx-autoscale` with a `minReplicas` count of `1`, a `maxReplicas` count of `5`, and `targetCPUUtilizationPercentage` set to `50` in the `hpa/hpa-nginx.yaml` path:

```
apiVersion: autoscaling/v1
kind: HorizontalPodAutoscaler
metadata:
  name: nginx-autoscale
  namespace: default
spec:
  scaleTargetRef:
    apiVersion: apps/v1
    kind: Deployment
    name: nginx-hpa
  minReplicas: 1
  maxReplicas: 5
  targetCPUUtilizationPercentage: 50
```

6. Execute the following command to create the deployment:

```
$ kubectl apply -f hpa-nginx.yaml
```

7. Confirm that our HPA is successfully created:

```
$ kubectl get hpa
NAME              REFERENCE             TARGETS
MINPODS   MAXPODS   REPLICAS    AGE
nginx-autoscale   Deployment/nginx-hpa  0%/50%   1
5         0         15s
```

8. The output of the preceding command should look as follows:

```
NAME             REFERENCE             TARGETS   MINPODS   MAXPODS   REPLICAS   AGE
nginx-autoscale  Deployment/nginx-hpa  0%/50%    1         5         0          15s
```

Figure 8.5 – HPA monitoring for CPU metrics to scale the application

In the preceding example, we used CPU utilization as our metric. HPA can use multiple metrics, including CPU, memory, and other custom external metrics such as service latency and I/O load, using **custom metrics adapters**. In addition to HPA, we can use **Pod Disruption Budgets** (**PDBs**) to avoid voluntary and involuntary disruptions to provide higher availability. You can read more about specifying a PDB for your application at `https://kubernetes.io/docs/tasks/run-application/configure-pdb/`.

Summary

In this chapter, we explored the components of container images, best practices for creating container images, and choosing the right base image type. We reduced our container image size by removing unnecessary files and using multistage builds. We learned how to scan our container images for vulnerabilities proactively. We learned about application deployment strategies to test and roll out new features and releases of our applications. We created an HPA to scale our applications. All the recommendations and best practices mentioned in this chapter help us reduce the attack surface and increase stability to improve efficiency in our production environment.

In the next chapter, we will learn about Kubernetes observability and key metrics to monitor in production. We will learn about the tools and stacks to use or build, compare the best tools in the ecosystem, and learn how to deal with observability from a site reliability perspective.

Further reading

You can refer to the following links for more information on the topics covered in this chapter:

- *A Practical Introduction to Container Terminology*: `https://developers.redhat.com/blog/2018/02/22/container-terminology-practical-introduction/`

- Open Container Initiative: `https://opencontainers.org/`

- *Hardening ELF binaries using Relocation Read-Only (RELRO)*: `https://www.redhat.com/en/blog/hardening-elf-binaries-using-relocation-read-only-relro`

- *A Comparison of Linux Container Images*: `http://crunchtools.com/comparison-linux-container-images/`

- *Alpine makes Python Docker builds way too (50×) slower, and images double (2×) larger*: `https://lih-verma.medium.com/alpine-makes-python-docker-builds-way-too-50-slower-and-images-double-2-larger-61d1d43cbc79`

- *Why Elastic moved from Alpine to CentOS base images*: `https://www.elastic.co/blog/docker-base-centos7`

- *Introducing multi-architecture container images for Amazon ECR*: `https://aws.amazon.com/blogs/containers/introducing-multi-architecture-container-images-for-amazon-ecr/`

- How to use distroless Docker images: `https://github.com/GoogleContainerTools/distroless`

- *Best practices for building containers*: `https://cloud.google.com/solutions/best-practices-for-building-containers`

- *Automated rollback of Helm releases based on logs or metrics*: `https://blog.container-solutions.com/automated-rollback-helm-releases-based-logs-metrics`

- *Kubernetes – A Complete DevOps Cookbook* (*Chapter 7, Scaling and Upgrading Applications*): `https://www.packtpub.com/product/kubernetes-a-complete-devops-cookbook/9781838828042`

9

Monitoring, Logging, and Observability

In previous chapters, we learned about application deployment best practices on Kubernetes to modernize our architecture. We learned how Kubernetes creates an abstraction layer on top of a group of container hosts that makes it easier to deploy applications and, at the same time, changes development teams' responsibilities compared to traditional monolithic applications. Adopting microservice architectures requires implementing new observability practices to efficiently monitor the layers introduced by the Kubernetes platform. Whether you plan to expand your existing monitoring stack to include Kubernetes or are looking for a complete cloud-native solution, it is essential to know the critical metrics to monitor and create a strategy to enhance observability to troubleshoot and take effective action when needed.

In this chapter, we will discuss the vital infrastructure components and Kubernetes object metrics. We will understand how to define production **service-level objectives (SLOs)**. We will learn about monitoring and logging stacks and solutions available in the market and when to use each of them. We will learn how to deploy the core observability (monitoring and logging) stacks for our infrastructure, use dashboards, and fine-tune our applications' observability by adding new dashboards to use with visualization tools. By the end of this chapter, you will be able to detect cluster and application abnormalities and pinpoint critical problems.

In this chapter, we're going to cover the following main topics:

- Understanding the challenges with Kubernetes observability
- Learning site reliability best practices
- Monitoring, metrics, and visualization
- Logging and tracing

Technical requirements

You should have the following tools installed from previous chapters:

- `kubectl`
- **Helm 3**
- `metrics-server`
- **KUDO Operator**
- `cert-manager`
- A Cassandra instance

You need to have an up-and-running Kubernetes cluster as per the instructions in *Chapter 3, Provisioning Kubernetes Clusters Using AWS and Terraform.*

The code for this chapter is located at `https://github.com/PacktPublishing/Kubernetes-in-Production-Best-Practices/tree/master/Chapter09`.

Check out the following link to see the Code in Action video:

`https://bit.ly/36IMIRH`

Understanding the challenges with Kubernetes observability

In this section, we will learn the differences between monitoring and observability from a Kubernetes perspective. We will retain the key metrics we need to monitor to resolve outages quickly. Before discussing the best practices and getting into our monitoring options, let's learn what are considered important metrics in Kubernetes.

Exploring the Kubernetes metrics

When we explored the components of container images in *Chapter 8, Deploying Seamless and Reliable Applications*, we also compared the monolithic and microservices architectures and learned about the function of a **container host**. When we containerize an application, our container host (**2**) needs to run a container runtime (**4**) and Kubernetes layers (**5**) on top of our OS to orchestrate scheduling of the Pod. Then our container images are (**6**) scheduled on Kubernetes nodes. During the scheduling operation, the state of the application running on these new layers needs to be probed (see *Figure 9.1*):

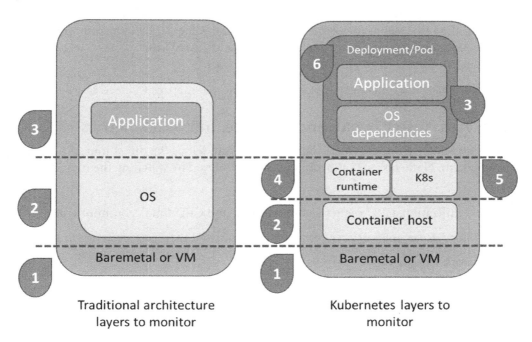

Figure 9.1 – Comparison of monolithic and microservices architecture monitoring layers

Considering all the new levels and failure points we have introduced, we can summarize the most important metrics into three categories:

- **Kubernetes cluster health and resource utilization metrics**
- **Application deployment and pods resource utilization metrics**
- **Application health and performance metrics**

It is quite common in production clusters to run into scheduling issues due to insufficient resources or missing labels and annotations. When scheduling issues happen, your applications can quickly get into an unstable state, directly impacting your service availability. Multiple reasons can trigger these issues, and the best way to start troubleshooting is by observing changes in critical cluster health and resource utilization metrics. Kubernetes provides detailed information at every level to detect the bottlenecks impacting our cluster performance.

Most of the useful metrics are available in real-time through the Metrics API and the / `metrics` endpoint of the HTTP server. It is recommended to scrape metrics regularly in a time series database similar to the Prometheus server in production. You can read more about the resource metrics pipeline at the official Kubernetes documentation site: `https://kubernetes.io/docs/tasks/debug-application-cluster/ resource-metrics-pipeline/`.

Here is a brief list of useful cluster resources and internal metrics we need to watch.

Kubernetes cluster health and resource utilization metrics

The number of active nodes is a crucial metric that can tell us the direct impact on cluster cost and health. Node resource utilization can be observed by watching the metrics listed here:

- CPU utilization, CPU requests commitment, and CPU limits commitment
- Memory usage, memory requests commitment, and memory limits commitment
- Network I/O pressure
- Disk I/O, disk space usage, and volume space usage

The Kubernetes control plane makes the critical scheduling decisions with the help of components including the Kubernetes API server (`kube-apiserver`), a highly available key-value store (`etcd`), a scheduler function (`kube-scheduler`), and a daemon that handles the Kubernetes control loop (`kube-controller-manager`). The Kubernetes control plane usually runs on dedicated master nodes. Therefore, the control plane's health and availability are critically important for our cluster's scheduling capabilities' core function. We can observe the control plane state by watching the metrics listed here:

- **API server availability and API server read/write Service-Level Indicators (SLIs)**
- **etcd uptime and etcd total leader elections**

- **Scheduler uptime, scheduling rate, POST request latency, and GET request latency**
- **Controller manager uptime, work queue add rate, and work queue latency**

All the metrics listed here collectively indicate the resource and control plane availability in our Kubernetes cluster.

Application deployment and pods resource utilization metrics

From application pod and deployment health monitoring perspectives, allocations are important to watch. We can observe the following metrics categorized in Kubernetes constructs such as pods, deployments, namespaces, workloads, and StatefulSets to troubleshoot pending or failed deployments:

- **Compute resources (by namespace, pod, and workload)**
- **StatefulSet-desired replicas and replicas of the current version**
- **Kubelet uptime, pod start duration, and operation error rate**

We should watch for abnormalities in the individual node resource utilization to maintain even pod distribution across nodes. We can also use resource utilization by namespaces or workloads to calculate project and team chargeback.

Application health and performance metrics

Pod and deployment resource utilization or even their states will not always provide us with a full view of the application. Every application comes with different expectations and, therefore, specific application-provided metrics to watch. As an example, for the **Prometheus** application, metrics such as target sync, scrape failures, appended samples, and uptime would be useful to watch. For other applications, as an example, **Cassandra**, we may want to watch metrics such as total node count, the number of nodes down, repair ratio, cluster ops, read and write ops, latencies, timeouts, and others. Later in this chapter, in the *Monitoring applications with Grafana* section, we will learn how to enable metric exporters for our applications and add their dashboards to Grafana to monitor.

Now, we have learned about some of the Kubernetes observability challenges and key metrics to watch. Let's look into how we can apply our knowledge to real production use cases using site reliability best practices.

Learning site reliability best practices

In this section, we will learn about considerations and best practices followed by the industry site reliability experts that handle technical site availability issues when observed.

Site Reliability Engineering (SRE) is a discipline introduced by the Google engineering team. Google's approach of operating their core services at scale still represents a model for SRE best practices today. You can read more about the foundations and practices on the Google SRE resources site at `https://sre.google/resources/`. Before we learn about the monitoring and metric visualization tools, let's learn about a few common-sense SRE best practices we should consider:

- **Automate everything possible and automate now**: SREs should take every opportunity to automate time-consuming infrastructure tasks. As part of a DevOps culture, SREs work with autonomous teams choosing their own services, which makes the unification of tools almost impossible, but any effort for standardizing tools and services can enable small SRE teams to support very large teams and services.

- **Use incremental deployment strategies**: In *Chapter 8, Deploying Seamless and Reliable Applications*, in the *Learning application deployment strategies* section, we learned about alternative deployment strategies for different services you can use to implement this practice.

- **Define meaningful alerts and set the correct response priorities and actions**: We can't expect different level response speeds from SREs if all our notifications and alerts go into one bucket or email address. Categorize alerts into a minimum of three or more response categories similar to *must react now* (pager), *will react later* (tickets), and *logs available for analysis* (logs).

- **Plan for scale and always expect failures**: Set resource utilization thresholds and plan capacity to address service overloads and infrastructure failure. Chaos engineering is also a great practice to follow to avoid surprises in production.

- **Define your SLO from the end user's perspective**: This includes taking the client-side metrics before server-side metrics. If the user-experienced latency is high, positive metrics measuring on the server side cannot be accepted alone.

Now we have learned about Kubernetes observability challenges and site reliability best practices. Let's look into how we can deploy a monitoring stack on Kubernetes and visualize metrics we collect from metrics exporters.

Monitoring, metrics, and visualization

In this section, we will learn about popular monitoring solutions in the cloud-native ecosystem and how to get a monitoring stack quickly up and running. Monitoring, logging, and tracing are often misused as interchangeable tools; therefore, understanding each tool's purpose is extremely important.

The most recent 2020 **Cloud Native Computing Foundation** (**CNCF**) survey suggests that companies use multiple tools (on average five or more) to monitor their cloud-native services. The list of the popular tools and projects includes Prometheus, OpenMetrics, Datadog, Grafana, Splunk, Sentry, CloudWatch, Lightstep, StatsD, Jaeger, Thanos, OpenTelemetry, and Kiali. Studies suggest that the most common and adopted tools are open source. You can read more about the CNCF community radar observations at `https://radar.cncf.io/2020-09-observability`.

Prometheus and Grafana used together is the most relevant combined solution for Kubernetes workloads. It is not possible to cover all the tools in this book. Therefore, we will focus on popular Prometheus and Grafana solutions. We will learn how to install the stacks to get some of the core cluster and application metrics.

Installing the Prometheus stack on Kubernetes

Prometheus is the most adopted open source monitoring and alerting solution in the ecosystem. Prometheus provides a multi-dimensional data model and uses a flexible query language called **PromQL** to take advantage of its dimensionality. The Kubernetes Prometheus stack includes multiple components to properly monitor your cluster, including Prometheus Operator, highly available Prometheus, Alertmanager, Prometheus Node Exporter, Prometheus Adapter for Kubernetes Metrics APIs, `kube-state-metrics`, and Grafana. You can read more about Prometheus and its concepts on the official Prometheus documentation site at `https://prometheus.io/docs/introduction/overview/`.

Now, let's install Prometheus using `kube-prometheus-stack` (formerly Prometheus Operator) and prepare our cluster to start monitoring the Kubernetes API server for changes:

1. Create a namespace called `monitoring`:

    ```
    $ kubectl create ns monitoring
    ```

2. Add the `kube-prometheus-stack` Helm Chart repository to your local repository list:

    ```
    $ helm repo add prometheus-community https://prometheus-
    community.github.io/helm-charts
    ```

3. Add the Helm `stable` chart repository to your local repository list:

    ```
    $ helm repo add stable https://charts.helm.sh/stable
    ```

4. Update Helm Chart repositories:

    ```
    $ helm repo update
    ```

5. Install `kube-prometheus-stack` from its Helm repository:

    ```
    $ helm install --namespace monitoring prometheus
    prometheus-community/kube-prometheus-stack
    ```

6. Verify successful installation by executing the following command:

    ```
    $ kubectl get pods -n monitoring
    ```

7. The output of the preceding command should look as follows:

```
NAME                                                          READY   STATUS    RESTARTS   AGE
alertmanager-prometheus-kube-prometheus-alertmanager-0        2/2     Running   0          66s
prometheus-grafana-59bfb6b6bf-tflwn                           2/2     Running   0          71s
prometheus-kube-prometheus-operator-58778957c9-8699x          1/1     Running   0          71s
prometheus-kube-state-metrics-c65b87574-hh98m                 1/1     Running   0          71s
prometheus-prometheus-kube-prometheus-prometheus-0            2/2     Running   1          66s
prometheus-prometheus-node-exporter-2jvlh                     1/1     Running   0          71s
prometheus-prometheus-node-exporter-6k4hb                     1/1     Running   0          71s
prometheus-prometheus-node-exporter-8ww6b                     1/1     Running   0          71s
prometheus-prometheus-node-exporter-d46lr                     1/1     Running   0          71s
prometheus-prometheus-node-exporter-nvt5m                     1/1     Running   0          71s
```

Figure 9.2 – List of the Prometheus pods running after successful installation

8. Now we have `kube-prometheus-stack` installed. Let's access the included Grafana service instance. Create port forwarding to access the Prometheus interface and Grafana dashboards locally:

```
$ kubectl port-forward -n monitoring svc/prometheus-k8s
9090
```

```
$ kubectl port-forward -n monitoring svc/grafana 3000
```

> **Important note**
>
> Instead of port forwarding Prometheus and Grafana service IPs, you can choose to expose service IPs externally through your cloud provider's load balancer options, changing the service type from `NodePort` to `LoadBalancer`.

9. Verify service IPs by executing the following command:

```
$ kubectl get svc -n monitoring
```

10. The output of the preceding command should look as follows:

```
NAME                                         TYPE           CLUSTER-IP      EXTERNAL-IP
   PORT(S)                             AGE
alertmanager-operated                        ClusterIP      None            <none>
   9093/TCP,9094/TCP,9094/UDP          18h
prometheus-grafana                           LoadBalancer   100.71.40.196   a724ff8566efb4c63b8f69f9f9b9b2cf-2054523943.us-east-1.elb.amazonaws.com
   80:31322/TCP                        18h
prometheus-kube-prometheus-alertmanager      ClusterIP      100.65.57.162   <none>
   9093/TCP                            18h
prometheus-kube-prometheus-operator          ClusterIP      100.66.40.29    <none>
   443/TCP                             18h
prometheus-kube-prometheus-prometheus        LoadBalancer   100.68.100.42   a78fe3811a4ee4dea8c333e5deb06ef9-1220794032.us-east-1.elb.amazonaws.com
   9090:30318/TCP                      18h
prometheus-kube-state-metrics                ClusterIP      100.68.57.63    <none>
   8080/TCP                            18h
prometheus-operated                          ClusterIP      None            <none>
   9090/TCP                            18h
prometheus-prometheus-node-exporter          ClusterIP      100.67.63.189   <none>
   9100/TCP                            18h
```

Figure 9.3 – List of the services exposed in the monitoring namespace

11. If you used port forwarding, you can access the service interface on your host using `http://localhost:9090` (for Prometheus) and `http://localhost:3000` (for Grafana). If you used `LoadBalancer` instead, then use the external IP from the output of the `kubectl get svc -nmonitoring` command with the port address. You will get to a Grafana login screen similar to the following:

Figure 9.4 – Grafana service login screen

12. Use the default `admin` Grafana username and the `prom-operator` password to access the Grafana dashboards. If you have used a custom password, you can always get it from its secret resource by executing the following command:

```
$ kubectl get secret \
    --namespace monitoring prometheus-grafana \
    -o jsonpath="{.data.admin-password}" \
    | base64 --decode ; echo
```

13. Click on the **Search** button on the upper-left corner of the dashboard to search the available dashboards and select the dashboards you want to view. You can see the cluster resource consumption used by pods in namespaces similar to what is displayed in the following screenshot by selecting the **Kubernetes / Compute Resources / Cluster** dashboard:

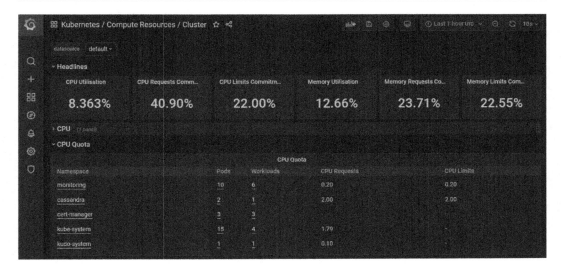

Figure 9.5 – Kubernetes cluster resources dashboard in Grafana

As part of the `kube-prometheus` stack, there are around 20 dashboards you can immediately start monitoring. A list of important dashboards is as follows:

- **etcd**

- **Kubernetes: API server**

- **Kubernetes / Compute Resources / Cluster - Namespace (pods), Namespace (Workloads), Node (pods), Pod, Workload**

- **Kubernetes / Controller Manager**

- **Kubernetes / Kubelet**

- **Kubernetes / Networking / Cluster - Namespace (Pods), Namespace (Workloads), Pod, Workload**

- **Kubernetes / Persistent Volumes:**

- **Kubernetes / Proxy**

- **Kubernetes / Scheduler**

- **Kubernetes / StatefulSets**

- **Nodes**

We have now learned how to get essential components to get our Prometheus-based monitoring stack running on our Kubernetes clusters. Let's add new dashboards to our Grafana instance to monitor our applications.

Monitoring applications with Grafana

Grafana is an open source observability platform. It is used to visualize data provided from various databases with plugins. Grafana is very often used in combination with Prometheus to visualize metrics provided from Kubernetes endpoints. Grafana's large community makes it very easy to start composing observability dashboards or use its official and community-driven dashboards. Now, we will learn how to add additional dashboards to the Grafana interface to observe our application state.

You can read more about Grafana and its concepts on the official Grafana documentation site at `https://grafana.com/docs/grafana/latest/`.

In *Chapter 7, Managing Storage and Stateful Applications*, in the *Stateful workload operators* section, we deployed a Cassandra instance using the KUDO. Here, we will use our existing instance and add a dashboard to Grafana to monitor its state. If you don't have a Cassandra instance deployed, you can follow the instructions in *Chapter 7, Managing Storage and Stateful Applications*, to provision it or use these instructions as a guideline to monitor other applications.

Now, enable the Prometheus exporter on our existing Cassandra instance and add the dashboard:

1. By default, the Prometheus exporter on our KUDO-operated application instance is disabled. We can enable the metric exporter by executing the following command:

    ```
    $ kubectl kudo update \
        -p PROMETHEUS_EXPORTER_ENABLED=true \
        --instance $instance_name -n $namespace_name
    ```

2. Update the `servicemonitor` labels to fetch the metrics from our Prometheus instance:

    ```
    $ kubectl label servicemonitor cassandra-monitor \
        -n $namespace_name release=prometheus --overwrite
    ```

3. Click on the + button on the upper-left corner of the Grafana interface and select **Import**:

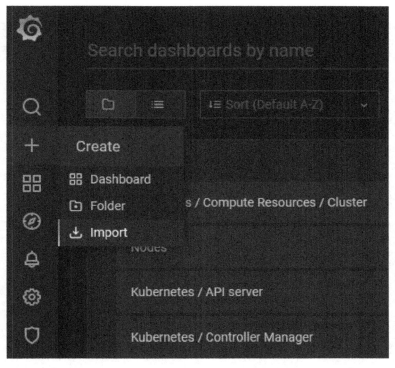

Figure 9.6 – Import menu view to add new Grafana dashboards

4. Paste the `https://grafana.com/api/dashboards/10849/ revisions/1/download` link into the **Import via garafana.com** field and click on the **Load** button.

5. On the next screen, select **Prometheus** as the data source and click on the **Import** button to load the dashboard, similar to the screen shown in the following screenshot:

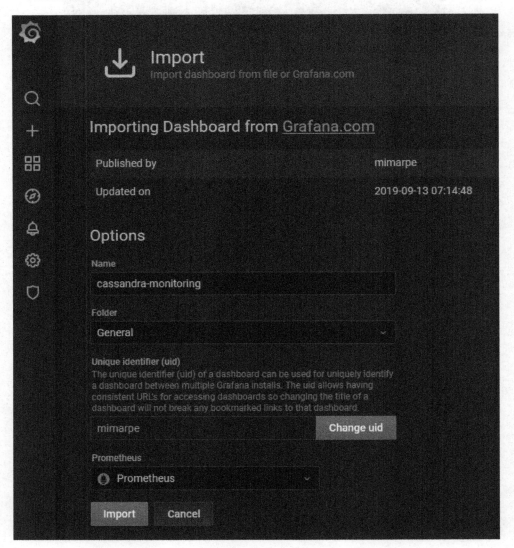

Figure 9.7 – Importing new dashboards from Grafana.com

Now, we've learned how to add custom dashboards to monitor our applications' state in Kubernetes. Similarly, you can find community-built dashboards on the Grafana website at https://grafana.com/grafana/dashboards to monitor your applications and common Kubernetes components.

Logging and tracing

In this section, we will learn about the popular logging solutions in the cloud-native ecosystem and how to get a logging stack quickly up and running.

Handling logs for applications running on Kubernetes is quite different than traditional application log handling. With monolithic applications, when a server or an application crashes, our server can still retain logs. In Kubernetes, a new pod is scheduled when a pod crashes, causing the old pod and its records to get wiped out. The main difference with containerized applications is how and where we ship and store our logs for future use.

Two cloud-native-focused popular logging stacks are the **Elasticsearch, Fluentd, and Kibana (EFK)** stack and the **Promtail, Loki, and Grafana (PLG)** stack. Both have fundamental design and architectural differences. The EFK stack uses Elasticsearch as an object store, Fluentd for log routing and aggregation, and Kibana for the visualization of logs. The PLG stack is based on a horizontally scalable log aggregation system designed by the Grafana team that uses the Promtail agent to send logs to Loki clusters. You can read more about Loki at `https://grafana.com/oss/loki/`.

In this section, we will focus on the EFK stack as our centralized logging solution. We will learn how to install the stack to store and visualize our logs.

Installing the EFK stack on Kubernetes

Let's follow these steps to get our logging solution up and running. We will start with installing Elasticsearch using the Elasticsearch Operator, then deploy a Kibana instance, and finally, add Fluent Bit to aggregate our logs:

> **Important note**
>
> You can find the complete source code at `https://github.com/PacktPublishing/Kubernetes-in-Production-Best-Practices/blob/master/Chapter09/logging/eck/elastic.yaml`.

1. Add the `elastic` Helm Chart repository to your local repository list:

   ```
   $ helm repo add elastic https://helm.elastic.co
   ```

2. Update Helm Chart repositories:

   ```
   $ helm repo update
   ```

3. Install `eck-operator` and its **Custom Resource Definitions (CRDs)** from its Helm repository:

```
$ helm install eck-operator \
     elastic/eck-operator --version 1.3.1
```

4. Verify that the CRDs have been created and installation is successful by executing the following command:

```
$ kubectl get pods,crds -nelastic-system|grep elastic
```

> **Important note**
>
> Logs are the best place to start troubleshooting when we run into an issue with deploying applications on Kubernetes. If the deployment of ECK pods cannot complete, review the logs by executing the `kubectl -n elastic-system logs -f statefulset.apps/elastic-operator` command.

5. The output of the preceding command should look as follows:

```
pod/elastic-operator-0   1/1      Running   0          5m14s
customresourcedefinition.apiextensions.k8s.io/apmservers.apm.k8s.elastic.co                           2021-01-06T09:10:50Z
customresourcedefinition.apiextensions.k8s.io/beats.beat.k8s.elastic.co                               2021-01-06T09:10:51Z
customresourcedefinition.apiextensions.k8s.io/elasticsearches.elasticsearch.k8s.elastic.co           2021-01-06T09:10:51Z
customresourcedefinition.apiextensions.k8s.io/enterprisesearches.enterprisesearch.k8s.elastic.co     2021-01-06T09:10:51Z
customresourcedefinition.apiextensions.k8s.io/kibanas.kibana.k8s.elastic.co                           2021-01-06T09:10:51Z
```

Figure 9.8 – List of the ECK pods running and CRDs created after successful installation

6. Create a namespace called `logging`:

```
$ kubectl create ns logging
```

7. Create an Elasticsearch instance manifest named `elastic` with the desired number of nodes, with `NodeSets.count` set to 3 in the `logging/eck/elastic.yaml` path. Make sure to replace `version` if you would like to deploy a newer version:

```
apiVersion: elasticsearch.k8s.elastic.co/v1
kind: Elasticsearch
metadata:
  name: elastic
  namespace: logging
spec:
  version: 7.10.1
```

```
nodeSets:
- name: default
  count: 3
  config:
    node.store.allow_mmap: false
```

8. Execute the following `kubectl` command to create an Elasticsearch instance in the cluster:

```
$ kubectl apply -f elastic.yaml
```

9. Verify the state of the Elasticsearch nodes we have created by executing the following command:

```
$ kubectl get pods -n logging
```

10. The output of the preceding command should look as follows:

```
NAME      HEALTH   NODES   VERSION   PHASE   AGE
elastic   green    3       7.10.1    Ready   8m8s
```

Figure 9.9 – Status of all Elasticsearch nodes in the ready state

11. We can verify the state of Elasticsearch pods by executing the following command:

```
$ kubectl get elasticsearch -n logging
```

12. The output of the preceding command should look as follows:

```
NAME                   READY   STATUS    RESTARTS   AGE
elastic-es-default-0   1/1     Running   0          17m
elastic-es-default-1   1/1     Running   0          17m
elastic-es-default-2   1/1     Running   0          17m
```

Figure 9.10 – All Elasticsearch pods are ready and running

13. Store the credentials created for the `elastic` user in a variable called ES_ PASSWORD:

```
$ ES_PASSWORD=$(kubectl get secret \
    elastic-es-elastic-user -n logging \
    -o go-template='{{.data.elastic | base64decode}}')
```

14. Get the list of services created in the logging namespace:

```
$ kubectl get svc -n logging
```

15. The output of the preceding command should look as follows:

```
NAME                   TYPE        CLUSTER-IP      EXTERNAL-IP   PORT(S)    AGE
elastic-es-default     ClusterIP   None            <none>        9200/TCP   4h10m
elastic-es-http        ClusterIP   100.64.42.161   <none>        9200/TCP   4h10m
elastic-es-transport   ClusterIP   None            <none>        9300/TCP   4h10m
```

Figure 9.11 – List of services created by the Elasticsearch Operator

> **Important note**
>
> When accessing from our workstation, we can create port forwarding to access the service endpoint locally by creating a port forwarding to localhost using the following command: $ kubectl port-forward service/elastic-es-http 9200.

16. Get the address of the Elasticsearch endpoint using the password we have saved and the service name by executing the following command:

```
$ curl -u "elastic:$ES_PASSWORD" \
    -k https://elastic-es-http:9200
```

17. The output of the preceding command should look as follows:

```
{
  "name" : "elastic-es-default-2",
  "cluster_name" : "elastic",
  "cluster_uuid" : "RwaujlTRQwK-MizxCxJ7gA",
  "version" : {
    "number" : "7.10.1",
    "build_flavor" : "default",
    "build_type" : "docker",
    "build_hash" : "1c34507e66d7db1211f66f3513706fdf548736aa",
    "build_date" : "2020-12-05T01:00:33.671820Z",
    "build_snapshot" : false,
    "lucene_version" : "8.7.0",
    "minimum_wire_compatibility_version" : "6.8.0",
    "minimum_index_compatibility_version" : "6.0.0-beta1"
  },
  "tagline" : "You Know, for Search"
}
```

Figure 9.12 – List of services created by the Elasticsearch Operator

> **Important note**
>
> You can find the complete source code at https://github.com/PacktPublishing/Kubernetes-in-Production-Best-Practices/blob/master/Chapter09/logging/eck/kibana.yaml.

18. Now we have our Elasticsearch instance deployed. Let's deploy a Kibana instance and bundle it with our existing Elasticsearch instance. Create a Kibana instance manifest named `kibana` with a desired number of nodes of 3 in the `logging/eck/kibana.yaml` path. Make sure to replace `version` if you would like to deploy a newer version when available:

```
apiVersion: kibana.k8s.elastic.co/v1
kind: Kibana
metadata:
  name: kibana
  namespace: logging
spec:
  version: 7.10.1
  count: 3
  elasticsearchRef:
    name: elastic
```

19. Execute the following `kubectl` command to create a Kibana instance in the cluster:

```
$ kubectl apply -f kibana.yaml
```

20. Verify the state of the Kibana nodes we have created by executing the following command:

```
$ kubectl get kibana -n logging
```

21. The output of the preceding command should look as follows:

```
NAME     HEALTH   NODES   VERSION   AGE
kibana   green    3       7.10.1    3m53s
```

Figure 9.13 – Status of all Kibana nodes in a healthy state

22. We can verify the state of associated Kibana pods by executing the following command:

```
$ kubectl get pods -n logging \
    --selector='kibana.k8s.elastic.co/name=kibana'
```

23. The output of the preceding command should look as follows:

```
NAME                            READY   STATUS    RESTARTS   AGE
kibana-kb-68596c8d86-cttzm      1/1     Running   0          5m57s
kibana-kb-68596c8d86-hcqpm      1/1     Running   0          5m57s
kibana-kb-68596c8d86-rdl4n      1/1     Running   0          5m57s
```

Figure 9.14 – All Kibana pods are ready and running

24. Get the list of services created in the logging namespace:

```
$ kubectl get svc -n logging \
    --selector='kibana.k8s.elastic.co/name=kibana'
```

25. When accessing from our local workstation, we can create port forwarding to access the service endpoint by creating port forwarding to localhost using the following command:

```
$ kubectl port-forward service/kibana-kb-http 5601
```

26. Get the elastic user password we previously obtained by executing the following command:

```
$ echo $ES_PASSWORD
```

27. Now, open https://localhost:5601 in your browser. Use the elastic user and the password we copied from the previous step to access the Kibana interface.

> **Important note**
>
> You can find the complete source code at https://github.com/
> PacktPublishing/Kubernetes-in-Production-Best-
> Practices/blob/master/Chapter09/logging/eck/
> fluent-bit-values.yaml.

28. Now, we have both Elasticsearch and Kibana instances installed. As the last step, let's deploy the fluent-bit instance to aggregate logs. Create a Helm configuration file named fluent-bit-values.yaml. Make sure to replace the host address and http_password parameters if necessary:

```
backend:
  type: es
  es:
    host: elastic-es-http
```

```
    port: 9200
    http_user: elastic
    http_passwd: ${ES_PASSWORD}
    tls: "on"
    tls_verify: "off"
parsers:
  enabled: true
  regex:
    - name: log_parser
      regex: ^(?<logtimestamp>[^ ]+)
(?<stream>stdout|stderr) (?<logtag>[^ ]*) (?<log>.*)$
      timeKey: logtimestamp
      timeFormat: "%Y-%m-%dT%H:%M:%S.%L%z"
input:
  tail:
    parser: log_parser
```

29. Add the Helm `stable` Chart repository to your local repository list:

```
$ helm repo add stable https://charts.helm.sh/stable
```

30. Update Helm Chart repositories:

```
$ helm repo update
```

31. Install `fluent-bit` from its Helm repository:

```
$ helm install fluent-bit stable/fluent-bit \
    -n logging -f fluent-bit-values.yaml
```

32. Verify a successful installation by executing the following command:

```
$ kubectl get pods -n logging
```

33. The output of the preceding command should look as follows:

```
NAME                             READY   STATUS    RESTARTS   AGE
elastic-es-default-0             1/1     Running   0          7h
elastic-es-default-1             1/1     Running   0          7h
elastic-es-default-2             1/1     Running   0          7h
fluent-bit-42bhv                 1/1     Running   0          7m48s
fluent-bit-6hh52                 1/1     Running   0          7m48s
fluent-bit-bfph6                 1/1     Running   0          7m48s
fluent-bit-xqcgf                 1/1     Running   0          7m48s
kibana-kb-57d99cd6d9-k8js7       1/1     Running   0          110m
kibana-kb-57d99cd6d9-n6kfc       1/1     Running   0          110m
kibana-kb-57d99cd6d9-ntpxt       1/1     Running   0          110m
```

Figure 9.15 – List of all necessary pods to complete our logging stack

34. Now, we will switch to the Kibana interface on our browser. If you closed the browser window, repeat *steps 26* and *27* to access the Kibana interface. Click on the **Kibana** icon on the dashboard.

35. On the Kibana getting started dashboard, click on the **Add your data** button. The dashboard should look similar to the following screenshot:

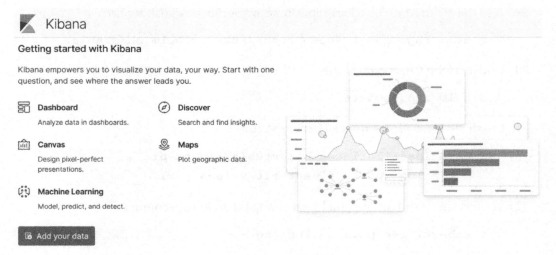

Figure 9.16 – Kibana's Getting started interface

36. Now, Kibana will detect data forwarded by Fluent Bit. On the next screen, click on the **Create index pattern** button to create an index pattern matching our indices.

37. As we can see in the following screenshot, Fluent Bit creates indices following the `kubernetes_cluster-YYY.MM.DD` pattern. Here, use `kubernetes_cluster-*` as our index pattern name and click on the **Next step** button to continue:

Create index pattern

An index pattern can match a single source, for example, `filebeat-4-3-22`, or **multiple** data sources, `filebeat-*`.
Read documentation ⎘

Step 1 of 2: Define an index pattern

Index pattern name

| kubernetes_cluster-*| | Next step > |

Use an asterisk (*) to match multiple indices. Spaces and the characters \, /, ?, ", <, >, | are not allowed.

◯ ✕   Include system and hidden indices

✓   Your index pattern matches 1 source.

kubernetes_cluster-2021.01.07   Index

Rows per page: 10 ✕

Figure 9.17 – Creating an index pattern on Kibana to match the source data

38. Finally, enter `@timestamp` in the **Time Filter** field and click on the **Create index pattern** button to complete indexing.

Now we have learned how to deploy a logging solution based on the ECK stack on our Kubernetes stack to aggregate and visualize our cluster logs. When running in production, make sure to separate the cluster running your logging stack from the clusters you collect logs from. We need to make sure that when clusters are not accessible for any reason, our logs and the logging stack that is necessary to troubleshoot issues are still accessible.

Summary

In this chapter, we explored important Kubernetes metrics and learned about the SRE best practices for maintaining higher availability. We learned how to get a Prometheus and Grafana-based monitoring and visualization stack up and running and added custom application dashboards to our Grafana instance. We also learned how to get Elasticsearch, Kibana, and Fluent Bit-based ECK logging stacks up and running on our Kubernetes cluster.

In the next and final chapter, we will learn about Kubernetes operation best practices. We will cover cluster maintenance topics such as upgrades and rotation, disaster recovery and avoidance, cluster and application troubleshooting, quality control, continuous improvement, and governance.

Further reading

You can refer to the following links for more information on the topics covered in this chapter:

- *CNCF End User Technology Radar: Observability*: https://www.cncf. io/blog/2020/09/11/cncf-end-user-technology-radar-observability-september-2020/

- *Hands-On Infrastructure Monitoring with Prometheus*: https://www. packtpub.com/product/hands-on-infrastructure-monitoring-with-prometheus/9781789612349

- *Prometheus official documentation*: https://prometheus.io/docs/ introduction/overview/

- *Learn Grafana 7.0*: https://www.packtpub.com/product/learn-grafana-7-0/9781838826581

- *Grafana official and community-built dashboards*: https://grafana.com/ grafana/dashboards

- *ECK Operator official documentation*: https://www.elastic.co/guide/en/ cloud-on-k8s/current/k8s-operating-eck.html

- *Logging in Kubernetes: EFK vs PLG Stack*: https://www.cncf.io/ blog/2020/07/27/logging-in-kubernetes-efk-vs-plg-stack/

10

Operating and Maintaining Efficient Kubernetes Clusters

In previous chapters, we learned about production best practices for automating Kubernetes and its infrastructure components. We discussed challenges with provisioning stateless workloads in our clusters, including getting persistent storage up and running, choosing container images, and deployment strategies. We also learned about important observability tools in the ecosystem and building monitoring and logging stacks in our cluster to provide a solid base for our troubleshooting needs. Once we have a production-ready cluster and have started to serve workloads, it is vital to have efficient operations to oversee the cluster maintenance, availability, and other **service-level objectives** (SLOs).

In this chapter, we will focus on Kubernetes operation best practices and cover topics related to cluster maintenance, such as upgrades and rotation, backups, disaster recovery and avoidance, cluster and troubleshooting failures of the cluster control plane, workers, and applications. Finally, we will learn about the solutions available to validate and improve our cluster's quality.

In this chapter, we're going to cover the following main topics:

- Learning about cluster maintenance and upgrades
- Preparing for backups and disaster recovery
- Validating cluster quality

Technical requirements

You should have the following tools installed from previous chapters:

- AWS CLI v2
- AWS IAM authenticator
- `kubectl`
- Terraform
- Helm 3
- `metrics-server`
- MinIO instance (optional as an S3 target for backups)

You need to have an up-and-running Kubernetes cluster as per the instructions in *Chapter 3*, *Provisioning Kubernetes Clusters Using AWS and Terraform*.

The code for this chapter is located at `https://github.com/PacktPublishing/Kubernetes-in-Production-Best-Practices/tree/master/Chapter10`.

Check out the following link to see the Code in Action video:

`https://bit.ly/3aAdPzl`

Learning about cluster maintenance and upgrades

In this section, we will learn about upgrading our Kubernetes clusters in production. Generally, a new major Kubernetes version is announced quarterly, and every minor version is supported around 12 months after its initial release date. Following the rule of thumb for software upgrades, it is not common to upgrade to a new version immediately after its release unless it is a severe time-sensitive security patch. Cloud providers also follow the same practice and run their conformance tests before releasing a new image to the public. Therefore, cloud providers' Kubernetes releases usually follow a couple of versions behind the upstream release of Kubernetes. If you'd like to read about the latest releases, you can find the Kubernetes release notes on the official Kubernetes documentation site at `https://kubernetes.io/docs/setup/release/notes/`.

In *Chapter 3, Provisioning Kubernetes Clusters Using AWS and Terraform*, we learned about cluster deployment and rollout strategies. We also learned that cluster deployment is not a one-time task. It is a continuous process that affects the cluster's quality, stability, and operations, as well as the products and services on top of it. In previous chapters, we established a solid infrastructure deployment strategy, and now we will follow it with production-grade upgrade best practices in this chapter.

In *Chapter 3, Provisioning Kubernetes Clusters Using AWS and Terraform*, we automated our cluster deployment using Terraform. Let's use the same cluster and upgrade it to a newer Kubernetes release.

Upgrading kubectl

First, we will upgrade `kubectl` to the latest version. Your `kubectl` version should be at least equal to or greater than the Kubernetes version you are planning to upgrade to:

1. Download the latest `kubectl` binary and copy it to the `bin` directory:

```
$ curl -LO https://storage.googleapis.com/kubernetes-
release/release/$(curl -s https://storage.googleapis.com/
kubernetes-release/release/stable.txt)/bin/linux/amd64/
kubectl
$ chmod +x ./kubectl && sudo mv ./kubectl /usr/local/bin/
kubectl
```

2. Confirm that the `kubectl` binary is updated to the newer version by executing the following command:

```
$ kubectl version --short
Client Version: v1.20.1
Server Version: v1.15.12-eks-31566f
```

3. Now, check your node status and version by executing the following command:

```
$ kubectl get nodes
```

The output of the preceding command should look as follows:

```
NAME                        STATUS  ROLES     AGE   VERSION
ip-10-40-102-5.ec2.internal  Ready   <none>   11m   v1.15.12-eks-31566f
ip-10-40-74-21.ec2.internal  Ready   <none>   11m   v1.15.12-eks-31566f
```

Figure 10.1 – The kubectl command showing the node status and its version

Here, we have updated `kubectl` to the latest version. Let's move on to the next step and upgrade our cluster version.

Upgrading the Kubernetes control plane

AWS EKS clusters can be upgraded one version at a time. This means that if we are on version 1.15, we can upgrade to 1.16, then to 1.17, and so on.

> **Important note**
>
> You can find the complete source code at `https://github.com/PacktPublishing/Kubernetes-in-Production-Best-Practices/tree/master/Chapter10/terraform`.

Let's upgrade our controller nodes using the Terraform scripts we also used in *Chapter 3, Provisioning Kubernetes Clusters Using AWS and Terraform*, to deploy our clusters:

1. Edit the `terraform.tfvars` file under the `Chapter10/terraform/packtclusters` directory and increase the `cluster_version` value to the next release version number. In our example, we have increased the version from `1.15` to `1.16`:

```
aws_region = "us-east-1"
private_subnet_ids = [
  "subnet-0b3abc8b7d5c91487",
  "subnet-0e692b14dbcd957ac",
```

```
    "subnet-088c5e6489d27194e",
  ]
  public_subnet_ids = [
    "subnet-0c2d82443c6f5c122",
    "subnet-0b1233cf80533aeaa",
    "subnet-0b86e5663ed927962",
  ]
  vpc_id = "vpc-0565ee349f15a8ed1"
  clusters_name_prefix  = "packtclusters"
  cluster_version       = "1.16"        #Upgrade from 1.15
  workers_instance_type = "t3.medium"
  workers_number_min    = 2
  workers_number_max    = 3
  workers_storage_size  = 10
```

2. Run the `terraform plan` command to validate the planned changes before
    applying them:

    ```
    $ cd chapter-10/terraform/packtclusters
    $ terraform plan
    ```

    You will get the following output after the `terraform plan` command completes
    successfully. There is one resource to change. We are only changing the cluster
    version:

    ```
    Plan: 0 to add, 1 to change, 0 to destroy.
    ------------------------------------------------------------------
    Note: You didn't specify an "-out" parameter to save this plan, so Terraform
    can't guarantee that exactly these actions will be performed if
    "terraform apply" is subsequently run.
    ```

    Figure 10.2 – The terraform plan command output

3. Execute the `terraform apply` command. Enter `yes` when you get a prompt to
    approve the in-place update:

    ```
    $ terraform apply
    ```

While an upgrade is in progress, we can track the progress both from the command line or in the AWS console. The cluster status in the AWS console will look similar to the following screenshot:

Figure 10.3 – AWS console output showing the cluster status as Updating

You will get the following result after the `terraform apply` command completes successfully. By then, Terraform has successfully changed one AWS resource:

```
Plan: 4 to add, 0 to change, 0 to destroy.

Do you want to perform these actions?
  Terraform will perform the actions described above.
  Only 'yes' will be accepted to approve.

  Enter a value: yes

aws_dynamodb_table.clusters_vpc_dynamodb_tf_state_lock: Creating...
aws_dynamodb_table.clusters_dynamodb_tf_state_lock: Creating...
aws_s3_bucket.clusters_tf_state_s3_bucket: Creating...
aws_s3_bucket.clusters_vpc_tf_state_s3_bucket: Creating...
aws_dynamodb_table.clusters_dynamodb_tf_state_lock: Creation complete after 6s [id=packtclusters-terraform-state-lock-dynamodb]
aws_s3_bucket.clusters_vpc_tf_state_s3_bucket: Creation complete after 7s [id=packtclusters-vpc-terraform-state]
aws_s3_bucket.clusters_tf_state_s3_bucket: Creation complete after 7s [id=packtclusters-terraform-state]
aws_dynamodb_table.clusters_vpc_dynamodb_tf_state_lock: Creation complete after 10s [id=packtclusters-vpc-terraform-state-lock-dynamodb]

Apply complete! Resources: 4 added, 0 changed, 0 destroyed.
```

Figure 10.4 – The terraform apply command output

Here, we have updated our Kubernetes control plane to the next version available. Let's move on to the next step and upgrade our node groups.

Upgrading Kubernetes components

Upgrading the Kubernetes control plane doesn't upgrade the worker nodes or our Kubernetes add-ons, such as `kube-proxy`, CoreDNS, and the Amazon VPC CNI plugin. Therefore, after upgrading the control plane, we need to carefully upgrade each and every component to a supported version if needed. You can read more about the supported component versions and Kubernetes upgrade prerequisites on the Amazon EKS documentation site at `https://docs.aws.amazon.com/eks/latest/userguide/update-cluster.html`. The following figure shows an example support matrix table for the upgrade path we will follow in our example:

Kubernetes Version	1.18	1.17	1.16	1.15
Amazon VPC CNI plug-in	1.7.5	1.7.5	1.7.5	1.7.5
DNS (CoreDNS)	1.7.0	1.6.6	1.6.6	1.6.6
KubeProxy	1.18.9	1.17.12	1.16.15	1.15.12

Figure 10.5 – An example of a Kubernetes component support matrix

Some version upgrades may also require changes in your application's YAML manifest to reference the new APIs. It is highly recommended to test your application behavior using a continuous integration workflow.

Now that our EKS control plane is upgraded, let's upgrade `kube-proxy`:

1. Get the current version of the `kube-proxy` component by executing the following command:

   ```
   $ kubectl get daemonset kube-proxy --namespace kube-
   system -o=jsonpath='{$.spec.template.spec.containers[:1].
   image}'
   ```

   The output of the preceding command should look as follows. Note that your account ID and region will be different:

   ```
   123412345678.dkr.ecr.us-east-1.amazonaws.com/eks/kube-
   proxy:v1.15.11-eksbuild.1
   ```

2. Now, upgrade the `kube-proxy` image to the supported version from *Figure 10.5* by using the output of the previous command:

   ```
   $ kubectl set image daemonset.apps/kube-proxy \
       -n kube-system \
       kube-proxy=123412345678.dkr.ecr.us-west-2.amazonaws.
   com/eks/kube-proxy:v1.16.15-eksbuild.1
   ```

3. Run the command from *step 1* to confirm the version change. This time, the output of the preceding command should look as follows:

   ```
   123412345678.dkr.ecr.us-east-1.amazonaws.com/eks/kube-
   proxy:v1.16.15-eksbuild.1
   ```

4. Let's learn how we can upgrade `coredns` when needed. Note that only an upgrade from 1.17 to 1.18 requires the `coredns` version to be at 1.7.0. Confirm that your cluster uses `coredns` as the DNS provider by executing the following command:

   ```
   $ kubectl get pod -n kube-system -l k8s-app=kube-dns
   ```

The output of the preceding command should look as follows:

```
NAME                        READY   STATUS    RESTARTS   AGE
coredns-7cf87cdb56-29pfg    1/1     Running   0          3h58m
coredns-7cf87cdb56-ll2t7    1/1     Running   0          3h58m
```

Figure 10.6 – CoreDNS pods running on the Kubernetes cluster

5. Get the current version of the `coredns` component by executing the following command:

```
$ kubectl get deployment coredns --namespace kube-system
-o=jsonpath='{$.spec.template.spec.containers[:1].image}'
```

The output of the preceding command should look as follows. Note that your account ID and region will be different:

```
123412345678.dkr.ecr.us-east-1.amazonaws.com/eks/
coredns:v1.6.6-eksbuild.1
```

6. Now, upgrade the `coredns` image to the supported version from *Figure 10.5* by using the output of the previous command:

```
$ kubectl set image deployment.apps/coredns \
    -n kube-system \
       coredns=123412345678.dkr.ecr.us-west-2.amazonaws.com/
eks/coredns:v1.7.0-eksbuild.1
```

7. Run the command from *step 1* to confirm the version change. This time, the output of the preceding command should look as follows:

```
123412345678.dkr.ecr.us-east-1.amazonaws.com/eks/
coredns:v1.7.0-eksbuild.1
```

Here, we have updated our Kubernetes components to the next version available. Let's move on to the next step and upgrade our worker nodes.

Upgrading Kubernetes worker nodes

After upgrading AWS EKS controllers, we will follow with adding new worker nodes using updated AMI images. We will drain the old nodes and help Kubernetes to migrate workloads to the newly created nodes.

Let's upgrade our worker nodes:

1. Edit the `config.tf` file under the `Chapter03/terraform/packtclusters` directory and change the name of the workers AMI ID increased version from `1.15` to `1.16`:

```
terraform {
  backend "s3" {
    bucket           = "packtclusters-terraform-state"
    key              = "packtclusters.tfstate"
    region           = "us-east-1"
    dynamodb_table = "packtclusters-terraform-state-lock-dynamodb"
  }
  required_version = "~> 0.12.24"
  required_providers {
    aws = "~> 2.54"
  }
}


provider "aws" {
  region  = var.aws_region
  version = "~> 2.54.0"
}


data "aws_ssm_parameter" "workers_ami_id" {
  name            = "/aws/service/eks/optimized-ami/1.16/amazon-linux-2/recommended/image_id"
  with_decryption = false
}
```

2. Edit the `terraform.tfvars` file under the `Chapter03/terraform/packtclusters` directory and increase `workers_number_min` if you like:

```
aws_region = "us-east-1"
private_subnet_ids = [
  "subnet-0b3abc8b7d5c91487",
  "subnet-0e692b14dbcd957ac",
  "subnet-088c5e6489d27194e",
```

```
]
public_subnet_ids = [
   "subnet-0c2d82443c6f5c122",
   "subnet-0b1233cf80533aeaa",
   "subnet-0b86e5663ed927962",
]
vpc_id = "vpc-0565ee349f15a8ed1"
clusters_name_prefix   = "packtclusters"
cluster_version        = "1.16"
workers_instance_type  = "t3.medium"
workers_number_min     = 2
workers_number_max     = 5
workers_storage_size   = 10
```

3. Run the terraform plan command to validate the planned changes before applying them:

```
$ cd chapter-10/terraform/packtclusters
$ terraform plan
```

You will get the following output after the terraform plan command completes successfully. There is one resource to change. We are only changing the cluster version:

```
Plan: 0 to add, 1 to change, 0 to destroy.
--------------------------------------------------------
Note: You didn't specify an "-out" parameter to save this plan, so Terraform
can't guarantee that exactly these actions will be performed if
"terraform apply" is subsequently run.
```

Figure 10.7 – The terraform plan command output

4. Execute the terraform apply command. Enter yes when you get a prompt to approve the in-place update:

```
$ terraform apply
```

You will get the following output after the terraform apply command completes successfully. By then, Terraform has successfully changed one AWS resource:

```
Do you want to perform these actions in workspace "prod1"?
  Terraform will perform the actions described above.
  Only 'yes' will be accepted to approve.

  Enter a value: yes

module.packtcluster.module.workers.aws_autoscaling_group.workers: Modifying...
module.packtcluster.module.workers.aws_autoscaling_group.workers: Modifications
m]
Apply complete! Resources: 0 added, 1 changed, 0 destroyed.
```

Figure 10.8 – The Terraform command output after changes are applied

5. Execute the `kubectl get nodes` command to get the name of your old nodes.
    You will get the following output and as we can see, two out of three nodes in our
    cluster are still on v1.15.12:

```
NAME                        STATUS   ROLES    AGE    VERSION
ip-10-40-102-5.ec2.internal Ready    <none>   5h7m   v1.15.12-eks-31566f
ip-10-40-74-21.ec2.internal Ready    <none>   5h7m   v1.15.12-eks-31566f
ip-10-40-87-72.ec2.internal Ready    <none>   6m9s   v1.16.15-eks-ad4801
```

Figure 10.9 – The kubectl output showing node names and version

6. Now that we've confirmed one new node is added to our cluster, we need to move
    our pods from the old nodes to the new nodes. First, one by one, taint the old nodes
    and drain them:

```
$ kubectl taint nodes ip-10-40-102-5.ec2.internal
key=value:NoSchedule
```

```
node/ip-10-40-102-5.ec2.internal tainted
```

```
$ kubectl drain ip-10-40-102-5.ec2.internal --ignore-
daemonsets --delete-emptydir-data
```

7. Then, remove the old nodes from your cluster. New nodes will be automatically
    created and added to our cluster. Let's confirm all nodes are upgraded by executing
    the `kubectl get nodes` command. The output of the command should look as
    follows:

```
NAME                         STATUS   ROLES    AGE    VERSION
ip-10-40-66-90.ec2.internal  Ready    <none>   4m     v1.16.15-eks-ad4801
ip-10-40-87-72.ec2.internal  Ready    <none>   29m    v1.16.15-eks-ad4801
ip-10-40-96-218.ec2.internal Ready    <none>   106s   v1.16.15-eks-ad4801
```

Figure 10.10 – The kubectl output showing updated node version

We have now learned how to upgrade the Kubernetes control plane and workers using
Terraform. It is a production best practice to have a regular backup of persistent data and
applications from our clusters. In the next section, we will focus on taking a backup of
applications and preparing our clusters for disaster recovery.

Preparing for backups and disaster recovery

In this section, we will be taking a complete, instant, or scheduled backup of the applications running in our cluster. Not every application requires or can even take advantage of regular backups. Stateless application configuration is usually stored in a Git repository and can be easily deployed as part of the **Continuous Integration and Continuous Delivery (CI/CD)** pipelines when needed. Of course, this is not the case for stateful applications such as databases, user data, and content. Our business running online services can be challenged to meet legal requirements and industry-specific regulations and retain copies of data for a certain time.

For reasons external or internal to our clusters, we can lose applications or the whole cluster and may need to recover services as quickly as possible. In that case, for disaster recovery use cases, we will learn how to use our backup data stored in an S3 target location to restore services.

In this section, we will use the open source Velero project as our backup solution. We will learn how to install Velero to take a scheduled backup of our data and restore it.

Installing Velero on Kubernetes

Traditional backup solutions and similar services offered by cloud vendors focus on protecting node resources. In Kubernetes, an application running on nodes can dynamically move across nodes, therefore taking a backup of node resources does not fulfill the requirements of a container orchestration platform. Cloud-native applications require a granular, application-aware backup solution. This is exactly the kind of solution cloud-native backup solutions such as Velero focus on. Velero is an open source project to back up and restore Kubernetes resources and their persistent volumes. Velero can be used to perform migration operations and disaster recovery on Kubernetes resources. You can read more about Velero and its concepts on the official Velero documentation site at `https://velero.io/docs/main/`.

> **Information**
>
> You can find the complete source code at `https://github.com/PacktPublishing/Kubernetes-in-Production-Best-Practices/tree/master/Chapter10/velero`.

Now, let's install Velero using its latest version and prepare our cluster to start taking a backup of our resources:

1. Let's get the latest release version tag of `velero` and keep it in a variable called `VELEROVERSION`:

    ```
    $ VELEROVERSION=$(curl -silent "https://api.github.com/
    repos/vmware-tanzu/velero/releases/latest" | grep '"tag_
    name":' | \
          sed -E 's/.*"v([^"]+)".*/\1/')
    ```

2. Now, download the latest `velero` release binary and install by executing the following command:

    ```
    $ curl --silent --location "https://github.com/vmware-
    tanzu/velero/releases/download/v${VELEROVERSION}/velero-
    v${VELEROVERSION}-linux-amd64.tar.gz" | tar xz -C /tmp
    $ sudo mv /tmp/velero-v${VELEROVERSION}-linux-amd64/
    velero /usr/local/bin
    ```

3. Confirm that the `velero` command can execute:

    ```
    $ velero version
    Client:
            Version: v1.5.2
            Git commit:
    e115e5a191b1fdb5d379b62a35916115e77124a4
    <error getting server version: no matches for kind
    "ServerStatusRequest" in version "velero.io/v1">
    ```

4. Create the credentials file for Velero to access your S3 target in this `chapter10/velero/credentials-velero` path. Replace `aws_access_key_id` and `aws_secret_access_key` with your AWS ID and access key and save the file:

    ```
    [default]
    aws_access_key_id = MY_KEY
    aws_secret_access_key = MY_ACCESS_KEY
    ```

5. Before you run the following command, update `s3Url` with your AWS S3 bucket address or S3-compatible object storage, such as a MinIO object storage server address. Install the Velero server components by executing the following command:

```
$ velero install \
    --provider aws \
    --plugins velero/velero-plugin-for-aws:v1.0.0 \
    --bucket velero \
    --secret-file ./credentials-velero \
    --use-restic \
    --backup-location-config
region=minio,s3ForcePathStyle="true",s3Url=http://
abcd123456789-1234567891.us-east-1.elb.amazonaws.com:9000
```

The output of the preceding command should look as follows:

```
VolumeSnapshotLocation/default: created
Deployment/velero: attempting to create resource
Deployment/velero: created
DaemonSet/restic: attempting to create resource
DaemonSet/restic: created
Velero is installed! ⚠ Use 'kubectl logs deployment/velero -n velero' to view the status.
```

Figure 10.11 – Velero installer output showing successful installation

6. Confirm that the Velero server components are successfully installed by executing the following command:

```
$ kubectl get deployments -l component=velero -n velero
```

The output of the preceding command should look as follows:

```
NAME      READY   UP-TO-DATE   AVAILABLE   AGE
velero    1/1     1            1           3m23s
```

Figure 10.12 – Velero deployments status showing ready

Now we have Velero installed and configured to take a backup of resources to an S3 target. Next, we will learn how to take a bundled backup of Kubernetes resources.

Taking a backup of specific resources using Velero

Let's follow the steps here to get a backup of Kubernetes resources we would like to protect. For this example, we will need a stateful application. We will deploy a MinIO object storage workload, upload some files on it, and take a backup of all resources to demonstrate the backup and restoration capabilities. You can apply the same steps to any application you wish:

> **Information**
>
> You can find the complete source code at `https://github.com/PacktPublishing/Kubernetes-in-Production-Best-Practices/tree/master/Chapter10/velero/backup`.

1. If you already have a stateful application with persistent volumes to protect, you can skip to *step 4*. Otherwise, execute the following command to deploy a MinIO instance to continue with the scenario:

```
$ kubectl apply -f https://raw.githubusercontent.com/
PacktPublishing/Kubernetes-Infrastructure-Best-Practices/
master/Chapter10/velero/backup/deployment-minio.yaml
```

2. Verify that MinIO pods, service, and persistent volumes are created by executing the following command:

```
$ kubectl get pods,svc,pvc -nminio-demo
```

The output of the preceding command should look as follows:

```
NAME                             READY   STATUS      RESTARTS   AGE
pod/minio-569464db84-b6rst       1/1     Running     0          7m5s
pod/minio-setup-m2jg9            0/1     Completed   2          7m4s

NAME                TYPE           CLUSTER-IP      EXTERNAL-IP
 PORT(S)          AGE
service/miniodemo   LoadBalancer   172.20.243.26   a4dbf6bfd29214b4791215b34d5e2457-135578941.us-east-1
.elb.amazonaws.com   9000:31864/TCP   7m4s

NAME                                     STATUS   VOLUME                                     CAPACITY   A
CCESS MODES   STORAGECLASS   AGE
persistentvolumeclaim/minio-pv-claim     Bound    pvc-6bf98751-feca-4b6f-9a47-9d5970a13105   10Gi       R
WO            gp2            7m5s
```

Figure 10.13 – Status of the MinIO pods, service, and persistent volume

3. Now, we will create a backup for all resources that have the label `app=minio`. Make sure to match the selector if you are using different labels. Execute the following command to create a backup:

```
$ velero backup create minio-backup --selector app=minio
```

> **Important note**
>
> To create scheduled backups, you can add a schedule parameter to the backup using a cron expression. For example, to create a daily backup, you can use either the `--schedule="0 1 * * *"` or `--schedule="@daily"` parameters. Later, you can get a list of scheduled backup jobs using the `velero schedule get` command.

4. Run the following command to verify that the backup job is completed:

```
$ velero backup describe minio-backup
```

5. As an alternative, we can back up resources in an entire namespace. Let's make another backup, this time using a namespace, by executing the following command:

```
$ velero backup create minio-backup-ns --include-
namespaces minio-demo
```

Now, we have learned how to create a backup of our first resource group and namespace in Kubernetes. Let's simulate a disaster scenario and test recovering our application.

Restoring an application resource from its backup using Velero

Let's follow these steps to completely remove resources in a namespace and restore the previous backup to recover them. You can apply the same steps on any application to migrate from one cluster to another. This method can also serve as a cluster upgrade strategy to reduce upgrade time:

1. Delete all resources in a namespace of your application by executing the following command:

```
$ kubectl delete ns minio-demo
```

2. Create a new namespace and execute the following command to restore the application and its resources from its backup:

```
$ kubectl create ns minio-demo
```
```
$ velero restore create –from-backup minio-backup
```

3. Wait for a couple of second for resources to be restored and verify that your MinIO pods, service, and persistent volume are restored by executing the following command:

```
$ kubectl get pods,svc,pvc -nminio-demo
```

4. The output of the preceding command should look as follows:

```
NAME                           READY   STATUS      RESTARTS   AGE
pod/minio-569464db84-b6rst     1/1     Running     0          7m5s
pod/minio-setup-m2jg9          0/1     Completed   2          7m4s

NAME                   TYPE            CLUSTER-IP       EXTERNAL-IP
                       PORT(S)                         AGE
service/miniodemo      LoadBalancer    172.20.243.26    a4dbf6bfd29214b4791215b34d5e2457-135578941.us-east-1
.elb.amazonaws.com     9000:31864/TCP  7m4s

NAME                                        STATUS   VOLUME                                       CAPACITY   A
CCESS MODES   STORAGECLASS   AGE
persistentvolumeclaim/minio-pv-claim        Bound    pvc-6bf98751-feca-4b6f-9a47-9d5970a13105     10Gi       R
WO            gp2            7m5s
```

Figure 10.14 – Status of the MinIO pods, service, and persistent volume

Now we have learned how to restore a resource group backup of the service in our production Kubernetes clusters. Let's take a look at how we can improve by continuously validating the quality of our clusters and troubleshooting issues.

Validating cluster quality

In this section, we will learn about some of the best practices and tools in the ecosystem to improve different aspects of our Kubernetes clusters. Continuous improvement is a wide-ranging concept that encompasses everything from providing a smooth platform to services on Kubernetes and setting a particular **Quality of Service (QoS)** for resources, to making sure resources are evenly distributed and unused resources are released to reduce the pressure on cluster resources and the overall cost of providing services. The definition of improvement itself is gradually getting more granular, and it is not limited to the practices that we will discuss here. Before we learn about the conformance and cost management tools, let's learn about a few common-sense quality best practices we should consider:

- **Generate state-of-cluster reports**: Although it is expected that Kubernetes clusters should behave the same whether it's a managed Kubernetes service provided by a public cloud provider, a distribution provided by a specific vendor, or a self-managed cluster based on upstream Kubernetes, the reality is there may be limitations and configuration differences that we should validate. Conformance testing is a great way to ensure that the clusters we support are properly configured and conform to official Kubernetes specifications.

- **Define QoS for pods**: Unless configured correctly, pods scheduled on Kubernetes clusters can consume all the resources available to them. When Kubernetes schedules a pod, it also assigns a QoS class. These classes can be either `Guaranteed`, `Burstable`, or `BestEffort`.

- **Reduce latency to closer to users' location**: There is a reason why cloud providers offer clusters in different geographic locations. It is common to start locally and observe end user latencies and traffic before spinning clusters in different geographies. Observe issues and bottlenecks, and expand to additional regions closer to users when needed.

- **Define storage classes with different QoSes**: In a Kubernetes cluster, the CPU, memory, and also to a degree, the network, QoS can be managed by Kubernetes. Storage QoS is expected to be handled by storage providers. Storage can be provided by the external storage of the cluster or hyper-converged **Container Attached Storage (CAS)** outside. A best practice is to abstract data management from specific storage vendors to provide vendor-agnostic service flexibility with storage classes. Different storage classes can be used to provide cold storage, SSD, or NVMe-backed storage depending on the application's needs. We learned about tuning Kubernetes storage and choosing the storage solution in *Chapter 7, Managing Storage and Stateful Applications*.

- **Optimize container images**: It is recommended to continuously monitor your cluster resources' top consumers, improve their consumption, and look for ways to optimize their consumption. Optimizing container images can have a significant impact on resource utilization and performance. You can read more about the challenges and best practices of improving container images in *Chapter 8, Deploying Seamless and Reliable Applications*.

- **Optimize cluster resource spend**: In theory, the only limit on the cloud provider's resources is your budget. It is recommended to monitor the cost of resources and project allocation to get the full cost of running a product.

Now we have learned the best practices for improving the quality of our cluster; we have touched on some of the topics in previous chapters. Let's look into the remaining areas that we haven't covered yet, including how we can validate cluster resources in a non-destructive manner and monitoring the cost of resources.

Generating compliance reports

There are many ways and tools to get a Kubernetes cluster up and running. It is an administrative challenge to maintain a proper configuration. Fortunately, there are tools to validate reports and detect configuration problems. Sonobuoy is one of the popular open source tools available to run Kubernetes conformance tests and validate our cluster's health. Sonobuoy is cluster-agnostic and can generate reports of our cluster's characteristics. These reports are used to ensure the best practices applied by eliminating distribution-specific issues and conforming clusters can be ported into our clusters. You can read more about custom data collection capabilities using plugins and integrated **end-to-end** (**e2e**) testing at Sonobuoy's official documentation site, https://sonobuoy.io/docs/v0.20.0/. Now, let's install the latest version of Sonobuoy and validate our cluster by running a Kubernetes conformance test:

1. Let's get the latest release version tag of Sonobuoy and keep it in a variable called SONOBUOYVERSION:

    ```
    $ SONOBUOYVERSION=$(curl -silent "https://api.github.
    com/repos/vmware-tanzu/sonobuoy/releases/latest" | grep
    '"tag_name":' | \
        sed -E 's/.*"v([^"]+)".*/\1/')
    ```

2. Now, download the latest sonobuoy release binary and install by executing the following command (https://github.com/vmware-tanzu/sonobuoy/releases/download/v0.20.0/sonobuoy_0.20.0_linux_amd64.tar.gz):

    ```
    $ curl --silent --location "https://github.com/vmware-
    tanzu/sonobuoy/releases/download/v${SONOBUOYVERSION}/
    sonobuoy_${SONOBUOYVERSION}_linux_amd64.tar.gz" | tar xz
    -C /tmp
    $ sudo mv /tmp/sonobuoy /usr/local/bin
    ```

3. Confirm that Sonobuoy is installed, and the command can execute:

    ```
    $ sonobuoy version
    Sonobuoy Version: v0.20.0
    MinimumKubeVersion: 1.17.0
    MaximumKubeVersion: 1.99.99
    GitSHA: f6e19140201d6bf2f1274bf6567087bc25154210
    ```

4. Make sure that the cluster has enough resources to execute all the tests. You can find a specific suggestion for every provider on Sonobuoy's source repository at `https://github.com/cncf/k8s-conformance/tree/master/v1.16`. For EKS, the suggested cluster size is 10 `c5.xlarge` worker instances. Start the conformance tests on your EKS cluster by executing the following command:

```
$ sonobuoy run --wait \
    --sonobuoy-image projects.registry.vmware.com/
sonobuoy/sonobuoy:v0.20.0
```

5. To shorten testing and validate the configuration rather than full certified conformance, we can run the test with the `--mode quick` option:

```
$ sonobuoy run --wait --mode quick
```

6. Validation will take up to an hour to complete depending on the tests executed on the cluster. Once finished, execute the following command to get the plugins' results and inspect the results for failures. For a detailed list of options to inspect results, see the documentation at `https://sonobuoy.io/docs/v0.20.0/results/`:

```
$ results=$(sonobuoy retrieve)
$ sonobuoy results $results
```

The output of the preceding command should look as follows:

```
Plugin: systemd-logs
Status: passed
Total: 3
Passed: 3
Failed: 0
Skipped: 0
```

Figure 10.15 – Sonobuoy validation results

7. Delete the Sonobuoy components from the cluster and clean up the resources:

```
$ sonobuoy delete --wait
```

Now we have learned how to validate our Kubernetes cluster configuration. Let's look into how we can detect overprovisioned, idle resources and optimize our cluster's total cost.

Managing and improving the cost of cluster resources

Monitoring project cost and team chargeback and managing total cluster spending are some of the big challenges of managing Kubernetes on public cloud providers. Since we have a theoretically unlimited scale available through cloud vendors, utilization fees can quickly go up and become a problem if not managed. Kubecost helps you monitor and continuously improve the cost of Kubernetes clusters. You can read more about the cost and capacity management capabilities of Kubecost at Kubecost's official documentation site: `https://docs.kubecost.com/`.

Now, let's install Kubecost using Helm and start analyzing cost allocation in our cluster:

1. Create a namespace called `kubecost`:

    ```
    $ kubectl create ns kubecost
    ```

2. Add the `cost-analyzer` Helm Chart repository to your local repository list:

    ```
    $ helm repo add kubecost \
            https://kubecost.github.io/cost-analyzer/
    ```

3. Update the Helm Chart repositories:

    ```
    $ helm repo update
    ```

4. Install `cost-analyzer` from its Helm repository:

    ```
    $ helm install kubecost kubecost/cost-analyzer \
        --namespace kubecost \
        --set
    kubecostToken="bXVyYXRhbWF5YWRhdGEuaW8=xm343yadf98"
    ```

5. Verify successful installation by executing the following command:

    ```
    $ kubectl get pods -n kubecost
    ```

    The output of the preceding command should look as follows:

    ```
    NAME                                                   READY   STATUS      RESTARTS   AGE
    cost-analyzer-checks-1610671200-2zwqw                  0/1     Completed   0          100s
    kubecost-cost-analyzer-f5bc9bd6-s2kkk                  3/3     Running     0          4m14s
    kubecost-grafana-6df5cc66b6-8n592                      3/3     Running     0          4m14s
    kubecost-kube-state-metrics-57d4dfc748-sgvzw           1/1     Running     0          4m14s
    kubecost-prometheus-alertmanager-7cdff76d5-vmtpv       2/2     Running     0          4m14s
    kubecost-prometheus-node-exporter-2xn6z                1/1     Running     0          4m14s
    kubecost-prometheus-node-exporter-hqf2b                1/1     Running     0          4m14s
    kubecost-prometheus-node-exporter-q66s6                1/1     Running     0          4m14s
    kubecost-prometheus-server-6f79df498c-8jhsk            2/2     Running     0          4m14s
    ```

    Figure 10.16 – List of the pods deployed by Kubecost after successful installation

> **Important note**
>
> Kubecost installs Prometheus, Grafana, and `kube-state-metrics` in
> the `kubecost` namespace. Your existing Prometheus and Grafana instance
> deployment of the `node-exporter` pod can get stuck in the pending state
> due to a port number conflict with the existing instances. You can resolve this
> issue by changing port number instances deployed with the Kubecost chart.

6. Now we have `cost-analyzer` installed. Let's access the Kubecost dashboard.
    Create port forwarding to access the Kubecost interface locally:

```
$ kubectl port-forward --namespace kubecost deployment/
kubecost-cost-analyzer 9090
```

> **Important note**
>
> Instead of port forwarding Prometheus and Grafana service IPs, you can
> choose to expose service IPs externally through your cloud provider's
> load balancer options, changing the service type from `NodePort` to
> `LoadBalancer`.

7. Open a browser window and visit `http://localhost:9090`, which is
    forwarded to the `kubecost-cost-analyzer` service running in the cluster. The
    dashboard will immediately show the running monthly cost of your cluster, similar
    to the following:

Figure 10.17 – Kubecost Available Clusters screen

8. Click on your cluster from the list and access the Kubecost dashboard. The top part
    of the dashboard will show a summary of the total cost and any potential identified
    savings, similar to that in the following screenshot:

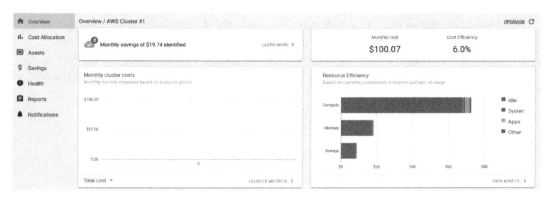

Figure 10.18 – Kubecost dashboard

9. Let's scroll down the dashboard screen to find a summary of the controller component and service allocation. At the bottom of the dashboard, we will see the health scores. A health score is an assessment of infrastructure reliability and performance risks:

Figure 10.19 – Kubecost dashboard showing the cluster health assessment score

10. The most important quick summary pages on the dashboard are the health assessment and estimated saving detail pages. Let's click on each to get to the areas where you can improve your cluster's cost and performance. In the following screenshot, we can see an example of a significant saving suggestion from Kubecost after analyzing our cluster:

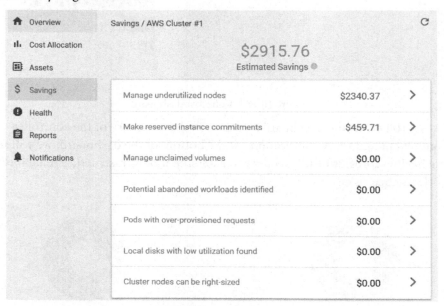

Figure 10.20 – Kubecost estimated savings dashboard

11. Click on the arrow button next to one of the saving categories and review the recommendations to optimize your cluster cost.

Now we have learned how to identify monthly cluster costs, resource efficiency, cost allocation, and potential savings by optimizing request sizes, cleaning up abandoned workloads, and using many other ways to manage underutilized nodes in our cluster.

Summary

In this chapter, we explored Kubernetes operation best practices and covered cluster maintenance topics such as upgrades, backups, and disaster recovery. We learned how to validate our cluster configuration to avoid cluster and application problems. Finally, we learned ways to detect and improve resource allocation and the cost of our cluster resources.

By completing this last chapter in the book, we now have the complete knowledge to build and manage production-grade Kubernetes infrastructure following the industry best practices and well-proven techniques learned from early technology adopters and real-life, large-scale Kubernetes deployments. Kubernetes offers a very active user and partner ecosystem. In this book, we focused on the best practices known today. Although principles will not change quickly, as with every new technology, there will be new solutions and new approaches to solving the same problems. Please let us know how we can improve this book in the future by reaching out to us via the methods mentioned in the *Preface* section.

Further reading

You can refer to the following links for more information on the topics covered in this chapter:

- *Amazon EKS Kubernetes release calendar*: `https://docs.aws.amazon.com/eks/latest/userguide/kubernetes-versions.html#kubernetes-release-calendar`

- Disaster recovery for multi-region Kafka at Uber: `https://eng.uber.com/kafka/`

- *Disaster Recovery Preparedness for Your Kubernetes Clusters*: `https://rancher.com/blog/2020/disaster-recovery-preparedness-kubernetes-clusters`

- The official website of the Velero project: `https://velero.io/`

- The official website of the Sonobuoy project: `https://sonobuoy.io/`

- KubeDR, an alternative open source Kubernetes cluster backup solution: `https://github.com/catalogicsoftware/kubedr`

- Kasten, an alternative Kubernetes backup, disaster recovery, and mobility solution: `https://www.kasten.io/`

Subscribe to our online digital library for full access to over 7,000 books and videos, as well as industry leading tools to help you plan your personal development and advance your career. For more information, please visit our website.

Why subscribe?

- Spend less time learning and more time coding with practical eBooks and Videos from over 4,000 industry professionals

- Improve your learning with Skill Plans built especially for you

- Get a free eBook or video every month

- Fully searchable for easy access to vital information

- Copy and paste, print, and bookmark content

Did you know that Packt offers eBook versions of every book published, with PDF and ePub files available? You can upgrade to the eBook version at packt.com and as a print book customer, you are entitled to a discount on the eBook copy. Get in touch with us at customercare@packtpub.com for more details.

At www.packt.com, you can also read a collection of free technical articles, sign up for a range of free newsletters, and receive exclusive discounts and offers on Packt books and eBooks.

Other Books You May Enjoy

If you enjoyed this book, you may be interested in these other books by Packt:

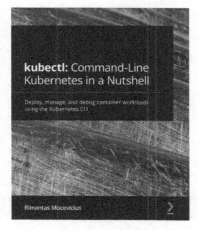

kubectl: Command-Line Kubernetes in a Nutshell

Rimantas Mocevicius

ISBN: 978-1-80056-187-8

- Get to grips with the basic kubectl commands
- Delve into different cluster nodes and their resource usages
- Understand the most essential features of kubectl
- Discover how to patch Kubernetes deployments with Kustomize
- Find out ways to develop and extend kubectl tools with their own plugins
- Explore how to use Helm as an advanced tool for deploying apps

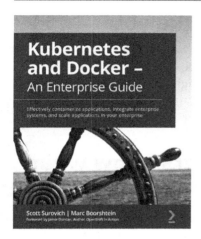

Kubernetes and Docker - An Enterprise Guide

Scott Surovich and Marc Boorshtein

ISBN: 978-1-83921-340-3

- Create a multinode Kubernetes cluster using kind

- Implement Ingress, MetalLB, and ExternalDNS

- Configure a cluster OIDC using impersonation

- Map enterprise authorization to Kubernetes

- Secure clusters using PSPs and OPA

- Enhance auditing using Falco and EFK

- Back up your workload for disaster recovery and cluster migration

- Deploy to a platform using Tekton, GitLab, and ArgoCD

Packt is searching for authors like you

If you're interested in becoming an author for Packt, please visit `authors.packtpub.com` and apply today. We have worked with thousands of developers and tech professionals, just like you, to help them share their insight with the global tech community. You can make a general application, apply for a specific hot topic that we are recruiting an author for, or submit your own idea.

Leave a review - let other readers know what you think

Please share your thoughts on this book with others by leaving a review on the site that you bought it from. If you purchased the book from Amazon, please leave us an honest review on this book's Amazon page. This is vital so that other potential readers can see and use your unbiased opinion to make purchasing decisions, we can understand what our customers think about our products, and our authors can see your feedback on the title that they have worked with Packt to create. It will only take a few minutes of your time, but is valuable to other potential customers, our authors, and Packt. Thank you!

Index

main resources 65, 66
output values 68
security groups 66
Elastic Block Store (EBS) 8
Elastic File System (EFS) 8
Elastic Kubernetes Service
(EKS) 11, 35, 45, 111
Elasticsearch, Fluentd, and
Kibana (EFK) stack 223
end-to-end (e2e) testing 251
ExternalDNS
configuring 120-123

F

Falco
reference link 153
runtime, monitoring 152, 153
Firecracker 188
Flagger
about 201
reference link 201

G

General Availability (GA) 178
Google Kubernetes Engine (GKE) 11, 45
Google SRE resources site
reference link 214
Grafana
about 215, 220
reference link 220
used, for monitoring
applications 220-222

H

hard multi-tenancy
implementing 144
Helm
about 163
installing 163
higher availability
achieving 204-207
highly available (HA) cluster 33
Horizontal Pod Autoscaler (HPA)
about 25, 204
reference link 25
hybrid cloud clusters 33
hyperconverged storage solutions 176

I

Identity and Access Management
(IAM) 5, 97
Infrastructure as a Service (IaaS) 13
infrastructure as Code (IaC) 31
infrastructure resources
cleaning up 82
destroying 82
International Data Corporation (IDC) 3
IP Address Management (IPAM) 114

K

k8s module
reference link 102
Kata 188
kernel space 187